S0-BSY-722

THE BIBLE AND THE
HERMENEUTICS OF LIBERATION

REGIS COLLEGE LIBRARY
100 Wellesley Street West
Toronto, Ontario
Canada M5S 2Z5

Society of Biblical Literature

Semeia Studies

Gale A. Yee, General Editor

Editorial Board:

Jione Havea

Jennifer L. Koosed
Tat-siong Benny Liew
Jeremy Punt
Erin Runions
Ken Stone
Caroline Vander Stichele
Elaine M. Wainwright

Number 59

THE BIBLE AND THE
HERMENEUTICS OF LIBERATION

THE BIBLE AND THE
HERMENEUTICS OF LIBERATION

Edited by

Alejandro F. Botta and Pablo R. Andiñach

BT
83.57
B53
2009

REGIS COLLEGE LIBRARY
100 Wellesley Street West
Toronto, Ontario
Canada M5S 2Z5

Society of Biblical Literature
Atlanta

THE BIBLE AND THE
HERMENEUTICS OF LIBERATION

Copyright © 2009 by the Society of Biblical Literature

All rights reserved. No part of this work may be reproduced or transmitted in any form or by any means, electronic or mechanical, including photocopying and recording, or by means of any information storage or retrieval system, except as may be expressly permitted by the 1976 Copyright Act or in writing from the publisher. Requests for permission should be addressed in writing to the Rights and Permissions Office, Society of Biblical Literature, 825 Houston Mill Road, Atlanta, GA 30329 USA.

Library of Congress Cataloging-in-Publication Data

The Bible and the hermeneutics of liberation / edited by Alejandro F. Botta and Pablo R. Andiñach.
    p. cm. — (Society of Biblical Literature semeia studies ; no. 59)
    Includes bibliographical references.
    ISBN 978-1-58983-241-1 (pbk. : alk. paper)
    1. Liberation theology. 2. Liberty—Biblical teaching. I. Botta, Alejandro F., 1960– II. Andiñach, Pablo R.
    BT83.57.B53 2009
    230'.0464—dc22   2009022438

17 16 15 14 13 12 11 10 09   5 4 3 2 1
Printed in the United States of America on acid-free, recycled paper conforming to ANSI/NISO Z39.48-1992 (R1997) and ISO 9706:1994 standards for paper permanence.

To the memory of our teacher and friend, José Severino Croatto

Contents

ACKNOWLEDGMENTS

Several colleagues and institutions provided support, inspiration, and encouragement for this project. Abraham Smith (Perkins School of Theology, Southern Methodist University) first suggested to us the topic for this volume and was instrumental in its forthcoming. Abe read the manuscript thoroughly and offered many valuable suggestions that improved the book considerably. We are very grateful for his continuous encouragement and support. The project began to take shape during Pablo Andiñach's visiting professorship at Perkins School of Theology, where Alejandro Botta was teaching before he moved to Boston University. We are thankful to ISEDET for providing Pablo a sabbatical leave and to Dean William D. Lawrence and Marjorie Procter-Smith (then Associate Dean for Academic Affairs at Perkins) for welcoming Pablo at Perkins in such a graceful way and for their continuous support and encouragement of Alejandro's work. We also want to thank Alejandro's Research Assistant at Boston University School of Theology, Ms. Rachel Vogelzang, for her help in the formatting and style correction of the manuscript and her enthusiasm with the project.

Several libraries provided us the necessary resources for our research: we want to express our thanks to the library of ISEDET in Buenos Aires, to Bridwell Library (Perkins School of Theology), to Boston University School of Theology Library, and to Andover-Harvard Theological Library (Harvard University Divinity School). We also want to express our gratitude to Dean Ray Hart and his successor at Boston University School of Theology, Dean Mary Elizabeth Moore, for their continuous support of Alejandro's research.

We also want to thank the Semeia Studies board and Gale Yee (general editor) for accepting this volume for the prestigious Semeia Studies series. Our thanks to all those who participated in this project; we hope that the liberating words of the Bible continue to be challenging to them as well as to the readers of this volume.

Finally, we dedicate this volume to the memory of our teacher at ISEDET, José Severino Croatto, whose life commitments and engaged scholarship are still an inspiration for us.

ABBREVIATIONS

AB	Anchor Bible
ABD	*The Anchor Bible Dictionary*. Edited by David Noel Freedman. 6 vols. New York: Doubleday, 1992.
Bib	*Biblica*
BibInt	*Biblical Interpretation*
BibOr	Biblica et orientalia
BZ	*Biblische Zeitschrift*
ChrCent	*Christian Century*
EKKNT	Evangelisch-katholischer Kommentar zum Neuen Testament
EstTeo	*Estudios teológicos*
FOTL	Forms of the Old Testament Literature
HBT	*Horizons in Biblical Theology*
HTR	*Harvard Theological Review*
IB	*Interpreter's Bible*. Edited by G. A. Buttrick et al. 12 vols. New York: Abingdon, 1951–57.
IBC	Interpretation: A Bible Commentary for Teaching and Preaching
ICC	International Critical Commentary
IDB	*The Interpreter's Dictionary of the Bible*. Edited by G. A. Buttrick. 4 vols. Nashville: Abingdon, 1962.
Int	*Interpretation*
JAAR	*Journal of the American Academy of Religion*
JBL	*Journal of Biblical Literature*
JBQ	*Jewish Bible Quarterly*
JR	*Journal of Religion*
JSOT	*Journal for the Study of the Old Testament*
JTS	*Journal of Theological Studies*
JTSA	*Journal of Theology for Southern Africa*
NCBC	New Cambridge Bible Commentary
NIB	*The New Interpreter's Bible*. 12 vols. Nashville: Abingdon.
OTL	Old Testament Library
RIBLA	*Revista de interpretación bíblica latino-americana*
SBB	Stuttgarter biblische Beiträge

SBLGPBS	Society of Biblical Literature Global Perspectives on Biblical Scholarship
SBM	Stuttgarter biblische Monographien
SemeiaSt	Semeia Studies
TDOT	*Theological Dictionary of the Old Testament.* Edited by G. J. Botterweck and H. Ringgren. Translated by J. T. Willis, G. W. Bromiley, and D. E. Green. 15 vols. Grand Rapids: Eerdmans, 1974–2006.
TRE	*Theologische Realenzyklopädie.* Edited by Gerhard Krause and Gerhard Müller. 36 vols. Berlin: de Gruyter, 1976–2004.
USQR	*Union Seminary Quarterly Review*
VT	*Vetus Testamentum*
VTSup	Supplements to Vetus Testamentum
WBC	Word Biblical Commentary
WMANT	Wissenschaftliche Monographien zum Alten und Neuen Testament
WUNT	Wissenschaftliche Untersuchungen zum Neuen Testament
ZAW	*Zeitschrift für die alttestamentliche Wissenschaft*

Introduction: The Bible and the Hermeneutics of Liberation: Worldwide Trends and Prospects

Pablo R. Andiñach and Alejandro F. Botta

An isolated consideration of the three central words of our title would yield diverse social and linguistic realities, each of which could be considered to be unrelated to the other. "The Bible" directs us to the universe of sacred texts, religions, and foundational stories of the Jewish-Christian faith. It is a set text, objective, transcendent of time and culture, rising as a fountain of inspiration for those who consider it their sacred text. For hermeneutics, however, we find something quite different; the word "hermeneutics" allows us to consider an aspect of contemporary philosophy, linguistics, semiotics, and the science of reading texts. It is an academic discipline in constant transformation; its postulates are a matter of debate in every place where texts, history, or life itself are interpreted. It is not a word of common usage—it refers us to the expression of intellectual circles rather than everyday feeling and expressions. Finally, the word "liberation" has political and social connotations—and as we will see in this book, it has biblical and religious ones as well—and is associated with revolutionary processes, with actions in favor of human rights and the dignity of people. It urgently refers us to reality, to what is pressing, because it involves the simple and elemental rights to justice and dignity. A naïve reflection could come to the conclusion that, by putting these three words together in a unique discourse, they are redefined, acquiring a different sense and thus creating a new linguistic and theological universe. There is some truth in this: when they are combined they acquire a sense enriched by their relation. However, reality is rather more complex; these three words working together in a unique universe—which we can call "theologies of liberation"—are redefined, without losing the main nuance of their original definition. In this new theological space the Bible does not cease to belong to or cease to direct us to the religious world that shaped it and in which it reaches its maximum value. Hermeneutics continues to be an area of philosophy and linguistics, the area from which it emerges and in which it nurtures and expands. Liberation continues to evoke the process by which the oppressed seek to overcome their social and political condition and to find the dignity of which they are deprived. At the same time, these three individual disciplines—biblical universe, hermeneutical reflection, and liberating action—all mutually contribute to the creation of a determinate and integrated way to interpret reality and life, which provides a sense of faith to believers.

1. The Beginnings

Although it would not be fair to say that, as discussed above, the biblical discourse *is and continues to be* theological and that it uses the other two spheres instrumentally, as external agents that do not pepper their own identity, this would be true in a traditional way of doing theology. In the beginning of what would later be called theology of liberation in Latin America, there was a deep awareness that a new way of doing theology was in the making. Back in the 1960s the first suggestions that theological thinking should make the effort to gain insight from other disciplines emerged, focused particularly on those insights that explained the oppressive social reality of Latin America. Until that point we can safely say that theology only joined in conversations with philosophy and, to a lesser degree, with psychology. In this way theology presented itself as the religious expression of a philosophy of the time, sometimes as a direct product of those philosophies and other times as a reaction or answer. Martin Heidegger's existentialism provided the tools that Rudolf Bultmann and Paul Tillich elaborated in their own theologies; Ernest Bloch's philosophy of hope constituted the raw material for Jürgen Moltmann and his theology of hope. A combination of postwar feminist thinking together with strong secularization in Europe invited Dorothee Sölle to produce her influential work. Elements of classical Marxism appear in the works of Richard Schaull, whose reflection from the early 1960s was occasionally called a theology of revolution (see Vendrell 2008).

In Latin America it was quite different. Due to the influence of Marxism—a philosophy that presented itself as both *anti*philosophical and the end of philosophy—theological thinking transferred the classical concern from understanding reality and answering intellectual challenges to a new concern, more profound and disturbing: how to transform reality. Nevertheless, it would be a mistake to suppose that this movement came into existence as a consequence of the new scenario in academic philosophical discussions or in specialized journals This novel object of theology emerged as the result of the actions of committed Christians in social and political struggles, as well as the consequences for the pastoral ministry of such commitments. Due to these commitments, one of the axioms of liberation theology is that it is a "second act." This is a concept that is not always well understood. In the classical form of doing theology, thinkers develop their thoughts and then apply them to reality, to the church, to preaching. First they think theologically, and then they apply this theology to reality. Quite differently, in what was called theology of liberation, the first act is the commitment to modify reality, thus seeking a more just and humane society. Once one is immersed in this world of struggles and social relations, then one thinks theologically and establishes priorities and themes, which must be thought out theologically. Questions emerge from a situation of oppression and subjugation, and those who suffer seek answers from a Christian faith. In this sense theology is a "second act" that follows the commitment for liberation.

This sequence, sociopolitical commitment followed by theological reflection, explains the essential component of doing theology "from praxis," in which dialogue with theology and other disciplines begins to direct the theologian toward the science that supports those commitments and expectations. In this way the discussion left the academic cloisters—accustomed only to philosophy and morals—and came closer to the social sciences, particularly sociology, economy, and politics. This knot needed to be untied, and instead of knitting words together it sought to produce concrete actions that would modify the reality of oppression and provide hope. Those who sought tools to change the world discovered in that search and action that those tools changed theology as well. Instead of using the social sciences as external tools and instruments, the social sciences were incorporated to the discourse and were considered more and more as constituent of the theological task itself, thus marking a deep epistemological severance with the other way of doing theology. However, sociology did not stop being an autonomous discipline, nor did politics abandon its earthly aims; rather, theology incorporated these instruments of analysis and transformation of social reality and made them actors within its own discourse. These were the first works of a Latin American theology that may be referred to as "liberation theology," which included strong components of social analysis and a critique of the traditional way of doing theology.[1]

Biblical theology accompanied this development of liberation theology. Probably the first work of this characteristic view of theology that reached widespread coverage was a small book written by José Severino Cro-

---

1. The first work published that included the concept "theology of liberation" was by a Presbyterian Brazilian theologian, Rubem Alves (1969); other works followed: Gutiérrez 1973a; Bonino 1975.

atto, called *Liberación y Libertad* (Croatto 1973; 1981b). Croatto presented the exodus from Egypt as a paradigm of liberation from slavery as well as a key for reading the whole Bible. In this book Croatto develops the ideas that already existed in embryonic form in his earlier work, *Historia de la Salvación*—with its successive re-editions and revisions carried out by the author—which became the most read and reedited Latin American book of biblical theology (1995). In this book he points to a crucial concept in Latin American hermeneutics: that the exodus was not only an event in biblical history but rather is a foundational event of everything that follows. From this one event one should understand the prophets, psalms, wisdom literature, and a good part of the New Testament. In his understanding, Exodus is read both on a symbolic level and in its social and political dimensions. Thus, to recognize that the text speaks of slaves who cried out to God in their pain and were liberated, without taking into account whether it is possible historically to reconstruct the historicity of the event, speaks loudly of the God of the Bible and God's project for humanity. The collective memory of the people of Israel—who developed these texts—assumed that in the beginning their ancestors suffered oppression by a foreign power. The will of God opposed this suffering to the point of doing everything possible to free them from the yoke and provided them with a land where they could grow and develop their lives in peace.

This hermeneutics of liberation comes together in dialogue with the hermeneutical works of Paul Ricoeur,[2] who proposed that a text is an unfathomable place of encounter with semantic worlds. In this sense texts are not exhausted in the simple reading; rather, they are placed in the context of life—which is the only place where it is possible to read texts—where multiple readings may be opened up due to the polysemic nature of the accounts and the reservoir of sense hidden in their words. Ricoeur contributed to Latin American hermeneutics by opening up texts to a new dimension of reading that would overcome serious and scientific readings done by the historical-critical methods of biblical analysis. Latin American hermeneutics did not reject those methods; rather, it tended to relativize them and put them next to other approaches that in the final moment would contribute to the hermeneutical "leap" by which the message was placed above any other language dimension (Ricoeur 1976a). Today this is an everyday occurrence in many schools of interpretation, though it is interesting to observe that this atti-

---

2. The principle work for this matter is his *El conflicto de las interpretaciones* (Ricoeur 1976b), though the rest of his writings should also be considered of significance for Latin American hermeneutics.

tude which values the final text, sometimes called "canonical," other times identified with the received text, materialized about thirty years ago in Latin America. However, it did not develop through academic assurance but rather as a demand of a reality that, when confronting the biblical text with an experience of oppression and subjugation of human rights, imposed a reading that would privilege sense and message.

Simultaneously—and in no contradiction with the above—sociological readings of biblical texts were also being explored at this time. The development of disciplines such as biblical archaeology, advances in critical history, and sociology applied to the analysis of ancient societies began to cause an impact in biblical studies. It could not be ignored that the history of ancient Israel literally understood as narrated in the Bible was in conflict with some of the results of ongoing archaeological research, such as, for example, that the destruction of Jericho had not happened as narrated in Josh 5 (Kenyon 1957, 256–65). While these archaeological findings led in the northern Atlantic centers of learning to a series of modifications in the understating of the relationship between biblical stories and factual happening—which had sent the "maximalist" archaeological school of William Foxwell Albright (1940; 1963) and John Bright (1962) into a crisis (see also Davies 2004)—in Latin America, this type of conclusion and work would impact indirectly and in a different sense. Rather than create a crisis in an archaeological school, it awoke the possibility of radical critique of the theological vision of the entire biblical history. If those texts were not a literal reflection of the facts, then it was necessary to address the ideologies that constituted those narratives and revise the social and political concepts sustaining their particular understanding of the past. It was possible—and also the duty to get to the heart of the message—to read the reverse of the texts seeking their material base, the social and ideological context in which they emerged.[3]

Thus, in the middle of the 1970s there was a firm purpose in both the general theological field[4] and biblical theology in favor of getting involved with

---

3. This search was expressed from what is called the "popular" reading (see the work of Carlos Mesters) to the academic production in the materialistic reading of biblical texts supported by Michel Clévenot (1978).

4. In Latin American theology there has existed and still exists a certain apprehension to speak of "systematic theology," due to the strong critique of all closed systems in which the classical systematic thinking was understood as enclosing the theological discourse. This way there were compulsory issues to be resolved and exposed that emerge from the "system" and not as demands of reality. On the contrary, the liberationist theological task was understood as an open space of reflection on those issues that the reality of struggle for liberation proposed.

social sciences in order first to understand reality and then to commit to the struggles to modify it so that oppression and injustices may be overcome.[5]

2. The Expansion toward Other Areas of Reality

The first hints of a liberationist hermeneutic had an outlook concentrated on direct and immediate problems. The challenges were pressing, and there was not much time to waste in excessive considerations: being overcareful in the reflective process could result in some sort of social paralysis or in establishing a distance from the social process. In spite of the risks involved, the process could be delayed no longer. As a consequence, it became quite clear that, perhaps due to Marxist influence, reflection was limited to the liberation analysis of the classical political processes, whether by armed struggles or through popular electoral processes. With a certain naiveté it was argued that, when the oppressed masses reached victory, all forms of oppression would fall by their own weight. However, this argument did not conform to the vast social sectors that did not clearly identify with a class structure; rather, it crossed over all social classes in a horizontal manner. Still, on the whole these classes were part of the vast oppressed sectors of society. Their struggles did not always coincide with the traditional social struggles, and in many cases their interests included aspects that were not taken into account by the revolutionaries who represented them. This conscious awareness within the social and political sphere soon fertilized the theological reflection of Christians involved in those sectors who were committed to the liberation of their sisters and brothers. In this way the Christians who were within the indigenous movements began to realize that biblical hermeneutics allowed them to see beyond the class struggle and to understand themselves as part of a sector of oppressed people who at the same time suffered from the oppression of their class-mates. In other words, it showed them that as poor they too were discriminated against and that the triumph of the future revolution would not assure them their own dignity as indigenous people. In a similar way, the struggles for equality between races revealed a parallel picture.

Women discovered that the Bible could provide them with tools to seek their own identity and place in relation to an andocentric society. Those people involved in ecological issues discovered that Scripture sustained their struggles for the preservation of life and the defense of a real future for cre-

---

5. By this time works such as Juan Luis Segundo's *Liberación de la Teología* (1975); José Míguez Bonino's *Christians and Marxists* (1976); and Hugo Assman's *Teología desde la praxis de liberación* (1973) had all been published.

ation. However, it would not be correct to say that prior to that point the liberating value of the Bible had remained undiscovered. Those who believe that liberation as a biblical theme was discovered over forty years ago in Latin America demonstrate laziness and ignorance, not an experience of the people of God over the centuries. It is only in the last centuries that we find valuable antecedents in the so called social gospel of Walter Rauschenbusch in the United States and in authors such as Hermann Kutter and Leonhard Ragaz in Europe, who founded Christian Socialism, clearly pointing to the gospel consequences for a social ethic. Indeed, *Negro spirituals* have been sung about this for over two centuries, and thousands of women have survived humiliation by finding strength in reading Scripture. The novelty of a hermeneutic of liberation lies in the fact that Christian communities are collectively reading the Bible in the midst of their struggle with eyes wide open to a liberating message. It became increasingly less a text for an illuminated group of isolated fighters and more a book that oriented Christian communities in their search for justice, peace, and dignity for the people of which they were an inextricable part. It seems quite an irony of history that this same book that so often was invoked to sustain exploitation of an entire people—of women by men, of black by white, of poor by rich—now has become the source of inspiration for all who rebel against oppression and seek to overcome all injustice. The oppressor's instrument has now been turned against the oppressor and has nurtured the dreams and hopes of the oppressed.

In the middle of the 1980s a sectarian hermeneutics exploded onto the scene: we were enriched by feminist, ecological, postcolonial, indigenous, and popular thought. This volume is an example of the explosion that readers can explore; the breadth of this hermeneutical outgrowth can be observed simply by examining the index. Each and every one of these hermeneutics seeks to render a reality of oppression and represent biblical responses to concrete situations that believers demand the Bible to face. Each hermeneutic develops from the intimate conviction that the text is best understood when it is read in the midst of a community of believers and is set in the midst of the challenges of life.

In our understanding, there are three challenges that must be addressed by all these different ways to approach the Bible. (1) How does each hermeneutic take into account the problems of the other ones? There is a tendency for each sector to struggle for their rights without being fully aware of the impact they have on the rest of the "community of the oppressed." This problem, which was originally a social-dynamic problem, can also create a too-sectarian biblical hermeneutic. An indigenous hermeneutic must also refer to its understanding of women in its vision of the world and of faith. A feminist hermeneutic— whose problematic is usually considered to be multiclass—must give account of the meaning of women's liberation for the poorest of women and also for those marginalized by the economic system. This demand is not only a political and ethical demand, of searching for real justice that is efficient for all people, but also a concern that emerges principally from the integrity of the biblical message that calls us to understand reality as a whole and not compartmentalized and unconnected from everything else.

(2) The second challenge is confronting the place each hermeneutic provides for self-criticism. All the reflections emerging from communities and from their commitment to transforming reality must be ready for changes that are part of the social processes and that also reflect changes in our thought and reflection. All human institutions tend to become rigid and try to preserve their mechanisms, even though after a certain time these institutions often turn against the principles that originated them. Theology and biblical reflection are no exception to this rule. The hermeneutical field must be aware that, because of its very nature—the polysemic nature of texts, the necessary flexibility of thought, and the passion to preserve what has been discovered—it may lose part of its charm. If this happens, the consequence is fatal for our hermeneutical task: it stops being relevant for readers and all those who seek orientation for their faith. Thus, each hermeneutic must consider the mechanisms for renewal of its thought and action.

(3) We would like to point out one final aspect, that, although it may seem more theoretical, is no less concrete and real: each particular hermeneutic is accountable to the general discourse of the church. We do not mean to synchronize hermeneutics with denominational documents or theologies proper of each ecclesial tradition, which sometimes contribute and other times are obstacles for a creative reading of the biblical text. We refer instead to the church as a community of women and men of all races, cultures, ages, ideologies, nations, and so on who gather around Scripture to receive guidance for their lives and hopes. Understood as such by believers, the church expresses human diversity while simultaneously expressing unity. The question is: How does our contextual hermeneutic support the universality of discourse of which it is a part? How can it express itself so that the theological and hermeneutical discourse, which necessarily is contextual and sectarian, does not lose the sense of being part of the word that "remains for ever" (Isa 40:8), which gave sense to the lives of our grandparents and will continue to do so for our children?

3. The Essays That Constitute This Volume

Although this is not the place to summarize the content of the volume, we can offer readers the necessary information to understand how this collection of essays came to be and the reasons for their selection. You will find that we offer two contributions from Africa (Musa Dube and Gerald West), three from the United States (Theodore Jennings, Alejandro F. Botta, who immigrated from Argentina, and Ada María Isasi Díaz, who immigrated from Cuba), three European authors (Luise Schottroff, Hans de Wit, and Erhard Gerstenberger), one by a native of Tonga but now living in Australia (Jione Havea), and one author from Argentina (Mercedes García Bachmann). They represent not only diverse geographical areas but also diverse social sectors, which superimpose and coincide following the dictates of reality in various cases. The contributions from Dube, Isasi Díaz, Schottroff, and García Bachmann explore texts from the perspective of women. Havea explores the impact of biblical narrative in communities in which the oral tradition is more significant than the written one. De Wit offers a discussion on the methodological presuppositions in liberation hermeneutics, offering both a critique of and proposals to overcome the presuppositions. Gerstenberger follows a similar way when researching European hermeneutics and the possible consequences for biblical interpretation in the current German context. Jennings explores texts in the context of the imperial reality in which they were produced and sheds light on the new—and often old—forms of imperial exploitation. Botta proposes to reread the doctrine of universal sin from a Latin perspective within the United States, while West raises questions on the liberationist discourse in a country that reached democracy and today faces new challenges.

The coordinates crisscross: feminist from Africa with Latinos/as in the United States; the Latin American discourse with the German; Holland crosses with Australia and Argentina with South Africa. This is an enriching panorama, a coming and going of ideas and readings that mutually nurture each other. They are all centered on how to read the Bible as a key to liberation, not through a philosophical or theological pose, but rather because they seek to be faithful to the internal coordinates of the texts themselves.

The volume is structured in three sections. The first one comprises three contributions that present regional overviews of liberating struggles and liberation hermeneutics: "Liberation Hermeneutics after Liberation in South Africa," by Gerald West; ""It Should Be Burned and Forgotten!" Latin American Liberation Hermeneutics through the Eyes of Another," by Hans de Wit; and "Liberation Hermeneutics in Old Europe, Especially Germany," by Erhard Gerstenberger. The second section engages the biblical text from various liberationist perspectives. Three essays analyze texts from the Hebrew Bible: "Releasing the Story of Esau from the Words of Obadiah," by Jione Havea; "How to Hide an Elephant on Fifth Avenue: Universality of Sin and Class Sin in the Hebrew Scriptures," by Alejandro F. Botta; "True Fasting and Unwilling

Hunger (Isaiah 58)," by Mercedes García Bachmann; four engage texts from the New Testament: "Talitha Cum Hermeneutics of Liberation: Some African Women's Ways of Reading the Bible," by Musa W. Dube; "Paul against Empire: Then and Now," by Theodore W. Jennings; "The Kingdom of God Is Not Like You Were Made to Believe: Reading Parables in the Context of Germany and Western Europe," by Luise Schottroff; and "A Mujerista Hermeneutics of Justice and Human Flourishing," by Ada María Isasi Díaz.

The last section comprises readers' responses. We have selected three reactors who complete the announced diversity: Mortimer Arias from Uruguay; Monica J. Melanchthon from India; and Lai Lang Elizabeth Ngan, an Asian American. Their opinions will help us see the presentations from a distance.

We hope the reading of these pages will encourage our own hermeneutics, leading us to think and act in a way that allows the texts to fulfill in us the reason for which they were created.

OVERVIEWS

Liberation Hermeneutics after Liberation in South Africa

Gerald O. West

1. Introduction

We have recently celebrated ten years of liberation, ten years of democracy, and in May 2006 we have celebrated ten years of our new Constitution. Much has been accomplished in these ten years. As our chief justice, Pius Langa, said, reflecting on the tenth anniversary of the Constitution:

> A number of factors indicate that our democracy is alive and well. The multiparty parliamentary system has fared reasonably well and structures have been set up to hold MPs and other public representatives and officials to account; regular elections, which have been free and fair, have been held; institutions to facilitate the advancement and protection of fundamental rights and equality have been set up; the media and other organs of civil society go about their work freely and, to a large extent, effectively. (Langa 2006)

Langa continues by placing emphasis on one particular institution, that of the courts, and their role in upholding our law in general and our Constitution and our Bill of Rights in particular. "As an institution, the courts," he continues:

> whose function is to resolve legal disputes and to ensure that the extensive powers of government are not abused, are carrying out their tasks effectively. This has been possible because of the guarantees of a legal system that provides for an independent judiciary, which commands the respect both of government and the general population. (Langa 2006)

In my view, Langa is right to place emphasis on our legal accomplishments over the past ten years. Writing on the eve of our liberation, James Cochrane and I argued that, because a "public discourse about the nature and conditions of society has been denied the bulk of the population for so long,"

> [t]o resolve the problem of violence requires the construction of adequate patterns of discourse, which will take the root conditions of past violence into account. To demand reconciliation when adequate patterns of discourse are not yet in place merely demonstrates a hidden agenda.... In other words, the task is not just a matter of defining an adequate framework for the future, but also of incorporating the effects of the past into the constitution of a renewed society. (Cochrane and West 1993, 33)

We envisaged this task as one that should be taken up "in the construction of a new Constitution and system of law in South Africa" (Cochrane and West 1993, 33; see also Cochrane 1991, 64–73).

Langa is right, then, when he says, citing the late Ismail Mahomed, a former chief justice, that our Constitution is a "mirror reflecting the national soul." The product of national consensus, "a joint project of the South African people," our Constitution gives us, "for the first time in our history,"

> a foundational document that legitimately constitutes the basis upon which all governmental authority must be exercised.... The "national soul" that we see reflected in this mirror is one that espouses non-racism and non-sexism, that upholds the rule of law, democratic ideals and the foundational values of human dignity, the achievement of equality and the advancement of human rights and freedoms. (Langa 2006)

While stating that "these are the ideals we have committed ourselves to," Langa immediately notes that we "are, however, a society in transition, hopefully moving toward the full realization of these ideals." His qualification is based on two factors. First, there is the question of "the pace at which we are moving and the distance that still remains before we reach the desired destination, when the reality of our everyday lives will fully match the reflection in the mirror" (Langa 2006). Second, and related, is our current reality, in which "we still suffer from massive problems. Poverty and unemployment, crime and corruption, HIV/AIDS and lack of basic resources are but a few of the evils that continue to delay fulfillment of our constitutional dream" (Langa 2006).

In the rest of his article Langa goes on to argue that "[i]t is in this context that the principle of an independent judiciary goes to the very heart of sustainable constitutional democracy based on the rule of law." However, in his concluding call to action, without diminishing the rule of law, Langa identifies both the limits and the potential of our legal transformation embodied in our Constitution:

> Despite its centrality to our young country, the wisdom of its provisions and
> its power as an instrument for change, the Constitution is not a magic wand
> that can sweep away the evils that history has burdened us with without any
> effort on our part. The Constitution is a call and a guide to a better place.
> But we must follow it with the same energy and commitment with which we
> fought apartheid. (Langa 2006)

We have undergone a fundamental transformation in South Africa, one that
can appropriately be designated as "liberation." Is there any further role, then,
for liberation theologies and hermeneutics in South Africa? Or, more collo-
quially, as one of my colleagues asked me with a mischievous smile on the day
of our liberation, "What will you now do, Gerald?"

My response to my colleague, also with a smile, was a biblical one: "Jesus
said, 'You always have the poor with you'" (Matt 26:11; Mark 14:7; John 12:8).
Jesus, I hope, was not being fatalistic about the abiding presence of the poor
for all time, and neither was I. Like Pius Langa, I am something of an ideal-
ist and have not given up on utopian visions (though such visions have not
been as prevalent in South African liberation theologies as they have in Latin
American liberation theologies). My snappy reply to my colleague was, however, more than teatime banter. My understanding of liberation theology is
fundamentally formed by the late Per Frostin's analysis, in which he argues
that liberation theology (and neither he nor I are wedded to this term) should
be defined "with methodology and not content as the distinguishing characteristic" (Frostin 1988).

In the next section I will revisit Frostin's formulation before going on to
use this formulation to interrogate our current context in South Africa. In
so doing I will address the question of the place of liberation hermeneutics
after liberation.

"Liberation Theology"

Writing in the late 1980s and drawing on a range of liberation theologies
(including African theologies, South African black theology, Tanzanian
Ujamaa theology, Asian theologies, feminist theologies, and even First World
liberal-political theologies), Frostin's analysis of liberation theologies finds
"five interrelated emphases: the choice of 'interlocutors', the perception of
God, social analysis, the choice of theological tools, and the relationship
between theory and practice" (Frostin 1988, 6).

With respect to the first, the choice of interlocutors, Frostin argues that
the emphasis in liberation theologies (I prefer the plural, though Frostin uses
the singular) has been on social relations, not ideas, as has been the tendency
in post-Enlightenment Western theology. This emphasis, Frostin goes on to

argue, leads to a new question: "Who are the interlocutors of theology? Or, Who are asking the questions that theologians try to answer?" (1988, 6). This new question is given a decisive answer by liberation theologies (and by me to my colleague during teatime): "a preferential option for the poor" (1988, 6). This choice of interlocutors is more than an ethical commitment, it is also an epistemological commitment, requiring a theological starting point within the social analysis of the poor themselves.

The other four emphases of liberation theologies each flow from this first, which is why it has been so informative in my own work and why I invoked Jesus' words in reply to my colleague. As long as the poor are with us (which, I hope, will not be "always"), there is work for liberation theologies. This is what I was trying to say.

As Frostin goes on to say, turning to his second emphasis, the choice of interlocutors "has important consequences not only for the interpretation of social reality but also for the understanding of God" (1988, 7). As the Ecumenical Association of Third World Theologians (EATWOT) so aptly expressed it, "the question about God in the world of the oppressed is not knowing whether God exists or not, but knowing on which side God is" (cited in Frostin 1988, 7). Put differently, in liberation theologies "the search for the true God and the struggle against the idols become central tasks of theology" (1988, 7).

The third emphasis, that of social analysis, also derives from the first, for "the option for the poor as the chief interlocutors of theology is based on a conflictual perception of the social reality, affirming that there is a difference between the perspectives of the privileged 'from above' and of the poor 'from below'" (Frostin 1988, 7–8). EATWOT reports characterize the world as "a divided world" where doing theology can only be done "within the framework of an analysis of these conflicts" (cited in Frostin 1988). The poles of conflict or "struggle" (to use the term common in South African liberation theologies; I. Mosala 1989; Nolan 1988) included, according to Frostin's summary of EATWOT's analysis, rich-poor (economic), capitalists-proletariat (classist), north-south (geographic), male-female (sexist), white-black (ethnic/racist), dominant-dominated cultures (cultural) (1988, 8). While EATWOT, one of the major sources of Frostin's analysis, consistently stressed the interrelatedness of these struggles, many of the debates within EATWOT centered around the priority given to and the relationship between different levels of oppression. "Generally speaking," says Frostin, "the discussion has followed continental lines of divisions, where Latin Americans have emphasized the value of socioeconomic analysis while Africans and Asians have tended to stress religio-cultural analysis," and where women from each of these continents have emphasized, increasingly, gender analysis (1988, 8).

The fourth emphasis in Frostin's analysis of the methodology of liberation theologies has to do with the relationship between the social sciences
and theology. "With a different interlocutor and a different perception of
God, liberation theologians need different tools for their theological reflection" (1988, 9). There is a shift in liberation theologies from philosophy as the
primary cognate discipline alongside theology to the social sciences. Among
the first tasks of a theological deployment of the social sciences is the identification of "the poor." As Frostin notes, this involves more than economic
statistics; rather, "the term denotes the underprivileged in the different power
structures and must be clarified [with the poor as interlocutors] by means of
social analysis" (1988, 9). As Frostin goes on to argue, economic analysis is "a
necessary dimension of the theo-logical discernment between God and idol"
(1988, 9). Significantly, Frostin states in passing that the kind of alliance liberation theologies forge between theology and the social sciences differentiates
it from "a Western sociology of knowledge (Marxist or non-Marxist)" precisely "in the insistence on the poor as the interlocutors of theology" (1988,
9). Again, the primacy of the first condition, namely, the poor as interlocutors, is evident.

Given that power relations are central to the analysis of all liberation
theologies, Marxist modes of analysis are "a generally accepted dimension,"
though "the actual use of Marxist analysis differs from group to group,"
depending on the form of oppression that is the focus of a particular liberation theology (Frostin 1988, 9). However, even those African forms of
liberation theology that emphasize socioeconomic oppression do so in
ways that are more nuanced than classical Marxism. First, African liberation theologies define the main contradiction in society as more complex
than does classical Marxism. "In classical Marxism the main contradiction is
analyzed in terms of classes, which are defined by their roles in production.
Hence, capital and labor are the two opposite poles in the analysis of the
contemporary 'class struggle'" (Frostin 1988, 182). Even though capital labor
is clearly one dimension of their analysis of the African struggle, African
liberation theologies adopt a multidimensional analysis of the relationship
between oppressor and oppressed, which includes race, gender, and culture
(1988, 182). Second, "the cultural dimension of oppression is emphasized
in [African] liberation theology far more than in classical Marxism" (1988,
182), which is what unites African forms of liberation theology. Third, while
classical Marxism maintains that "material production conditions human
thought," African theologies of liberation emphasize "the creativity of the
oppressed in a way that differs fundamentally from classical Marxism. The
difference is especially striking when compared with the Marxist-Leninist
theory of party, where the cadres, the 'conscious' elite, is seen as necessary

tools to inculcate the masses with a revolutionary consciousness" (1988, 182–83). In the words of the African American public intellectual and theologian Cornel West:

> Though Marxists have sometimes viewed oppressed people as political or economic agents, they have rarely viewed them as *cultural* agents. Yet without such a view there can be no adequate conception of the capacity of oppressed people—the capacity to change the world and sustain the change in an emancipatory manner. And without a conception of such capacity, it is impossible to envision, let alone create, a socialist society of freedom and democracy. It is, in part, the European Enlightenment legacy—the inability to believe in the capacities of oppressed people to create cultural products of value and oppositional groups of value—which stands between contemporary Marxism and oppressed people. (cited in Frostin 1988, 183; C. West 1984, 17)

Frostin's fifth and final emphasis is the dialectics between praxis and theology. In liberation theologies, theology is "a second act" (1988, 10). The first act is the praxis of action and reflection. The action is actual action in a particular struggle; integrally related to this action is reflection on the action, and integrally related to this action-induced reflection is further action, refined or reconstituted by the reflection on and reconsideration of theory (and so on goes the cyclical process). Out of this first act of praxis, second-order liberation theologies are constructed. How they are constructed and by whom is the subject of ongoing debate. Frostin favors a strong role for theologians and organic intellectuals in assisting the poor to break their silence and "create their own language" (1988, 10), though his sustained emphasis on the poor as primary *interlocutors* poses serious questions to this position (as I have argued; see G. West 1995; 2003a).

I will return to these constituent elements of liberation theologies in the discussion that follows, though in a more focused form as I discuss South African liberation theologies. I have used Frostin's analysis of liberation theologies in general because it draws on a wide range of related liberation theologies in dialogue. The data Frostin uses is drawn substantially from the self-constituted dialogue of Third World theologians working together in forums such as EATWOT. What I have summarized above are "the family resemblances" (to use Ludwig Wittgenstein's phrase; 1958, §65) among liberation theologies, and they provide a useful preface to the analysis that follows. In the next section I will discuss four or five strands of liberation theology in South Africa, before, in the final section of this essay, offering some reflection on "matters arising."

Liberation Theologies in South Africa

There are five or six main strands of liberation theology in South Africa. These include black theology, African theology, contextual theology, confessing theology, African women's theology, and HIV-positive theology. Though some historical perspective will be necessary, my concern is to examine each of these liberation theologies in the period after liberation. Though I will try to discuss them holistically, my analysis will concentrate on their biblical hermeneutics

Black Theology

Though the roots of black theology could be traced back to the very first encounters between southern African indigenous peoples and Bible-bearing missionary/colonial forces (G. West 1995, 52–55; 2004a), black theology as such emerged in the context of the rise of the black consciousness movement in the late 1960s and early 1970s (De Gruchy and De Gruchy 2004, 144–64; Kretschmar 1986, 58–68; Kritzinger 1988, 57–91; I. Mosala 1989, 1; Nolan 1988, 3–4).

Tinyiko Maluleke, the most productive black theologian at present, identifies three phases of South African black theology. Though Maluleke's phases follow a chronological periodization, he stresses the continuity between the phases:

> The first phase starts with the formation of the Black Theology Project by the University Christian Movement in 1970, while the second starts in 1981 with the establishment of the Institute for Contextual Theology. In phase one, Black Theology, though acknowledging Blackness to be a state of mind, nevertheless took objective Blackness as its starting point in such a way that all Black people were the focus of liberation and the whole Bible (Christianity) could be used for liberation. In phase two, objective Blackness, in and of itself, is no longer sufficient. Not all Black people are the focus of Black Theology. Not all theology done by Black people is Black Theology and not all the Bible (Christianity) is liberating. Furthermore, while phase one Black Theology was closely linked to the Black Consciousness philosophy, phase two Black Theology recognized a wider ideological ferment within the Black Theology movement. Most distinctive of the second phase has been the increasing introduction of Marxist historical materialism in the hermeneutic of Black Theology. (Maluleke 1998b, 61)

In terms of biblical hermeneutics, phase one is characterized by a hermeneutics of trust. The overall interpretive orientation toward the Bible is one of trust. A hermeneutics of trust is evident in a number of respects. First, as in much of African theology (and African American black theology and Latin American liberation theology), the Bible is considered to be a primary source of black theology (see Mbiti 1977). The Bible belongs to black theology in the sense that doing theology without it is unthinkable. Second, the Bible is perceived to be primarily on the side of the black struggle for liberation and life in South Africa. The Bible belongs to black theology in the sense that the struggle for liberation and life is central to them both (see Tutu 1983, 124–29).

While there is definitely an awareness that there are different, sometimes complementing and sometimes contradicting, theologies in the Bible, this is understood as evidence of the thoroughly contextual nature of the Bible, and, because the pervasive theological trajectory is one of liberation, the plurality of theologies in the Bible is unproblematic for black theology (Tutu 1983, 106). Those who use the Bible against black South Africans are therefore misinterpreting the Bible, because the Bible is basically on the side of black theology.

The biblical hermeneutics of phase two black theology inaugurates one of the most significant contributions to liberation theologies. While the "external" problem of the misuse of the Bible by oppressive and reactionary white South African Christians remains, phase two black theology identifies a more fundamental problem: the "internal" problem of the Bible itself. Takatso Mofokeng is critical of those who concentrate only on the external problem, those who accuse "oppressor-preachers of *misusing* the Bible for their oppressive purposes and objectives" and "preachers and racist whites of not practising what they preach." It is clear, Mofokeng maintains, that these responses are "based on the assumption that the Bible is essentially a book of liberation." While Mofokeng concedes that these responses, so characteristic of phase one–type biblical hermeneutics, have a certain amount of validity to them, the crucial point he wants to make is that there are numerous "texts, stories and traditions in the Bible which lend themselves to only oppressive interpretations and uses because of their inherent oppressive nature." What is more, he insists, any attempt "to 'save' or 'co-opt' these oppressive texts for the oppressed only serves the interests of the oppressors" (Mofokeng 1988, 37–38). Itumeleng Mosala is the clearest of phase two black theologians on this matter. In an early essay on "The Use of the Bible in Black Theology," he is the first black theologian to question in print the ambiguous ideological nature of Bible itself (I. Mosala 1986c; 1989, 1–42). Mosala's basic critique is directed at black theology's exegetical starting point, which "expresses itself in the notion that the Bible is the revealed 'Word of God'" (I. Mosala 1989, 15). He traces this view of the

Bible as an "absolute, non-ideological 'Word of God'" back to the work of James Cone.[1]

Mosala's contention is that most of the Bible "offers no certain starting point for a theology of liberation within itself." For example, he argues that the biblical book of Micah "is eloquent in its silence about the ideological struggle waged by the oppressed and exploited class of monarchic Israel." In other words, "it is a ruling-class document and represents the ideological and political interests of the ruling class." As such, there "is simply too much de-ideologization to be made before it can be hermeneutically straightforward in terms of the struggle for liberation" (I. Mosala 1986c, 196; 1989, 120–21). The Bible, therefore, cannot be the hermeneutical starting point of black theology. Rather, those committed to the struggles of the black oppressed and exploited people "cannot ignore the history, culture, and ideologies of the dominated black people as their primary hermeneutical starting point" (I. Mosala 1986c, 197).

However, this does not mean that Mosala totally rejects the Bible. While the Bible cannot be the primary starting point for black theology, "there are enough contradictions within the book [of Micah, for example] to enable eyes that are hermeneutically trained in the struggle for liberation today to observe the kin struggles of the oppressed and exploited of the biblical communities in the very absences of those struggles in the text." Because the Bible is "a product and a record of class struggles" (I. Mosala 1986c, 196), black theologians are able to detect "glimpses of liberation and of a determinate social movement galvanized by a powerful religious ideology in the biblical text." But, he continues, the "existence of this phenomenon is not in question; rather, the problem here is one of developing an adequate hermeneutical framework that can rescue those liberating themes from the biblical text" (I. Mosala 1989, 40).

Mosala goes on in his work to offer an adequate hermeneutical framework for black theology (phase two), proposing a dialectic between an appropriation of black culture and experience and an appropriation of the Bible (I. Mosala 1986a, 119). Central to Mosala's hermeneutics of liberation is the search for a theoretical perspective that can locate both the Bible and the black experience within appropriate sociohistorical contexts. Historical-critical tools (to delimit and historically locate texts), supplemented by sociological resources (including a historical-materialist understanding of

---

1. For a discussion of the role of James Cone in South African black theology, see the important book by Per Frostin (1988, 89–90). Frostin may be overstating this role (see Kee 2006, 71–97).

struggle), provide the theoretical perspective for Mosala's treatment of texts; historical-materialism, particularly its appropriation of "struggle" as a key concept, provides the sociological categories and concepts necessary to read and critically appropriate both black history and culture and the Bible. "The category of struggle becomes an important hermeneutical factor not only in one's reading of his or her history and culture but also in one's understanding of the history, nature, ideology, and agenda of the biblical texts" (I. Mosala 1989, 9).

In order to undertake this kind of analysis, Mosala argues, black interpreters must be engaged in the threefold task of Terry Eagleton's "revolutionary cultural worker": a task that is projective, polemical, and appropriative. While Mosala does not doubt that (phase one) black theology is "projective" and "appropriative" in its use of the Bible, it is "certainly *not* polemical—in the sense of being critical—in its biblical hermeneutics" (I. Mosala 1989, 32). Black theology has not interrogated the text ideologically in class, cultural, gender, and age terms. Black theology has not gauged the grain or asked in what code the biblical text is cast and so has read the biblical text as an innocent and transparent container of a message or messages (I. Mosala 1989, 41).

Returning to Maluleke's analysis, the contours of the third (postliberation) phase of black theology are more difficult to discern, because "we are living in and through it" (Maluleke 1998b, 61). Nevertheless, he does offer a tentative sketch of the third phase.[2] Repudiating allegations of black theology's "death" after liberation, Maluleke argues that the third phase of black theology draws deeply on resources within earlier phases of black theology and elaborates these formative impulses into the future.

First, while the plurality of ideological positions and political strategies in the construction of black theology has been acknowledged since the early 1980s, the ideological and political plurality within black theology in the 1990s is more marked and brings with it a new 1990s-type temptation that must be refused. Ideological and political plurality in postapartheid (and postcolonial) South Africa must avoid both the temptation of an uncommitted play with pluralism and the temptation of a despairing paralysis (perhaps even an abandonment) of commitment. Despite the pressures of ideological and political plurality, commitment remains the first act in black theology, whatever the particular brand (Maluleke 1998b, 61).

---

2. The paper of Maluleke I am referring to here is a brief "concept paper," so I am sometimes making fairly bold inferences from the available clues. Wherever possible, I have used Maluleke's other published work to enhance my understanding of the moves he makes in the concept paper.

Second, if race was the central category in the first phase of black theology, and if the category of class was placed alongside it in the second phase of black theology, then gender as a significant category has joined them in the third phase of black theology. But, once again, the tendency to minimize the foundational feature of black theology, namely, race, must be resisted, argues Maluleke. Gender, like class, in South Africa always has a racial component. Furthermore, warns Maluleke, in a context "where race is no longer supposed to matter" (1998b, 61), racism often takes on different guises and becomes "more 'sophisticated'" (1998b, 62).

The third and final feature of phase three black theology has three related prongs, each of which might be considered as a separate element. Here, however, I want to stress their connectedness, as does Maluleke, and so will treat them as subelements of a formative feature of the third phase of South African black theology. The formative feature of phase three black theology is the identification of African traditional religions (ATRs) and African independent/instituted/initiated churches (AICs) as "significant" (perhaps even primary?) dialogue partners (Maluleke 1998b, 62).[3]

Subsumed under this general feature, the first of the three prongs has to do with culture. Whereas phase one black theology "ventured somewhat into cultural … issues," phase two "became more and more concerned with the struggle of black people against racist, political and economic oppression" (Maluleke 1998a, 133). However, "[at] crucial moments connections with African culture would be made—provided that culture was understood as a site of struggle rather than a fixed set of rules and behaviours" (Maluleke 1998a, 133). Culture remains problematized in phase three, but the envisaged rapprochement with ATRs and AICs that characterizes phase three foregrounds culture in a form not found in phase two.

The second prong has to do with solidarity with the poor. In each of its phases, black theology "has sought to place a high premium on *solidarity with the poor* and not with the state or its organs, however democratic and benevolent such a state might be." While such a position "must not be mistaken with a sheer anti-state stance … Black Theology is first and foremost not about the powerful but about the powerless and the silenced." And, and I stress this

---

3. Implicit in this formulation is my tentative analysis that locates ATRs and AICs along a continuum. At one end of the continuum would be ATR as a distinct "faith." I am not sure what would stand at the other end of the continuum, but along the way would be various manifestations of what we call AICs, gradually becoming less and less (primally) African. My play on "primal" here is deliberate, alluding to the "translation" (see Maluleke 1996) trajectory in African theology articulated by Lamin Sanneh (1989) and Kwame Bediako (1995) and the high place it accords ATR as primal religion.

conjunction, "serious interest" in ATRs and AICs affords black theology in phase three "another chance of demonstrating solidarity with the poor—for ATRs is [*sic*] the religion of the poor in this country" (Maluleke 1998b, 62).

Closely related to the first and second prongs, but particularly to the first, is a third. By making culture a site of struggle, black theology "managed to relativise the Christian religion sufficiently enough to encourage dialogue not only with ATRs but with past and present struggles in which religions helped people to take part, either in acquiescence or in resistance" (Maluleke 1998a, 133). If, as Itumeleng Mosala has argued (1986b), African culture can be a primary site of a hermeneutics of struggle for African theology, supplemented only with a political class-based hermeneutics, then Christianity is not a necessary component in a black theology of liberation (Maluleke 1998a, 133). A key question, therefore, for the third phase of South African black theology is, "Have black and African theologies made the necessary epistemological break from orthodox or classical Christian theology required to effect 'a creative reappropriation of traditional African religions' (I. J. Mosala 1986b:100)?" (Maluleke 1998a, 135).

Speaking to his own question, Maluleke argues that South African black theology has tended to use "classical Christian tools, doctrines and instruments—for example the Bible and Christology" for its purposes. The challenge that black theology of liberation faced was to enable black people to use the Bible to "get the land back and to get the land back without losing the Bible" (I. Mosala 1989, 153).

> Realizing that Christianity and the Bible continue to be a "haven of the Black masses" (Mofokeng 1988:40), black theologians reckoned that it would not be advisable simply "to disavow the Christian faith and consequently be rid of the obnoxious Bible." Instead the Bible and the Christian faith should be shaped "into a formidable weapon in the hands of the oppressed instead of just leaving it to confuse, frustrate or even destroy our people" (Mofokeng 1988:40). Preoccupation with Christian doctrines and ideas was, for black theology therefore, not primarily on account of faith or orthodoxy considerations, but on account of Christianity's apparent appeal to the black masses. (Maluleke 1998a, 134).

Given this analysis, Maluleke goes on to argue,

> What needs to be re-examined now [in phase three] however, is the extent to which the alleged popularity of Christianity assumed in South African black theology is indeed an accurate assessment of the religious state of black people. If it were to be shown that ATRs are as popular as Christianity among black South Africans then in not having given much concerted attention to them, black theology might have overlooked an important

resource. There is now space for this to be corrected by making use of alternative approaches. (Maluleke 1998a, 134).

As I have shown, via Maluleke's analysis, one of the important features of phase three black theology is the recognition, recovery, and revival of its links with ATRs and AICs, and in so doing renewing its dialogue with African theology in its many and various forms. In other words, Maluleke could be said to be revisiting and questioning Mofokeng's assertion that "African traditional religions are too far behind most blacks" (Mofokeng 1988, 40). Is this actually the case, asks Maluleke? Gabriel Setiloane asks the question even more starkly: "why do we continue to seek to convert to Christianity the devotees of African traditional religion?" (Setiloane 1977, 64, cited in Maluleke 1997a, 13). "This," says Maluleke, "is a crucial question for all African theologies [including South African black theology] as we move into the twenty-first century" (Maluleke 1997a, 13).

Alongside this question, of course, looms the related question, prompted by Maluleke's analysis, of whether black theology can be done without the Bible.[4] If it is true, as is claimed by both Mofokeng and Mosala, that the Bible is primarily of strategic, not substantive (see Cady 1986; G. West 1995, 103–30), importance to black theology—a claim that is vigorously rejected by Desmond Tutu (see Tutu 1983), Boesak (1984), Simon Maimela (1991a), and many other black theologians—then there are good grounds for a black theology without "the Book."

However, Maluleke, like Mofokeng, doubts whether "pragmatic and moral arguments can be constructed in a manner that will speak to masses without having to deal with the Bible in the process of such constructions." The Bible remains in the 1990s, and probably into the millennium, a "haven of the Black masses," and as long as it is a resource, it must be confronted, "precisely at a hermeneutical level" (Maluleke 1996, 14). Quite what Maluleke means by this is not yet clear, but he does offer some clues that emerge in his dialogue with the biblical hermeneutics of African women's theology (1997a, 14–16).

He agrees with Mercy Amba Oduyoye, who speaks with many African women (see below), when she says that the problem with the Bible in Africa is that "throughout Africa, the Bible has been and continues to be absolutized: it is one of the oracles that we consult for instant solutions and responses"

---

4. Randall Bailey puts the question slightly differently, but in a closely related sense, when he argues "that unless one is aware of one's own cultural biases and interests in reading the text and appropriating the tradition, one may be seduced into adopting another culture, one which is diametrically apposed to one's own health and well-being" (1998, 77).

(Oduyoye 1995, 174, cited in Maluleke 1997a, 15). "However," continues Maluleke, while many African biblical scholars and theologians are locked into a biblical hermeneutics that makes "exaggerated connections between the Bible and African heritage," "on the whole, and in practice, [ordinary] African Christians are far more innovative and subversive in their appropriation of the Bible than they appear" (1997a, 14–15). Although they "may mouth the Bible-is-equal-to-the-Word- of-God formula, they are actually creatively pragmatic and selective in their use of the Bible so that the Bible may enhance rather than frustrate their life struggles" (1996, 13). The task before black theology, then, is "not only to develop creative Biblical hermeneutic methods, but also to observe and analyze the manner in which African Christians 'read' and view the Bible" (1996, 15).

This task lies before us, and there are signs that it is being taken up (G. West 2004b). As the work of Mofokeng and Mosala has hinted, ordinary black South Africans have adopted a variety of strategies in dealing with an ambiguous Bible, including rejecting it (Mofokeng 1988, 40) and strategically appropriating it as a site of struggle (Mofokeng 1988, 41; I. Mosala 1986c, 184). But, as I have argued (G. West 2004b), in order to do justice to Maluleke's project in our postliberation context, much more detailed case studies need to be done. This descriptive task is as important as reappropriating Mosala's sociohistorical materialist biblical hermeneutics in our postliberation context. Much has changed, but much remains the same. As Alistair Kee recognizes, one of the most significant contributions of South African black theology has been in "tracing the origins of oppression back to interest and relations of power"—a contribution he attributes to Mokgethi Motlhabi (1973)—and in so doing rooting "oppression in the economic base of society," a contribution exemplified by Mosala (Kee 2006, 87) and given fresh analytical rigor by Sampie Terreblanche's work on South Africa's history and present as one characterized by economic inequality (2002). In summary, the biblical hermeneutic task after liberation is both polemical and descriptive of what actually happens with the Bible among African Christians.

From the perspective of black theology, then, there is still plenty on the agenda to do. Though our postliberation context has drawn many of our most productive black theologians into governmental and educational leadership, the trajectories established by black theology remain intact, though the capacity to develop them has been somewhat diminished.

African Theology

Black theology has always considered itself an African theology, though this has sometimes been contested by African theologians in the rest of the

African continent (for various typologies of African theologies, see Frostin 1988; Maluleke 1996; 1997a). When South African black theology emerged during the early 1970s, "some African theologians squarely declared that this new brand of theology [with its strong sociopolitical emphasis and biblical hermeneutic of suspicion] could not be regarded as a branch of African theology" (Frostin 1988, 176). Some black theologians "were equally sharp in their criticism of the narrowness of the first endeavors of African theology, finding it too pre-occupied with a static, pre-colonial culture" (Frostin 1988, 176). Desmond Tutu, among others, said that he feared that African theology "had failed to produce a sufficiently sharp cutting edge," arguing that African theology had to recover its prophetic calling and be more "concerned for the poor and the oppressed" (Tutu 1979, 490; see also Frostin 1988, 176).

Since South African black theology has been the predominant form of African theology in South Africa, I will not say too much more about African theology, except to point to a resurgence in the domain that is usually associated with African theology, namely, the sociocultural domain. As Maluleke's analysis of phase three black theology clearly shows, African religion and culture have moved from the periphery to the center within black theology after liberation. While liberation in 1994 ushered in substantial sociopolitical liberation, the ravages of centuries of colonialism and decades of apartheid on African religious and cultural life had hardly been addressed. Prioritizing the sociopolitical was a deliberate strategy of black theology, and though its responses to religio-cultural concerns may at times have seemed ambiguous at best (Chikane 1985; B. Mosala 1985; I. Mosala 1986b; Motlhabi 1986; Tlhagale 1985) to AIC practitioners and their associated theologians (Ngada 1985; J. De Gruchy 1985; Scofield 1985; Setiloane 1977), both black theology and contextual theology (Petersen 1995) proponents have returned to religio-cultural concerns after liberation.

From the perspective of biblical hermeneutics, the liberation of South Africa has ushered in sustained dialogue and hermeneutical exchange between the sociopolitical emphasis of South African biblical hermeneutics and the religio-cultural emphasis of African biblical hermeneutics to the north of us (Ukpong, 2000a; 2000b; G. West, 2004b; 2005b). Certainly the Limpopo River is no longer a barrier between these different emphases. Indeed, much that is innovative in African biblical scholarship derives its energy from the deliberate dialogue that is taking place in African biblical hermeneutics (see, e.g., West and Dube 2000).

CONTEXTUAL THEOLOGY

The South African apartheid state, with its overt theological foundation, demonized liberation theology and relentlessly detained anyone associated with such forms of theology. The term "contextual theology" was coined to subvert the apartheid state's efforts and became "an umbrella term embracing a variety of particular or situational theologies" in South Africa (Speckman and Kaufmann 2001a, xi). Unfortunately, however, because of a lack of sustained collaboration between Latin American–derived contextual theologies and black theology–derived liberation theologies (Cochrane 2001, 70–73; Maluleke 2001b, 368), "contextual theology" also came to be considered as another, separate, form of liberation theology.

In its particular form, contextual theology clusters around at least four poles. The first is the work of Albert Nolan, who drew on elements of Latin American liberation theology and recontextualized and popularized them in South Africa (Kaufmann 2001; see Nolan 1976; 1988). The second coordinating point for contextual theology has been the Institute for Contextual Theology (ICT), an institution with whom Nolan worked for many years but that included the contributions of a host of church leaders and Christian activists of all kinds (Cochrane 2001). At its inaugural conference in 1982, Albert Nolan characterized the vision of the Institute for Contextual Theology and in doing so provided a foundational understanding of contextual theology itself. The ICT, Nolan said,

> wants to do theology quite explicitly and consciously from within the context of real life in South Africa. It wants to start from the fundamentally political character of life in South Africa. It wants to take fully into account the various forms of oppression that exist in South Africa: racial oppression, the oppression of the working class and the oppression of women. And finally it wants to start from the actual experience of the oppressed themselves. (cited in Kaufmann 2001, 23–24)

The third pole around which contextual theology in its particular form has located itself is *The Kairos Document* (Kairos theologians 1986). *The Kairos Document* was important both as a process and a product. As a product, *The Kairos Document* articulated "theology" as contested. *The Kairos Document* identified and analyzed three contending theologies in South Africa: state theology, church theology, and prophetic theology. Briefly, state theology is the theology of the South African apartheid state, which "is simply the theological justification of the status quo with its racism, capitalism and totalitarianism. It blesses injustice, canonizes the will of the powerful and reduces the poor to passivity, obedience and apathy" (Kairos theologians

1986, 3). Church theology is in a limited, guarded, and cautious way critical of apartheid. "Its criticism, however, is superficial and counter-productive because instead of engaging in an in-depth analysis of the signs of our times, it relies upon a few stock ideas derived from Christian tradition and then uncritically and repeatedly applies them to our situation" (Kairos theologians 1986 9). *The Kairos Document* moves toward a prophetic theology, a theology that "speaks to the particular circumstances of this crisis, a response that does not give the impression of sitting on the fence but is clearly and unambiguously taking a stand" (Kairos theologians 1986, 18).

While *The Kairos Document* had a number of shortcomings, especially its failure to engage overtly with South African black theology, it did make a massive impact on how we thought about religion, particularly Christianity, during the struggle for liberation. Roundly and publicly condemned by the apartheid state, *The Kairos Document* was also rejected by many of the institutional churches, including the so-called English-speaking churches. The initial wave of responses from the churches questioned the process of the theological analysis contained in *The Kairos Document* (van der Water 2001, 36–43). Theology that was made in the streets rather than in ecclesiastically controlled sites could not be proper theology, they claimed. Subsequent responses were more considered, but their spokesmen (mainly) still found it difficult to acknowledge that the theology of the church had failed to read "the signs of the times," a key concept in *The Kairos Document*. That the public theology of the churches, Theology with a capital T, was merely a form of either state theology or church theology struck a theological nerve, and the value of the analysis remains relevant for our postliberation context.

The fourth pole around which contextual theology could be said to cluster is its most important contribution. As a liberation theology, theological process was of particular importance to contextual theology. Describing the process that produced *The Kairos Document*, Nolan emphasized that "it was not planned or foreseen by the staff of ICT. It simply happened as a result of ICT's method of doing theology." Nolan goes on to briefly characterize this method, saying that ICT "simply enables people to do their own theological reflection upon their own praxis and experience" by "bringing Christians together, facilitating discussion and action, recording what people say, and doing whatever research may be required to support the reflections, arguments and actions of the people" (Nolan 1994, 212). Using this method, two ICT staff members facilitated a process, beginning in Soweto "one Saturday morning in July 1985," "to reflect upon South Africa's latest crisis, the recently declared State of Emergency" (Nolan 1994, 213). This led to *The Kairos Document*, a theological document that was vividly and dramatically contextual: it came straight out of the flames of the townships in 1985. Those who had no experience of the oppression, the repression, the suffering and the struggles of the peoples in the townships at the time were not able to understand the faith questions that were being tackled there, let alone the answers. (Nolan 1994, 213)

Elaborating on the process or method of contextual theology, James Cochrane, one of the founders of the ICT and both a proponent of and commentator on contextual theology, argues that "one of the basic genres of contextual theology propagated in South Africa, preeminently by Young Christian Workers, Young Christian Students and Albert Nolan, comes in the guise of the tripartite command to 'see-judge-act'" (Cochrane 2001, 76). In practice, McGlory Speckman and Larry Kaufmann tell us, this method "meant starting with a social analysis, then proceeding to the reading of the [biblical] text and then to action" (Speckman and Kaufmann 2001b, 4). "Seeing" involves careful social analysis of a particular context at a particular time, what was referred to as "reading the signs of the times." "Judging," which precedes acting but which is based on having acted already, "requires that we analyse the conditions of oppression in our context. The 'acting' that follows is enriched twice over by the first two discursive moves of seeing and judging. We assume that our action is both better informed as a result, and more effective" (Cochrane 2001, 77).

Developed by Fr. Joseph Cardijn in the 1930s in Belgium, where he was working as a chaplain among factory workers (S. De Gruchy undated), "See-Judge-Act" has been adopted and adapted in a range of Third World contexts, including South Africa. For example, among the Young Christian Workers (YCW), young workers begin by analyzing the conditions experienced by themselves and their friends at work, at home and at school (See). They assess the situation "in the light of the Gospel" (Judge), then try to improve the situation by taking appropriate action to change conditions (Act; Stevens 1985, 25–26). While contextual theology after liberation has produced nothing as prophetically seminal as *The Kairos Document*, and while the ICT is more or less defunct, its "See-Judge-Act" methodology remains relevant in addressing the postliberation context. Contextual theology has lent its name and its methodology to a form of collaborative and emancipatory Bible study known as Contextual Bible Study (G. West 1993; 2000; 2003a; 2006). Operating within the methodological framework of "See-Judge-Act," Contextual Bible Study (using the Ujamaa Centre for Community Development and Research in the University of KwaZulu-Natal as its institutional base) utilizes a four-phase interpretive process. It begins with a particular oppressed community's social concern (e.g., unemployment) and the analysis that informs this concern, which are then brought into dialogue with a particular biblical text (usually an unfamiliar text or an unfamiliar textual unit). The interpretations generated in this initial encounter between context and text are recorded. The second phase of the process then moves into a close and careful literary engagement with the text, using a range of literary-type questions (e.g., Who are the characters in this text, and what do we know about them?). A related third phase then shifts into a sociohistorical engagement with the text, using resources the community already has and/or input from biblical scholarship. Importantly, this third phase flows organically from phase two and is therefore shaped by the questions the text and context generate for the community. The fourth and final phase returns the focus of the process to the community's own knowledge and resources, reengaging with the initial community concern. The process begins, then, with what we call "community consciousness," moves through literary and sociohistorical forms of "critical consciousness," and concludes with "community consciousness." Throughout this process there is a collaborative reading relationship between the socially engaged biblical scholar and the community.

In this form, then, contextual theology, though many of its founding practitioners and institutions are no longer operative, still offers important methodological resources for working with the Bible in oppressed communities after liberation.

Confessing Theology

Again, I will not only deal with this strand briefly, for there has been considerable overlap with black theology and/or contextual theology. What makes this form of liberation theology worth mentioning in its own right is its location within particular church traditions.

In 1982 the South African Dutch Reformed Mission Church (DRMC), a predominantly black church, declared that the situation confronting the churches in South Africa constituted a *status confessionis*—a state of confession—in which the very truth of the gospel was at stake. Specifically, the DRMC drafted a confession of faith, which was fully endorsed in 1986, that set the DRMC apart from its "mother" church, the mainly white Afrikaner Dutch Reformed Church (DRC). The grounds for this separation were that the DRC had given theological, moral, and biblical sanction to the apartheid government (Cloete and Smit 1984).

What became known as "The Belhar Confession" (Cloete and Smit 1984, 1–6) remains a significant document, as Steve De Gruchy has pointed out to me, forming the guiding vision of the Accra confession of the World Alliance of Reformed Churches. While those who worked within this theological strand may not have seen themselves doing liberation theology in this particular confessional struggle, many of them were also active in both black and contextual theology (see, e.g., Boesak 1984; J. De Gruchy 1986; De Gruchy and Villa-Vicencio 1983; Villa-Vicencio 1988) and certainly used liberation theology methodology in their work.

Following the publication of *The Kairos Document*, two more confessional documents responded to its challenge from within the black evangelical and black Pentecostal churches, respectively: "Evangelical Witness in South Africa" and "Relevant Pentecostal Witness" (LaPoorta 1990). Again, many of those who made these confessions were active in black theology and/or contextual theology (Balcomb 1993).

Integral to each of these confessional forms of liberation theology (as well as *The Kairos Document*) was a detailed engagement with the Bible, for each saw itself as contesting for the truth of the Bible over against its appropriation by the apartheid state and its alliance churches. What marked this strand of liberation theology was its refusal to abandon the institutional church to forces of racial discrimination and death and its refusal to allow forces of discrimination and death, even within the church, to control biblical interpretation. The latter remains a significant feature of South African biblical scholarship.

African Women's Theology

African women's theology in South Africa both partakes of and contests "feminist" theology (see Haddad 2000, 142–75). It partakes of "feminist" theology in that it shares family resemblances with other forms of "feminist" theology, but it contests the dominant white feminist version. In particular, African women's theology includes and integrates the categories of race, class, and culture with that of gender (Haddad 2000, 145–56). As Beverley Haddad argues, quoting Obioma Nnaemeka, "a major flaw of feminist attempts to tame and name the feminist spirit in Africa is their failure to define African feminism on its own terms rather than in the context of Western feminism" (2000, 154, citing Nnaemeka 1998, 6). This is why the work of African women, such as that produced by the Association of African Woman Scholars and the Circle of Concerned African Women Theologians (which emerged as a gender caucus from within EATWOT) have marked "an important step in the process of African women defining feminist issues in their own terms" (Haddad 2000, 154).

Within South Africa more specifically, the debate about "feminism" has been strongly shaped by our apartheid history, so that "race and class divides prescribe the parameters" (Haddad 2000, 156).

This has resulted in a schism between academic feminists who have tended
to be white, middle class women who have to a large extent been inactive
in the political liberation struggle, and activists deeply committed to this
struggle who have tended to be black and working class. Human rights and
political liberation issues, strong on the activist agenda, hardly featured on
the academic agenda which instead focused on equality as understood by
first world feminists. (Haddad 2000, 156)

Throughout the 1980s and 1990s and into the present, the apartheid legacy
"haunts South African women in their dialogue and in their activist and academic practice" (Haddad 2000, 157).

As in all Third World contexts, whether supported by published work or
not (Jayawardena 1986; Wieringa, 1995; 1998), so in South Africa women's
resistance to oppression has been an enduring part of the previous century,
though usually in racially divided forms (Haddad 2000, 157–61). In the 1950s
there were serious organizational attempts to constitute a nonracial women's
movement, which had some success, particularly those associated with the
nonracialism political agenda of the African National Congress (ANC). However, with the banning of the ANC and the Pan Africanist Congress (PAC) in
1960, much of this nonracial momentum was lost, only to be reconstituted
within the Mass Democratic Movement in the 1980s (Haddad 2000, 159–60).
This nonracial strand within the women's project in South Africa "laid the
foundation for the launching of the Women's National Coalition in 1992,"
which was itself given impetus by the unbanning of the ANC and PAC in
1990 (Haddad 2000, 162). However, though the Women's National Coalition
"was an attempt to draw women together from different backgrounds of race,
class, religion, and political persuasion," "racial tensions persisted" (Haddad
2000, 162; see also Fester 1997).

In the postapartheid context, South African women were deeply aware
that debates between women over "perceived interests and very real differences," the lack of unity and "apparent failure to identify and struggle together
against a single patriarchy have led to a perception that South African wom-
en's struggles lack a feminist consciousness" (Haddad 2000, 167, citing Kemp
et al. 1995, 133). Writing from the perspective of black women, Amanda
Kemp, Nozizwe Madlala, Asha Moodley, and Elaine Salo identified three central assumptions that had shaped and should constitute the women's project:

First, our identities as women are shaped by race, class, and gender, and
these identities have molded our particular experiences of gender oppression. Second, our struggles as feminists encompass the struggles for national
liberation from a brutal white state. Third, we have to challenge and transform Black patriarchies even though Black men have been our allies in the

fight for national liberation. These three concerns are of equal importance and are often inextricably linked so that a theoretical perspective that insists on isolating certain issues as feminist and others as not is alienating. (cited in Haddad 2000, 167; Kemp et al. 1995, 133)

The situation was not that different in the women's theological project in South Africa, as Haddad shows.

In the early stages of the women's theological project in the 1980s, white women drew their impetus from feminist theological thinking from the first world. Black women increasingly aligned themselves with women theologians from the third world and African American women who had begun theologising their experiences as "womanist" theologians. (Haddad 2000, 195)

Indeed, what can be considered the first feminist theology conference in South Africa, hosted by the Institute for Contextual Theology (ICT) in 1984 under the title "Women's Struggle in South Africa: Feminist Theology," was attended almost entirely by black women activists from church-based and community-based organizations (Haddad 2000, 201). Within days of this conference, another conference was hosted, in the same region, by the University of South Africa, then a bastion of white (somewhat progressive) Afrikaner scholarship, under the title "Sexism and Feminism in Theological Perspective," which was attended largely by white, middle-class, academic women (Haddad 2000, 201). These two racial trajectories continued well into the 1980s and 1990s.

An emerging strand with the work of black South African women in the 1980s, Haddad argues (2000, 202–4), was a theological gender critique of black patriarchy in general and black theology in particular (Jordaan 1987; 1991; Mncube 1984; B. Mosala 1984; 1986), a critique that has been at least partially heard by black male theologians (Maimela 1991b; Maluleke 1997b; Mandew 1991; I. Mosala 1992). Though consistently subsumed by the larger black struggle for political liberation, and though hesitant to foreground gender concerns immediately after liberation when African culture was being recovered, African women's theology has worked with a steady beat (to borrow a phrase from African American biblical scholarship; Bailey 2003).

Located differently, one white strand situated predominantly in white academic institutions and shaped by white feminist discourse and one black strand situated predominantly in parachurch and other activist organizations and shaped by black consciousness, the two main strands of South African "feminist" discourse have found a further dialogue partner in the Circle of Concerned African Women Theologians (henceforth the Circle). The Circle has not only provided an institutional forum for individuals from these two strands to collaborate; it has also reconfigured the discourse of African women's theology.

The Circle arose out of a demand by women within the Ecumenical Association of Third World Women to be heard and their presence taken seriously (Fabella and Oduyoye 1988; Haddad 2000, 197–99; Oduyoye 1983). Meeting as a group for the first time in 1989 in Ghana, African women theologians, including two South African representatives, established the Circle (Haddad 2000, 198; Oduyoye and Kanyoro 1990). Constituted to include African women from the whole continent and of all faiths and with a specific agenda to publish African women's theology (Oduyoye 1990, 48; Phiri 1997, 69), the Circle "has been instrumental in linking women's theology in South Africa with the rest of Africa" (Haddad 2000, 200). While the Circle has not obliterated the differences that have constituted South African women's theology, it has provided an opportunity for these differences and their implications for future "feminist" work together "to be confronted and dealt with more openly" (Haddad 2000, 201), albeit in an institutional environment that privileges academic discourse.

Within these broader frameworks of "feminist" discourse in South Africa, South African women's biblical hermeneutics has made a substantial contribution. Among the most significant are the work of Madipoane (Ngwana' Mphahlele) Masenya (who has advocated a particularly African women's form of biblical hermeneutics known as *Bosadi* hermeneutics (Masenya 1997; 2001b), Musa Dube (who though from Botswana has had a major impact on South African biblical hermeneutics and who has pioneered an African women's postcolonial feminist biblical hermeneutics; Dube 1997, 2000), Gloria Kehilwe Plaatjie (who has posed the question of how black women in South Africa "read the Bible in light of the post-apartheid Constitution that gives her equality?"; 2001, 117), Sarojini Nadar (who has used womanist and literary hermeneutical categories to develop ways of working with the Bible among oppressed women, particular those in the South African Indian community; 2001; 2003), and Makhosazana K. Nzimande (who has advocated for a postcolonial *Imbokodo* biblical hermeneutics in postapartheid South Africa; 2005). Indeed, I agree entirely with Tinyiko Maluleke when he says, "African women's theologies [and their accompanying biblical hermeneutics] represent the most creative dimension of African theology during our times. There is no doubt that, in the past twenty years, no dimension of Christian theology in Africa has grown in enthusiasm, creativity, and quality like women's theology" (Maluleke 2001a, 237).

Maluleke then goes on to contrast the energy and creativity of African women's theology with the other forms of (traditionally male-dominated) theology we have been discussing, saying:

> At the start of the new millennium, there is a palpable sense of fatigue in male theology. At one level there is a frivolous search for new metaphors and new labels with very little in-depth engagement with substantial issues of methodology. At another level, African male theology appears to have lost its passion, its compassion, and its prophetic urge. African theology is bewildered and confused by the dismantling of apartheid, increased globalization, the forceful emergence of issues of gender, ecology, and human rights, and the irruption of a new world order. Admittedly, some male theologians have been trying to respond theologically to the new situation. But many of these responses lack the freshness, enthusiasm, creativity, and sharpness that one senses in the writing of African women. (Maluleke 2001a, 237–38)

Indeed, says Maluleke, "it is a cruel piece of irony that the foundation of creativity—African women's theology—is the place into which tired and frivolous African male theology will not look!" It is not surprising, therefore, that "there is little real innovation and change in mainstream African male theology" (Maluleke 2001a, 238).

Maluleke not only neatly summarizes the state of liberation theologies in South Africa after liberation; he also introduces some of the contextual features our liberation theologies are now facing.

HIV-Positive Theology

I hesitate to designate HIV-positive theology as a liberation theology in its own right. HIV and AIDS is an issue that we confront in South Africa and so should perhaps take its place among the other issues we face, such as unemployment, violence against women, ecological degradation, racism, and globalization. However, just as each of these "issues" has a theology that locates it as its theological locus (respectively, liberation/contextual/black theology, feminist/womanist/African women's theology, eco-/oiko- theology, black/contextual theology, and African/postcolonial theology), so we might envisage an HIV/AIDS theology. However, this is premature, for no such theological movement with a theological agenda set by those who are HIV-positive has yet emerged in South Africa. Instead, HIV and AIDS has addressed us all, generating some of the most creative and innovative work from each of the three main strands of liberation theology discussed in this essay. Even the lethargy Maluleke finds in the historically male-dominated forms of liberation theology—black theology, African theology, contextual theology, and confessing theology—has been partially dispelled by the urgent need to engage with HIV and AIDS theologically.

Indeed, HIV and AIDS is demanding that we bring every resource forged in all of our liberation theologies to bear on this devastating feature of our postliberation reality (see all the essays in Dube and Kanyoro 2004; Dube and Maluleke 2001; Phiri, Haddad, and Masenya 2003; Phiri and Nadar 2006; as well as Byamugisha et al. 2002; Gennrich et al. 2004; Haddad 2003; 2005; Kgosikwena 2001; Masenya 2001a; Stooss 2002; G. West 2003b; West and Zengele, 2004; 2006), and we are discovering both the capacity and the constraints of our existing resources (see, e.g., G. West 2009). Clearly the Bible is and will continue to be central to the task of working with those who are HIV-positive to construct relevant and redeeming liberating theology, for it is both a problem and a solution.

Other Issues, in Conclusion

There is not the space here to go into any depth about the other issues that confront South African liberation theologies, except to say that unemployment, globalization, gender violence, as well as concerns about land,[5] crime, corruption, the environment, and sexual orientation ensure that the poor, marginalized, and oppressed remain with us. As long as they do, there remains the need for theologies of liberation after liberation, whatever names we give them. There is also not the space here to examine the biblical hermeneutical challenges that our engagement with these contextual realities generates, except to say that they remain centered around the relationship between and the respective resources of socially engaged biblical scholars and those poor, marginalized, and oppressed communities they work with.

Our new Constitution and the other related structures that constitute our postliberation South Africa are indeed signs of hope, but only if we continue to fight for them and against the macro-economic (Terreblanche 2002) and macho-patriarchal systems that constantly threaten to co-opt and/or subsume them. There will be no abundant life (John 10:10) as long as these systems are in place. Finally, while the struggles of the past have been incorporated in our Constitution, they have not been adequately incorporated into the public theology of our churches (G. West 2005a). This task, too, remains before us.

---

5. Alistair Kee argues that Mosala's distinction between "the black working class" and the black "peasantry" (I. Mosala 1989, 21), though Mosala himself does not develop this distinction, is crucial for black theology's task after liberation, because, says Kee, they live in different worlds, "characterised in turn by capitalism and feudalism." According to Kee, "[t]he end of apartheid has been irrelevant to this fundamental division" (2006, 94), a fundamental division that can only be addressed by dealing with "the question of land" (Kee 2006, 95, 95–97). Kee goes on in the pages cited to make a number of controversial statements about the task of black theology with respect to the black "peasantry," saying that "urban blacks" must "liberate them" and "*redeem* them" (Kee 2006, 96).

The various liberation theologies that have emerged from our South African context provide us with a foundational trajectory for our present and future biblical and theological work.

"It Should Be Burned and Forgotten!" Latin American Liberation Hermeneutics through the Eyes of Another

Hans de Wit

Introduction

It happened in 1983, in Belo Horizonte, Brazil, during a CEBI meeting,[1] when one of the biblical scholars took a chip of wood, held it above a burning fire basket and exclaimed: "Everything we do with the Bible at the level of training, research, study, courses, projects, commentaries, if it is not at the disposal of the groups at the base, there where the word of God enters life, it must be burned and forgotten"—and he let the wood chip fall into the fire. (Mesters 2006, 86)

This anecdote is the model for the self-image of Latin American liberation hermeneutics. Its background is the heat of the last few decades of the past century, the time of military dictatorships, the "irrupción" of the poor in theological consciousness and discourse. In this contribution we will look back on the formulation of a number of basic patterns for these hermeneutics from a European perspective. What was it that biblical scholars had to forget and to burn as quickly as possible? To the benefit of what? Hermeneutics that are so radical in tone and design make themselves vulnerable. When we review these hermeneutics, the fate of which is so closely connected with the *effect* of reading the Bible, with praxis and social transformation, the question of how long its pretensions hold up is unavoidable. Which of its basic principles have also found response outside of Latin America? How was its reception in the Western context? What corrections can be made that originate from its own historic effect?

---

1. Centro de Estudos Bíblicos, Belo Horizonte, Brazil.

Conversion

The surge and development of Latin American liberation hermeneutics is a complex and multicolored process spanning three decades. There are various geographical focal points, differences in tone, pretensions, exegetical method, and depth (Comblin 1985; Gorgulho 1993; Richard 1982; 1988; Schwantes 1988; Croatto, 1978; 1981a; 1981b; 1994; 2002; see also de Wit 2002, 217–67.) What first asserts itself in a militant tone is later nuanced and softened (Richard 1988; 1998; Croatto 2002). Only some of the Bible scholars active in Latin America feel at home with these hermeneutics. The birth of this "mother of all genitive hermeneutics" bears the characteristics of a conversion history. It is fed by two penetrating moments of experience. On the one hand, there is the shocking confrontation with the intense suffering of the people and the powerlessness of the exegesis. "When confronted with the life of the suffering people, you don't know what to say as an exegete, you are forced to be silent.... become humble and begin to reflect" (Mesters 1977, 13–19). On the other hand, there is the discovery of a "new hermeneutical space" (Richard 1998, 275–77): the meeting between "the people and the Bible." In the initial phase, the enchantment with this encounter is expressed in a endless series of variations by Latin American biblical scholars (see de Wit 1991; 2002). Biblical scholars were confronted with what has been called *visceral memories*: memories of deep suffering, of innocent *and* faithful people whose blood was shed by other people. A process of "remembering" was set into motion over the past few decades in Latin America that has also been of essential importance to biblical studies. Fragmented experiences of torture, oppression, and disappearances became a coherent collective memory, fed by the dynamic relation with analogous memories found in the Scriptures. This process might be compared with what happened with the survivors of the concentration camps. Gérard Namer describes how the survivors of the camps were not capable of constructing a coherent whole of memories of their experiences until groups of survivors were formed. The fragmented, unspeakably traumatic experience of the camps became a coherent, articulable entirety via these groups (Namer 1987). Something like this appears to also have happened in circles of the Latin American Bible movement, both at the academic level and at that of the ordinary readers in their communities of faith (de Wit 2006).

The confrontation with this open suffering is the beginning of a completely new and extremely fertile and creative period. An overwhelming quantity of new publications appears, as well as new series of commentaries and new exegetical journals. New Bible centers are founded, new methods of reading the Bible in the basic groups are developed, people all over the continent are collecting the most impressive examples of grass-roots reading of the Bible. There is a need for constant and penetrating reflection on the role of the exegete in processes of social transformation, on the one hand, and the meaning of grass-roots reading of the Bible for exegesis, on the other.

The surge and development of the liberation hermeneutics are character-ized by an enormous feeling of urgency and optimism. The key terms are "the new humanity," "the great odyssey of *the oppressed people*" (Croatto 1981b, 10), "liberation," and "exodus." The conversion is radical, the tone fierce, the contrasts massive.

People

The *people* concept (Spanish *pueblo*, Portuguese *povo*) is a fundamental actor in liberation hermeneutics. *The people* is the new subject of these herme-neutics. Not too vague or diffuse, as happens so often in reader-response criticism, but concrete, to be encountered in living and suffering communities of faith where Bible and life are bound together. Popular reading of the Bible (*lectura popular de la Biblia*) becomes a source for hermeneutical reflection. It is something new and unprecedented when Bible scholars take a systematic look at what this large and *neglected* group of ordinary readers, mostly poor people, does with biblical texts. This is not yet happening anywhere else on this scale and with this intensity. The new commentaries, monographs, and articles in periodicals that began to appear in the 1980s made it clear to what extent biblical scholars were trying to make the perspective and questions of the communities their own in their theoretical praxis.[2] A study by Gersten-berger makes it clear that the differences between what occupied the minds of Latin American and European Bible scholars in those years were gigantic (Gerstenberger 1984).

Scripture

What *hermeneutical* aspects of that foundational and fundamental experi-ence—the encounter with the people—moved Latin American Bible scholars to a radical reorientation of their scholarly praxis? First of all, I identify the overwhelming confrontation with what Wilfred Cantwell Smith has called the most fundamental characteristic of *Scripture*, to wit, Scripture not as an object but as a process, as a human activity, Scripture as an expression of a special

---

2. See the central themes of *RIBLA* 1 ("Lectura popular de la Biblia"), 2 ("Violencia, poder y opresion"), and 30 ("Economía y Vida Plena").

relation between people, readers, and a text that is experienced as beneficent, as fundamentally good (W. Smith 1993, 232), Scripture as the surrender to a worldview, passed on to us not via philosophical or theological discourse but via a *story* (Ricoeur 1998, xvi).

A scriptural attitude becomes manifest in this surrender, especially noticeably in *communitarian* Bible reading, so characteristic for grass-roots reading of the Bible. Scriptural attitude is an attitude of trust, of recognition that this Scripture is a window to goodness, justice, and truth. The Bible as a window, as a breath of air, as a new perspective—this is what one encounters in the communities of faith (García Gutiérrez 1983, 29–30).

An ensuing component is praxis. The Bible and life are bound to each other in grass-roots reading practice, and there is a circularity that is fed from concrete life. Here we come across the importance of the praxeological dimension of the process of understanding. When Mesters totals up the balance of twenty years of Bible movement (*movimiento bíblico*) in Latin America, he points out this dimension:

> The Bible appears to be a spice, suitable for every meal. People use the Bible for everything....union conflicts and organizing strikes, building chapels and barracks together, for criticism of the clergy and their own lives, political and party meetings, the struggle for land and the defense of the Indian, letters to support people and demonstrations against injustice, processions with saints and protest marches...commemorative journeys and pilgrimages, workers strife and pickets at the gates of factories, hunger strike and resistance against the armed mercenaries (*pistoleiros*) of inhuman big land owners. (Mesters 1988, 2–3)

The *hermeneutical* implications of what just has been described dominated the hermeneutics of Mesters, Croatto, Schwantes, Richard, Pixley, and many others beginning in the 1980s (de Wit 1991; 2002). People are starting to reflect profoundly on the hermeneutical importance of "ordinary readers," the *foreground* of texts, the hermeneutical circulation, the praxis and the question of what exegetes can contribute to social transformation and liberation.

People as an Attitude

Before we analyze these hermeneutical subjects any further, we must first reflect a bit on the concept *people*. Anyone who sits at the feet of the people understands the enchantment of Latin American hermeneuts. However, *people* is an ambiguous and complex concept. Mesters writes, "I cannot say what I mean by 'people,' because only those who look at a tree from a distance can describe it. One who sits on one of the tree's branches is only capable of describing the scent of its leaves or the taste of its fruit" (1977, 27).

The concept is so heavily charged that it becomes impossible to handle and takes on reductionist and thus also normative features. Latin American biblical scholars should have used the hermeneutical dimension of the concept much more and should have exploited its power much more as an *attitude* toward the text: people *as a way of reading*, spontaneous, focused on appropriation, prefigurative, associative, like a game (Ricoeur 1986). A way of reading from the wounded heart, vulnerable and fragile in the face of the power and the systematics of exegesis (de Wit 2004c: 8–9). In liberation hermeneutics, *people* stands for the poor, for a social class, and is thus a descriptive concept. The concept quickly becomes normative. "The poor are the only ones who can save the Bible," says Pablo Richard (1988, 18). "The best qualified interpreters are, in our experience, workers and impoverished farmers," writes Milton Schwantes (1987, 8). This creates a peculiar circular reasoning that becomes particularly clear when one realizes that "people" has actually also become a reductionist concept. If one takes a good look, one sees that not all the poor belong to the group of most qualified interpreters, but rather the poor who match the profile of the ideal reader the hermeneutician cherishes. The poor Latin American hermeneuticians foster in particular are poor belonging to the Roman Catholic Church, participating in grass-roots communities, now politically aware and willing to participate in processes of social change (de Wit 1991). Many poor on the continent do not match this profile. What happens here is that this circle again returns the power to the exegete, robs "people" as a *uncontrollable* moment in the interpretation process *as opposed to* the exegesis of its hermeneutical power, and exposes the first signs of a hermeneutics that is little inclined to confrontation.

How is the turn to the people, which seems to have been halted halfway along its course, elaborated in liberation hermeneutics?

Hermeneutic Revolution

The reflection on the reading practice of the poor is given the predicate *liberation hermeneutics* by Pablo Richard. It is intended to be a militant hermeneutic. Its terms correspond with the conversion experience and are socially charged: struggle, conflict, rift, hermeneutic revolution (Richard 1988, 8–9; Silva Gotay 1981, 137–81). What is one breaking with? With all those mechanisms—fundamentalism, concordism, and historicism (Richard 1988, 19)—that are intended to chain the text to the past and strip from it all its current liberating force. One breaks with all those interpretations that deem processes of actualization, of current application, of social changes and prophetic protest against inequality and poverty as contamination. One provides the reading practice of the poor with theory formation. This is assisted by insights from modern European hermeneutics. The core question of liberation hermeneutics, as formulated by the Argentinean exegete Croatto, is how the text can be cut loose from its past and become liberating *message* (*mensaje*) for the oppressed again. In classic hermeneutics, Croatto observes, the biblical text is considered as a *depositum* that is definitely exhausted in its first production of a meaning (*producción de sentido*). However, texts also have a *foreground*. In the interpretation process, the text is liberated from the ballast of the situation-specific reference and remains as a polysemic, linguistic, and fundamentally open structure that is projected "forward" and demands manifestation of its *réserve-de-sens* (Croatto 1994, 33). This *réserve-de-sens* of the text is always made operational from a certain praxis. Each interpretation is made from a certain place and from a certain perspective. Hermeneutic circulation is created because events and texts from the past become important due to their "historic effect," meaning their effect on the practice of a certain group of people. It is not a causal relation between the original event and its interpretation, but rather a sense or meaning relation. The original event is interpreted and continued in a new event that does not absorb the original but rather considers it as foundational (*fundante*). The events in the past and their interpretation shed light on new events, on the basis of which the original events gradually acquire a "foundational nature" (Croatto 1985b, 77–78). From the background of Croatto's description of the hermeneutical circulation one can hear Ricoeur: "It is in interpreting the Scriptures in question that the community in question interprets itself. A kind of mutual election takes place here between those texts taken as foundational and the community we have deliberately called a community of reading and interpretation" (Ricoeur 1998, xvi).

The more new events start to become part of the meaning of the original event, the higher the accumulation of meaning that takes place with respect to the original event. However, at the same time meaning is also enriched in the reverse order. The meaning of the practice out of which the text is read is enriched by the original event. The *praxis* of the current reader is what enables the manifestation of the *réserve-de-sens* of a text and its subsequent hermeneutic circulation. "The key to reading texts is the praxis" (Croatto 1984, 222). "The correlation between the historic effect [*efecto histórico*] of the event and the effect of meaning [*efecto-de-sentido*] of the text is very tight and is prolonged in the relation between the praxis and reading of a tradition or a text" (Croatto 1985a, 61).

Thus the interpretation process of biblical texts should not be limited to the exploration of the historic meaning of the text, Severino observes, but should concentrate just as much on how the surplus of meaning of the text is made operational from the praxis in the interpretive communities. Croatto summarizes, "The not said [*lo no dicho*] of the said [*de lo 'dicho'*] of the text is said [*es dicho*] in the contextualized interpretation. This is the core of the hermeneutic act," (1981a, 55, 62; 1994, 75–76).

This formulates an elementary insight into liberation hermeneutics. "The not said of the text" that is found in the contextualized reading is not just a free-floating new meaning or a parasite on a flower; no, it *reorients, remodels, enriches the original*. It is precisely for this reason that biblical scholars must also be concerned with how the *foreground* of the text is explored in communities of faith.

The Problem of Praxis

The *praxis* component—of essential importance in liberation hermeneutics—deserves further analysis. Praxis is not a flat activism in liberation hermeneutics, as it is so often regarded in superficial criticism. In liberation hermeneutics, praxis is the space within which the humanizing and liberating potential of biblical texts is explored. Praxis is a continual process of searching, of transformation, of continually deciding, choosing, judging, and determining who we are and who we shall be—not as a private or an individual act but as a public and communal activity (Chopp 1986, 141–42). Hermeneutically speaking, praxis is the moment of appropriation where reading becomes an *event*, when the text is read as a letter addressed to you—the moment defined by Gadamer as the core of the interpretation process (1986, 301–2).

Chopp's concept of praxis has given rise to a great deal of criticism on liberation hermeneutics. The most significant reasons for this are the fact that continuing reflection on and varying interpretation of the concept has been involved (McGovern 1990, 32–35; van Nieuwenhove 1991, 199–202), that it sometimes seems as if all the themes from Christian tradition are classified under (liberation) praxis (de Wit 1991, 341–42), and that there is some hesitation among Latin American theologians to further analyze the praxis of the people since they have the feeling of treading on holy ground and running the risk of easily desecrating the mysticism surrounding "the people." The fact that the liberation hermeneuticians have been confronted with the demand for further definition of the concept of praxis mainly has to do with the fact that liberation hermeneutics, as a militant hermeneutics, also had to make a choice here and intends to speak of a *qualified* praxis. This involves liberation praxis as the access to the kerygma of the biblical texts.

> The texts that use liberation as a theme and are so easily condensed in the motif of the exodus have no better reader than the oppressed seeking their liberation.… the oppressed give us, from their praxis of liberation, the "not said" of what is said in the text, or rather its current kerygmatic value. (Croatto 1987, 113)

However, the concept of praxis becomes a problem when a certain *previously* qualified praxis is elevated to a normative factor in the interpretation process. If praxis is an open concept and points to a process of searching and feeling, "judging, and determining who we are and who we shall be," how is it possible that only one previously conditioned praxis can be considered as a norm for authenticity in interpretation? Does this not thereby give the hermeneutic circulation a closed and strictly utilitarian nature? Is it not reduced to finding the meaning that serves? Is it still possible to examine the hermeneutic circulation itself?

I see at least two pitfalls looming here: the empirical pitfall and the pitfall of successful *use* of the text. By empirical pitfall, I mean that, in much of what is written about the relation between reading and praxis, biblical texts and their effect, the suggestion is hidden that what one claims about it is based on empirical investigation. I wish to make a bold statement with respect to this: we hardly know anything about the effect of reading biblical texts on behavior, on praxis, on the awakening of people, and we know so little about it because we undertake no empirical studies. I think that we hit here upon one of the greatest aporia in all our statements about the effect of the Bible on social change, revolution, liberation. More than any place on earth, an impressive quantity of examples of grass-roots reading of the Bible has been collected in Latin America—fascinating, enriching, important. However, to the best of our knowledge, no real empirical research is being done on the question of exactly how readers make their way from interpretation to praxis and back again.

I quoted Carlos Mesters, who totals up the balance of twenty years of Bible movement in Latin America. In his initial words, Mesters refers to the second pitfall, the one of successful use of the Bible by the people: "The Bible seems like a spice, suitable for every meal. The people *use* the Bible for everything" (Mesters 1988, 2, emphasis added). The pitfall becomes clear when one joins Umberto Eco and others in detecting the difference between the *interpretation* and the *use* of texts (Eco 1997). Eco refers here to a tremendously complex and hardly ever empirically and systematically addressed relationship or perhaps even nonrelationship. *Use* of a text—action as result of a reading process—is not the same as a rhetorical reading: the way texts persuade or convince readers by means of their argumentative structure. "Use" many times takes place without any hermeneutical or interpretative mediation, just because of the status of the Bible as cultural heritage, fetish, exceptional object, holy book, and so on. We may think of the many instances in which the Bible as an *object* or as a *product*—its paper, its ink, the book as book, its covers, its images, its slogans, its magic—is used for health, success, bewitching, war, domination, oaths, conversion, and prosperity. Use is not always a natural sequel of interpretation; frequently use and interpretation contradict each other, do not coincide, are mutually excluding.

Summarizing, one could say that the way in which people and praxis are defined in liberation hermeneutics has a reductionist nature; it is focused on a wished-for praxis and takes little account of the fact of the irreducible plurivocity of texts. Indeed, it is rare that several communities *and* praxes are not engendered by one and the same text. In this sense, the plurivocity of the text and a plurality of readings are connected phenomena. Hence the text is not something unilinear, something it could be in virtue of the finality instituted by the presumed intention of the author, but multidimensional, as soon as it is not taken as something to be read on just one level but on several levels at the same time by a historical community marked by heterogeneous interests (Ricoeur 1998, xxx). The challenge in store for liberation hermeneutics here is how it can arrive at a liberating reading of the Bible without reducing the other, the other reading, the other praxis to an enemy a priori.

Exegete and Exegesis

Recognition of the hermeneutic competence of the people requires redefining the academic scholarly opinion of the task and rationality of exegesis. This has been expressed in all manner of ways since the 1980s. Exegetes are called upon to join the people and develop new methods. Not only the theology, but also the exegesis is a second step (*segunda lectura*). "The poor had to use all their spiritual and liberating power to salvage exegesis and the professional exegetes," Richard writes (1988), while reviewing the developments. The criticism of Latin American exegetes, only moderated somewhat at a later stage, is primarily focused on the historical-critical methods of exegesis. This is obvious for biblical scholars who are so interested in the *foreground*, the people, and current, liberating rereading of the text. Croatto summarizes the core of their criticism as follows:

> Those who wish to limit themselves to exploration of the primary explicit meaning of a text begin to hide the possibilities of the text (*ocultar*); the text is "specified" in such a way that it becomes rigid. One context is eternalized, namely the one that shaped the text. In other words: the text is exhausted. (Croatto 1978, 16)

No, in liberation hermeneutics more is demanded from the "ideal" exegete than an obsession with the past. Nothing less is demanded than an explicit contribution to the solution of the problems of the poor: "The exegete must be more than the gardener explaining to the hungry man how the tree may bear fruit, he must provide food for this person" (de Wit 1991, 260).

RELEVANCE

The subject under discussion here is the well-known problem of pertinence and relevance in exegesis (C. Boff 1980). The situation in which liberation hermeneutics is developing requires relevant results from the exegesis. It requires results that can relieve the pain and suffering of so many, that offer hope for a new future that can put an end to repression and exclusion. It is true that, from an epistemological point of view, there is not one single *scholarly* reason why exegetes should not be engaged in all that is now considered socially relevant. Just listening to the experiences of the poor and the willingness to have the exegetic agenda decided by their questions and perspective has resulted in an unimaginable wealth of new publications and insights into biblical texts in Latin America over the past few decades. This happened especially in places where people were convinced of the complexity of the relation between the old text and the new context, used not only the sociological method, and were modest in formulating the relevance of the results of the exegesis.

RELEVANCE FOR, NOT OF

However, the relation between pertinence (the questions stemming from the discipline itself) and relevance has not always been balanced. Schwantes's statement, which serves as the title for this contribution, is very revealing in this context. What must be burned and forgotten is "All that is not at the service of the basic groups, where the word of God enters life." But how can one determine what will eventually be and what will not be at the service of the basic groups within the space of *exegetical practice* itself? Could Gunkel, when developing his *formgeschichtliche Methode*, ever have imagined that this would at one time be embraced by Brazilian exegetes and basic groups seeking their liberation? No, the relation between the people and exegesis has not only been productive but all too often also suffocating and has led to stagnation and dependence.

This is evident in the use of methods. No matter how much about "rift" and the search for new methods has been spoken among Latin American exegetes, something like a specific Latin American exegetical method does not exist (de Wit 1991), and this may not be necessary either. My opinion is that the most impressive contributions to (Latin American) exegesis are produced where the biblical texts are questioned for their current relevance via a *plurality* of methods (e.g., Croatto 1997; Krüger 2003; Andiñach 2006; Wegner 1998). In places where *only* the sociological method is used—from the historical-critical arsenal and still the most popular one among Latin America liberation exegetes (!)—there is a risk of reducing the interpretation process even further, namely, to finding simple socioeconomic contrasts.

Too close a relation between the people and exegesis may paralyze exegesis. The people may require the exegesis to supply things that it does not have available, for example, "Evoking, generating, articulating and orienting the actions of the poor," as José Comblin would like (1985, 10–12). Here occurs what I would like to call the *epistemological pitfall*. The epistemological pitfall is probably the most frequently occurring pitfall in the discussion about exegesis and current praxis. This involves the insight that relevance is not an issue *of* the exegesis but *for* the exegesis. The extent to which application or appropriation of biblical texts is successful *now* is not a standard for the quality of the exegesis. The criterion on the basis of which is decided whether an exegetical investigation may be put into motion or has been "useful" cannot be the *praxis liberadora* of the people. The "benefit" or "usefulness" of a biblical commentary cannot be read from the degree to which this provides directives for the praxis, as Comblin would like. Such a presentation of issues does not take the epistemological statute of exegesis as a discipline into account. It is important to realize that neither the political destination of its results nor the social "place" of the exegete nor its thematic relevance decides the quality of the exegesis. The theories and instruments used by exegesis indicate the limits of its competence. The competence of exegesis applies to the text that was handed down to us. It intends to produce knowledge with respect to this text. This competence, however, does not naturally extend to the current sociopolitical reality. Not because the exegete is an exegete does he or she also have sufficient knowledge to give an adequate verdict on current economic, social, or political questions. Analytical reading of biblical texts, an activity intended to avoid the Scriptures functioning as a *Scriptura ex machina* (C. Boff), cannot be characterized as betrayal of the real or current meaning of texts. Biblical texts not only demand to be understood through appropriation but also demand to be explained by analytical approach. Furthermore, one has to ask if the study of part of a text that exposes the contours of the praxis that forms the basis for this text will be capable of putting an analogue praxis in motion by means of a *theoretical Putsch* (C. Boff 1980, 347, 350).

Permit me to show another result of too close an entanglement between *lectura popular* and exegesis. The terms *hermeneutic rift* and *hermeneutic fight* make it clear that a plurality of readings is not only undesirable in the most militant expressions of liberation hermeneutics but also unacceptable. This leads to the next pitfall, which I call the *pitfall of ownership* and clarify what I mean on the basis of a phrase by Richard: "The only ones who can save the Bible are the poor, because the people have deep faith. This salvation of the Bible by the faith of the poor is called 'hermeneutic struggle'" (Richard 1988, 18; de Wit 1991, 219–22). The argument, which can also be found in other genitive hermeneutics, is clear. The Bible is not a principally open text, accessible to everyone who can read, but produced by the poor and subsequently stolen by the dominant class. Today's poor appropriate what is theirs. In summary, the Bible is the book of the poor, and today's poor are the best interpreters of biblical texts (Richard 1982). The hermeneutic implication of this reasoning is that in the interpretation process no more space is offered for a critical dialogue between two *different* attitudes with respect to the text: explanation and understanding, exegesis and application. The exegete is required to be unconditionally faithful to the current "owners" of the biblical texts, the poor, who in fact frequently represent a *construct* that expresses the longings of liberation hermeneuticians themselves. Our answer to the question of ownership and which reader may do what with which biblical text can be short: texts have readers, texts have authors, but texts do not have owners. The claim of ownership does no justice to the polysemy of texts; it makes insufficient distinction between the message and the messenger and prevents the liberating potential of texts from completely unfolding.

The big challenge in store for liberation hermeneutics here is the question of how one can escape from this ghetto position. What can be the role of an exegete who really wants to serve the poor out of his or her own responsibility and space? Does the *fact* of the plurality of readings distract from liberation or lead to it? Many of the terms used in liberation hermeneutics—rift, fight, revolution—have to do with power. How can liberation exegetes become sensitive to their own power grabs and their own cultural definition?

DIFFERENCES

Liberation hermeneutics has also been influential outside Latin America. African and Asian genitive hermeneutics show traces of it. Its direct influence in the European context appears to have remained limited. For the German situation, the term *Nicht-Verhältnis* has been used to describe the relationship between Latin American and German biblical scholars (Huning 2005, 102–8). Latin American biblical scholars were blamed for *fundamentalist-*

ischer Unmittelbarkeit and the use of unscientific methods. For other Western European countries like the Netherlands, the same *Nicht-Verhältnis* can be found. A lot of reasons for this may be adduced. At a more formal level, one can think of the language question, access to international publication circles, and demarcation of disciplines in the theological curriculum—a great deal was left to practical theology and pedagogy of religion theory (Huning 2005, 100–101). However, the most significant reason is found in the area of social-cultural differences and the place of the Bible in the Western European context. Creating "a new hermeneutic space" in the European context, in keeping with liberation hermeneutics, requires that these differences be taken into account.

A Different Bible

Someone who comes from the Brazilian CEBs and looks at the place of the Bible in the Dutch and perhaps more general Western European context, gets an ice-cold bath. In order to describe the gigantic differences in context—something too often forgotten by Latin American biblical scholars—I will pass on a few data from a recent study on the possession and the use of the Bible in the Netherlands, the context in which I work. Such studies can set us with our feet on the ground and guard us from exaggerated ideas and romanticism (Stoffels 2004). One could say that those who read the Bible in the Netherlands are not the poor; the poor in the Netherlands do not read the Bible, but, if they do read religious texts at all, they read the Qur'an. Bible readers are chiefly to be found among a highly educated, Protestant minority. It seems that all those issues that appear essential for the "success" of contextual reading of the Bible in Latin America are lacking completely here.

The *statistics* offer the following picture. *Possession* and *use* of the Bible in the Netherlands is decreasing sharply. In the report the term "Bible fatigue" is used. People in the Netherlands read the Bible less all the time. Only 13 percent of the Dutch population regularly read the Bible. The number of Bible-reading Roman Catholics looks poor in comparison to even this number: only 8 percent of Roman Catholics in the Netherlands read the Bible at least once per week (Protestants 50 percent). From a hermeneutic point of view, it seems to apply that the Western Dutch secular and modernistic culture leaves an impressive mark on reading practices. The Bible suffers from a big image problem in the Dutch context: 87 percent of those who do not read the Bible do not want to read the Bible any longer. How one reads the Bible, what is regarded as its central message, the process of identification or appropriation, in what way the Bible is directive for the praxis of the readers—all that seems to be defined in a Western way. The Bible is not thought of as a current book (only 18 percent of the respondents); the Bible is a guideline for how to act to not even a quarter of those interviewed and a source of inspiration in daily life to even fewer respondents. What is called communal or "communitarian" reading in Latin America rarely takes place in the Western Dutch context: nearly half of the Bible readers read the Bible by themselves, individually; only 15 percent participate in some discussion group or another. When the question is asked why one reads the Bible and what is considered its central message, no one ever actually mentions themes such as social transformation, an end to inequality in the world, struggle or sociopolitical commitment, change, or liberation. Themes that are especially appealing to people are security, salvation, Jesus as the truth, Jesus as the light in the world, how one should live, a handhold, and a lesson for life.

The Project

What form can loyalty to liberation hermeneutics assume in the European context in this situation? What form can a project assume that, in keeping with liberation hermeneutics, is intended to involve the Bible and Bible readers in Europe in situations of manifest suffering, inequality, and globalization and avoid the pitfalls of liberation hermeneutics at the same time? Such a form was sought in the international project "Through the Eyes of Another: Intercultural Reading of the Bible" (de Wit, Jonker, Kool, and Schipani 2004). This is an international empirical project in which more than 125 groups from more than twenty-five different countries participated, read the same biblical text (John 4), and started to discuss its meaning. More than 70 percent of the participants considered themselves as belonging to the lower classes of society. The core question of the project was: What happens when Christians from radically different cultures and situations read the same Bible story and start talking about it with each other? Can joint, intercultural reading of Bible stories result in a new method of reading the Bible and communication of faith that is a catalyst for new, transborder types of dialogue and identity formation?

The *process* consisted of two basic phases, described in a protocol that was available to all groups. The text was first read in the intimacy of the small group. Reading was communitarian and done in the way participants were accustomed to read a Bible story. The group had the power. A report was made of every meeting. In addition to a presentation of the interpretation of the text, the reports also contain information about the group: the context of participants, personal information, their church backgrounds. Sometimes the reports contain attachments: photos of the group, videos of the meetings, pictures of the Samaritan woman, or songs composed especially for the occasion. The reports were then sent to the central coordination in Amsterdam and translated. On the basis of reports that were received and a number of previously established criteria, each group was linked to a partner group, and reports were sent to partner groups. Next, the *second* phase began. The group read the story once again, now through the eyes of the partner group. What were the similarities? What were the differences? What role did culture play in the reading? Could anything be learned from the partner group? Did people discover things in the text that had not been noticed at first? Did a change of perspective take place? A report was also made of the second phase. The group concluded the second phase with a response to the partner group, usually a letter.

In the *third* phase, the group responded to the responses of the partner group, looked back over the entire process, and reflected on the question of whether they wished to have further contact. An international group of scholars analyzed the more than three thousand pages of empirical material via the grounded-theory method (de Wit 2004a, 395–436).

In the project, which was designed by an international group, traces of elementary insights and emphases of liberation hermeneutics are clearly visible. The project focuses on the question of what "ordinary readers" do with Bible texts. Their reading practice is not regarded as a contamination process but as a hermeneutic reservoir, as a source; this focuses great attention on processes of appropriation and recontextualization, the *foreground* of the text; the participating groups read the text communally; "life," the direct context of the readers—often one of poverty, globalization, and exclusion—is involved in the discussion about the meaning of the text; narrativity plays an important role: groups can read their lives in the light of the story. However, the process also contains all kinds of elements that could count as a corrective for liberation hermeneutics. The weight of culture in interpretation processes is turned into a theme, and the cultural definition of interpretations is problematized in the interaction between groups; the underlying premise is not a rift, nor do we attempt to find homogeneous groups but rather to test the hermeneutic significance of confrontation; yes, confrontation is *organized*, is *sought for* between rich and poor, between different church backgrounds and social status, sex, level of education, cultural setting. Exegesis and scholarly reflection are a *second* act. Neither a dominant professional reader nor an "organic exegete" who could have an effect on the process is involved; empirical investigation is made of the question of what factors actually mediate in processes of actualization of texts, of the relation between reading and praxis.

LIBERATION HERMENEUTICS REVISITED "THROUGH THE EYES OF ANOTHER"

What do we see when we look back on liberation hermeneutics from its own *Wirkungsgeschichte*, of which the project Through the Eyes of Another is a part? What holds up, what correctives may apply? I will cite a few results from the empirical investigation.

The people. The fight for the right of ordinary readers for their own place in the understanding process is a crucial contribution to modern biblical scholarship from liberation hermeneutics. When leafing through the hundreds of pages of "popular reading" of John 4, it becomes clear why liberation hermeneutics is putting up such a strong fight. Those who attentively look at what ordinary readers do with biblical texts are struck by their spirituality, devotion, by the added value of religious texts—in brief, they *see* what Cantwell Smith means when he speaks about Scripture as process. Readers approach the text full of expectations. In the *communal* or *communitarian* Bible-reading process an interaction, indeed, a hermeneutic circulation, is created between the text and the readers that focuses on life, innovation, healing. This understanding from the wounded heart stands out as fragile and delicate, in contrast to the activity of professional readers. The effect on ordinary readers of dealing with the Bible in a scholarly way is often devastating, not because this is intended but because the instruments used to approach the text are so different: power and knowledge as opposed to expectation and hope. Ordinary readers often clam up like an oyster if any "experts" come forth in the groups. The slow, careful approach of the scholar is often difficult to understand in places where the quest for life is urgent.

The empirical material also gives rise to a significant nuancing of the people concept in liberation hermeneutics. We had our suspicions confirmed that the concepts of "people" or "ordinary reader" derive their strength from their *hermeneutic* dimension, as *attitude*, as a *way of understanding*, not from a socioeconomic dimension. No significant correlations were found between social status (e.g., poverty) and the interpretation *method* or the *result* of reading a biblical text. "People" is a way of reading, multifaceted, fascinating, and not only to be found in the southern hemisphere among the poor. As such, "people" is also a *quality* of the interpretation process that must be cherished in its multifacetedness and not be reduced to a *desirable* effect of the hermeneutic act. There is a dialectic relation between "people" and professional reading as spontaneous versus critical, prefigurative versus analytic. Indeed, the original, the model, is reoriented in the popular reading and its *réserve-de-sens* is explored in a way that may give professional readings something to think about and, yes, subject it to serious criticism. Spontaneous interpretations bring out meanings *of* the text that cannot be found in any commentary.

Exclusion of ordinary Bible readers, so common in modern biblical scholarship, is an anomaly not only from an ethical point of view but also from a hermeneutic and exegetic one.

The fact that exegetes are affected and transformed when they see ordinary readers read the Bible, that they cannot be spectators standing at a distance with clean hands (Levinas), that exegetes are converted to the people (Richard), that they are partially constituted by ordinary readers (G. West 1999), that they are prepared to burn everything and forget what does not serve (Schwantes)—or any metaphor whatsoever that one wishes to use for the meeting between exegesis and the people, the people are not the only actors in the game. They alone are not sufficient, and they know it and say so. Indeed, many groups wrestled with the narrative development of the text of the encounter at the well, the curious sequence of question, answer, and counterquestion, concepts, backgrounds, genre, and language that were not understood. Grass-roots reading of the Bible also shows superficiality, servitude to dominant reading traditions, servile repetition, in brief: fear of liberation. Exegetes who are after liberation sometimes do well in stopping their discussion with the people. Isn't there something like a difference between the *ethics of accountability for the historical past of the text* and the *ethics of accountability for its current relevance*? The task of the exegete to include the text in its "otherness" in the discussion is just as important as the task of applying the text now to the present moment.

No matter to what extent exegetes also have a responsibility of their own, there is no reason why they would exclude grass-roots reading of the Bible as a dialogue partner. Why is that relation between professional and popular reading of the Bible often so tense, unequal, fed by misunderstanding and contempt from both sides? I suspect that the reason is that power and play do not bear each other well. Classic exegesis—but not only there!—insufficiently recognizes that the dialogue with the text also bears the nature of the game, so emphasized by Gadamer and postmodern hermeneuticians. The mode of being of play does not allow the player to behave toward play as if toward an object (Gadamer 1989, 102–8). This is precisely one of the obstacles for the exegete who seeks distance from the text and coherent, controllable analysis of the text. The exegete prefers unambiguity. Unlimited creativity, as can be found in popular reading, is not useful in exerting power. Yet exegetes would be well off, as empirical study shows, if they were to pay careful attention to the game played with the text by ordinary readers. The game with the text could expose dimensions in it that would remain hidden from those exerting power over the text.

Culture. The culture component in interpretation processes has only been recognized as a theme and a problem by liberation hermeneutics in the past few years, especially due to the effect of feminist readings in Latin America. The empirical material makes it clear to what extent the ruling culture surrounding interpreters can lead to reproduction of what is acceptable within prevailing reading traditions. At the level of ordinary readers, culture—interpreted in keeping with Hofstede's definition of culture as mental programming, as *software of the mind* (1995, 13)—is extremely operative; however, hermeneutic designs do not escape *cultural bias* either. Liberation hermeneutics also shows strong masculine features with respect to what is considered relevant, to the way social transformation is thought, and then also to the way in which the exegetical agenda is set and the methods that are used. For example, one may wonder if the strong preference of liberation hermeneutics for the sociological method is not also determined very much by culture (de Wit 2000). Tight circulation between a culturally determined hermeneutic design and interpretation processes by ordinary readers in that same culture may reinforce captivity and intensify it. Authority has added value in the Latin American collectivist culture. This means that exegetes should consider very carefully their mode of reading "with" the nonprofessional readers. No matter how much one seeks to break with prevailing paradigms, rift is not sufficient to escape one's own *cultural bias*. This bias regards not only Eurocentric ways of reading but also liberation hermeneutics.

Praxis. We have seen that praxis plays an important role in liberation hermeneutics. Analysis of the empirical material makes it clear that further study precisely at the interface between interpretation and praxis is very necessary. A number of liberation hermeneutics spokespersons show the pretense that there might be a direct, problem-free relation between reading a biblical text and (social) transformation. The term *transforming reading* has been so generally adopted in hermeneutics that it is rarely problematized any longer (Thiselton 1992, 8–10). However, the relation between reading and praxis appears to be very complex and never immediate. It appears to be extraordinarily difficult to discover causal patterns in actualization processes. Sometimes, especially in Western groups, no actualization takes place at all. Direct actualization in the sense of identification with characters or situations in the story takes place directly and problem-free in non-Western groups. But even there, no simple causal contexts can be found, mainly because the actualization process is the product of a cocktail of factors that mediate in this. Socioeconomic, cultural, psychological, and ecclesiastical factors fight for preference and decide this process in a way that can scarcely be programmed. As different as the life stories and self-images of people are, so different also is the way people actualize the text. The most frequently occurring way of actualization is the one of tracing paper or the parallelism of terms (C. Boff

1980), in which the distance between the reader and the text often loses its critical function; little self-criticism is involved but immediate equalization between the Bible and the personal context: "We are the Samaritan woman." However, many self-critical moments of appropriation are also evident. The transformative power of texts is determined to a large extent by the prevailing reading tradition within which the text is read. The appropriation process among readers in a sociopolitically oriented community of faith usually does not leave much room for pietistic, psychologically oriented appropriation, even if the text provides room for it anyway. In reverse, the same is true. Empirical study shows that the weight of the dominant reading and church tradition one belongs to is many times greater than the social status of the reader. In other words, the fact that one belongs to a Pentecostal church is more defining to the way one actualizes than the fact that one is poor. In contrast to what is sometimes suggested by liberation hermeneuticians, it appears that there is no significant correlation between social status (poverty) and the manner of reading and actualizing (liberation praxis). "The poor" read the Bible in diverse ways, in which the church and reading tradition they belong to frequently is much more important than their social status.

That Bible reading is influenced by a certain praxis and worldview and that Bible reading also has an effect on how people think and act is evident. How precisely that circulation takes place is a complex question. For example, empirical studies make it clear that Bible reading seldom results in praxis, interpreted as direct action. To the surprise of participating scholars, it appeared that reading John 4 had incited only one group of the 130 to direct action (founding a committee against polygamy!), while all the others got stuck in the "We really should..." mode. The implication of all this to a hermeneutic design in keeping with liberation hermeneutics is important. The relation between interpretation and praxis, the area of empirical hermeneutics, is still undeveloped in biblical scholarship. The complex relation between the two is not done justice by the pretences of an immediate, causal relation sometimes found in genitive hermeneutics. In summary it can be said that, exactly because the relation between praxis and interpretation appears complex and scarcely programmable, it is very debatable whether a certain praxis, for example, a liberation praxis, could be an *intended* effect of Bible reading. It may have a heuristic effect but cannot be a standard or touchstone for good Bible reading.

ECCENTRICITY AND INTERACTIVE DIVERSITY

A great deal of the aforementioned discussion flows together in an important corrective for liberation hermeneutics. Genitive hermeneuticians by definition understand themselves as "alternative" to ruling hermeneutics. This position makes real, profound interaction difficult. Interaction, certainly when it ends up critical self-reflection, is easily interpreted as a betrayal of the issue of justice or liberation (de Wit 2002). Because of this, I repeat, genitive hermeneutics often end up maintaining a ghetto position. One cannot get into it. However, not one hermeneutic subject escapes cultural bias, exclusion, and seizure of power. To escape from that, another rift or embracing another new subject is not sufficient, but the willingness to be vulnerable and to have inter- action with other readers and readings are the conditions for this. Indeed, these two principles may serve as a normative criterion in the evaluation of hermeneutic designs. Interpretations differ in the degree in which they would learn from "foreign" interpretations. The more they do so, the more valuable they are. Interaction can be considered as the quality of the hermeneutic pro- cess and the condition for transformation (Kessler 2004; Kool 2004; Míguez 2004b; Riches 2004; Witvliet 2004). For this, I refer to two central concepts in culture studies: eccentricity and interactive diversity.

The (philosophical) concept of eccentricity has to do with something that is specific to the structure of human beings. It refers to "the insight that a human being is not only a body, but also has a body, is master and plaything of his psyche, product and producer of his culture" (Procee 1991, 207) One is and is related to that being. One never totally coincides with oneself. The eccentricity leads to the polymorphism of human individuals, as well as to the great diversity of cultural patterns. Some cultures are strongly focused on interactions, others just the opposite. Based on the same basic structure, it is possible to be open to new influences and exclude oneself from this as well. Eccentricity as a general human peculiarity means that interactions are essen- tial for human beings (Procee 1991, 205–15; de Wit 2004b). The theme of eccentricity can also be made fertile for intercultural hermeneutics. One is not only a product of one's biblical interpretation but also the producer of it. One can also examine other interpretations. However closed or reproductive interpretations of the Scripture may be, interpreters never totally coincide with them. Readers can objectify their own interpretation. Thus, the concept of eccentricity in hermeneutics leads to formulating a normative criterion: no exclusion and the willingness to stimulate interaction. Normative, because they indicate where the quality of interpretations lies, namely, in the possibil- ity for continuing discussion, in the ability to be vulnerable, the willingness not to exclude and to striving for consensus.

We do not demand genitive hermeneutics to give up what belongs to its own specificity, namely, the attention to the local situation, to the suffering *hic et nunc*, but to take a critical look at one's own types of exclusion and unwillingness for real interaction. Here interaction and self-criticism will have a complementary relationship: true interaction would also really expose possible types of exclusion. In such a model, the other is no longer the person with whom one has to break, the enemy, but, in keeping with Levinas, an *epiphanic space.*

LIBERATION?

Is the liberation hermeneutics' fear that the discussion in an open interaction between the most diverse groups in the north and south will no longer be about liberation or social change justified? Experience teaches something entirely different. It is exactly via this interaction that themes such as liberation and globalization come continuously under discussion. Mechanisms and experiences of repression and exclusion are not restricted to the Third World.

I refer to the following: the project Through the Eyes of Another connects the global and local aspects to one another in a simple and surprising manner. Participants are asked to get in contact with another small, local community of faith. In the interaction between "local" and "local," participants enter first of all into a discussion about each other's context. They will talk about legitimate differences, about contextual expressions of faith, about their own interpretation of the biblical text, about their own, current experiences of suffering and exclusion. However, they also speak about what goes beyond their own context and situation, influences from the outside, problems caused by *global* differences in wealth, power, and resources. This means that the discussion about "the global village" can be stripped of mystifying tendencies and become very concrete. After all, it is fed from the participant's own experience. Thus, groups will want to undertake concrete actions at the micro-level of *this* encounter, which is much more meaningful than general struggles against "globalization." In this manner, groups will be able to determine, together, what differences are legitimate and may continue to exist next to each other and where communal action for transformation is suitable. Participants discover that violence and repression take place more on the everyday level and are more culturally determined than is regarded by some liberation theologians. The area is extended in which liberation, justice, and wholeness of existence are searched for. Not only would it involve social and political structures in its analysis, but also those areas in which people are sacrificed to cultural values. The concept of liberation can also continue to fulfill here, in intercultural hermeneutics, a meaningful function as critical reflection on the transformative power of the word of the gospel, but now made fruitful in the broader context of human life itself and charged with the power to criticize also those theological models and interpretations of biblical texts that define themselves sometimes too hastily as liberative.

And the Text?

In conclusion, a word about the biblical text itself. In a project such as Through the Eyes of Another a last corrective is given here, again in keeping with Levinas. Much of what is done in liberation hermeneutics is an attempt to control the interpretation process. Its discussion with the text sometimes looks more like the interrogation of a prisoner than a real dialogue. Just as in classic exegesis, the texts are also here, in liberation hermeneutics, considered as objects over which, with the right means, power can be wielded. However, what a project in which profound interaction and confrontation is involved teaches about biblical texts is something entirely different. Texts are not objects but places of encounter. Biblical texts and Bible stories are a place where the readers' life stories flow together and seek a way to new life.

LIBERATION HERMENEUTICS IN OLD EUROPE, ESPECIALLY GERMANY

Erhard Gerstenberger

1. PRELIMINARIES

1.1. ORIGINS

Jewish-Christian tradition from the beginnings and throughout its history has been imbued with dissenting and opposing (prophetic) voices, more so, one may say, than other "religions of the book." About the reasons of this constant intrinsic challenge of dominant beliefs, practices, and structures we may speculate. The most likely ground may be a sociohistorical or political one: Those communities of old that brought together the existing canons of Old and New Testament writings were insignificant, widely spread and often disdained minorities in vast empires and influential cultures, the Persian and the Roman ones, respectively. They completely lacked the authority to enforce uniform doctrines and patterns of behavior among their own clientele of believers, and they constantly faced, in more or less crucial situations, the necessity to resist outside pressures on their own frames and paradigms of faith and order. We should put, therefore, all biblical hermeneutics of liberation into the contexts of confessional groups that, under outside or inside squeezes, had to struggle for their physical and spiritual survival. Liberation movements thus may be understood as individual and collective counteractions against dominant systems, inspired by critical evaluations of ongoing abuse of power. Critical reflection, furthermore, is hardly possible without harkening back to the just causes enshrined in one's own tradition, which for Christians include the kingdom of God, the preaching of Jesus Christ, and the sufferings of martyrs and saints.

As a rule, messages and practices of liberation are rooted in the better past, antedating present injustices. Christian liberationists have to resort to the Bible and to read it as a guidebook in the valleys of death.

1.2. HISTORY

"Impartial" historians that we want to be, we should try to look at liberation movements first from their own perspectives, leaving it to readers and critics to determine the validity of the claims raised. As always in scholarly reviews, however, we have to keep in mind that not all clamors for liberty are genuine or continue to be authentic in the course of events. Even Hitler used liberation rhetoric to propagate his goals. That means that humans are able to distort meanings, whether out of good or bad intention. Therefore we should be aware of the possible ambivalences of the language used. Christian struggle for recognition by the Roman authorities, for example, soon turned into a full-scale oppression of other religions, as soon their creed became sanctioned by the state. Virtually the same occurred with the Reformation, when it took over certain governments. Michael Servet, for example, was burned in Geneva as heretic (1553). Even the diverse monastic movements, which had sprung up forcefully in protest against too worldly attitudes of the general believers and their hierarchies (that is, against the bondages of mundane, sinful airs), quite often petered out to become the shallow waters of common, entangled ways of life. History thus teaches us to look at liberation movements as rather transitory phenomena and liberationist institutions as precarious efforts to give freedom a permanent shape and home.

2. LIBERATIONIST MOVEMENTS AND INSTITUTIONS

Delimitations of time and space always are arbitrary. We could start this historical purview in the eighth century C.E., when European tribal kingdoms became Christianized, follow up their trajectory through the Middle Ages and into the Renaissance period. It was primarily monastic movements that now and then challenged church and state, be it in terms of purity of evangelical lifestyle and/or seriousness of social consciousness over against *les miserables* or downtrodden people. The dawn of a new age since the beginning of sea-faring discoveries in the thirteenth century also brought about religious groups breaking away from the all-powerful Roman Catholic Church (e.g., the Albigenses or Cathari in France and Italy, who were established in 1167 C.E. and were fought by "crusaders" between 1209 and 1229; the Wyclifites in England, followers of the Bible translator John Wyclif, 1320–1384; the Hussites in Bohemia, named after Jan Hus, who was burned as a heretic in Konstanz in 1415). The dissenting confessional groups of pre-Reformation times would in fact yield rich material for the study of liberation movements and their interpretation of the Bible in central Europe. Lack of space precludes this early starting point.

2.1. THE SIXTEENTH TO EIGHTEENTH CENTURIES

The two movements of the Reformation, centered in Wittenberg as well as in Zurich and Basel, valued the idea of freedom from spiritual and partly also political oppression. In spite of crucial controversies with Roman Catholics (such as Erasmus of Rotterdam) about the freedom of human will, Martin Luther, basing himself on Scripture, fulminantly proclaimed independence of each individual Christian from every kind of ecclesial tutelage. His early writings (e.g., *Von der Freiheit eines Christenmenschen* [Of the Christian's Freedom], 1520) ignited a firestorm threatening every established order. Luther very soon made it clear that he wanted to liberate his contemporaries from spiritual bondage. He liked to speak of the "Babylonian captivity" of the church, not of the citizen. What he decidedly resented was to be a leader of a political revolution. Thus he fought enthusiasts and rebels with all his might. His stance in the peasants' uprisings of 1525 is exemplary. He condemned the revolutionaries and their middle-class leaders (e.g., Thomas Müntzer, 1490–1525, fervent preacher against the exploitation of the poor, leader of the Thuringian revolt, designer of the peasants rainbow-banner, and executed after the final battle)[1] and called on the state authorities, no matter of which confession, to smash them.

John Calvin took a slightly different position. For him, there was no fundamental division between the spiritual and the political realms. Freedom of faith for individuals called, ultimately, also for recognition of their basic equality and a reform of governmental institutions in a more aristocratic and rotating fashion (see his *Institutiones* 3.19 and 4.20, especially 4.20.8: Since monarchs are frail and limited, "it is much safer and more bearable, if a plurality of leaders holds the helm"). On the other hand, Calvin was also sharply opposed to civil disorder and confessional deviation. Both branches of Protestantism in the long run did not support a full-fledged freeing of humans from oppressive conditions but expelled all leftist and enthusiastic branches from their areas of influence. They emigrated mainly to the United States in search of true liberty (but some, ironically, founded repressive commonwealths themselves). The reformation movements impressively kindled many torches of spiritual, ecclesial, and partly social liberties in the early sixteenth century, in line with humanist and urbane reorganizations of commerce and culture. They heavily relied on biblical argumentation: humans are free before

---

1. Should not he and his coreligionists be considered the true liberation theologians of the time?

God and responsible only to God; forgiveness of sins does not have to be conditioned by hierarchical authorities.

Pietism and the Enlightenment in the seventeenth and eighteenth centuries both can be described as liberation movements of sorts in European history. Their protagonists wanted to break away from enslaving modes of believing and thinking. Within the Protestant churches pietism disdained sterile dogmatic discourses and heavy-handed hierarchical structures. Theologians such as Philipp Jakob Spener (1635–1705) and Nikolaus Ludwig Graf Zinzendorf (1700–1760) stressed the ideals of praxis-oriented Christian life of devotion and brotherly love. They felt very close to the beginnings of the church, preached the discipleship of Christ and communion among each other, and strengthened parish life and charitable activities, often in conflict with orthodox church leaders and theological schools. Separation from the forlorn world and expectancy of the last day of judgment also mark the piety of the newly born believers. Methodism in Great Britain was the parallel movement of renewal for individuals and faith communities.

The Enlightenment grew out of philosophical roots, predominantly in France and England, representing the liberation of intellectuals in the wake of modern sciences from "old-fashioned" worldviews and conceptualizations of life. It may be understood as a continuing emancipation of human rationality, including the capacity of mastering its own destiny. Immanuel Kant (1724–1804) called it "the exodus of the human being from its self-imposed wardship [*Unmündigkeit*]" (Kant 1784, 481). But this philosophical liberation influenced greatly some segments of Christianity. Biblical criticism became an important base for redefining faith in the context of modern, "natural," and "factual" worldviews (see Johann Salomo Semler, 1725–1791). The concept of "humanity" acquired a "progressive" meaning: the world, as it actually existed, had to be refined, modeled to perfection, including humanity itself. Pedagogical and ethical emphases, to be realized in daily life aiming at a complete transformation of social and political structures, were paramount in this liberationist movement (see Gotthold Ephraim Lessing, 1729–1781). The Declaration of Human Rights in the British colonies and the French revolution have been powerful manifestations of this spirit of enlightenment. In spite of wide differences between Pietism and the Enlightenment, both patterns of thinking and believing developed in distinct levels of society and did have liberationist effects in religious and political life; they tried to overcome barriers of human progress, rediscovered the blissful future as the ultimate goal (see John Bunyan, 1622–1688, and his *Pilgrim's Progress*, 1678), and nurtured strong ethical stances coached in continuous appeals to human will and resolve to really achieve the distant ideals. Biblical justification of attitudes to be taken was stronger in Pietism but did not go amiss in enlightened discourses. The interpretation of the Bible in the latter contexts, reducing miracles to rationally interpreted episodes, was part of the notorious wrestling with tradition.

2.2. THE NINETEENTH CENTURY

While France experimented with republican political systems, Germany remained under monarchic rule; here political and social unrest was successfully squelched by conservative forces. Nevertheless, socialist thinkers brought out the seeds of revolution (see Karl Marx, 1818–1823), partly and sometimes unconsciously influenced also by (prophetic) biblical concepts of justice and equality. The mainstream or "state" churches, however, stayed away from any form of criticism. German clergy usually preached obedience to political authorities and referred the discontent and miserable to transcendental bliss in the paradisiacal afterlife. Heavenly reward was to compensate all troubles experienced on earth. There were only a few Christians resisting that official doctrine, and most of them stayed well-protected under the cover of state-church institutions. Still, they fought complacency, lethargy, and bureaucratic routines within established church organizations. Thus, Johann Hinrich Wichern (1808–1881), stirred up by a kind of "social gospel," preached to "awakened" Christians in several parts of Germany; he gave a moving impromptu speech at the first *Kirchentag* (convention of Protestant churches seeking church unity) at Wittenberg in 1848, the same year the Communist Manifesto was published in London. Wichern pointed out the miserable social conditions of low-income urban populations and their growing alienation from the church. His presentation motivated the foundation of a "Central Committee for Internal Mission Work," the forerunner of later "Charitable Work" (*Diakonisches Werk*) for Germany. Like August Hermann Francke at Halle (1663–1727) and most adherents of pietistic awakening, Wichern dedicated himself intensely to the poor in the city of Hamburg (*Das Rauhe Haus*, a social and educative center for the underprivileged that is still operating), but with wide-ranging influences. Friedrich von Bodelschwingh (1831–1910), a nobleman by birth, experienced a conversion to the gospel, studied theology, and became involved in the charitable and missionary work of his church. He built up a formidable "City of Misericordia" near the industrial town of Bielefeld and named it "Bethel," which until this day serves disabled, homeless, and jobless persons. Theological and missionary tasks are integrated into this project. Thus, all these movements had their sociopolitical emphases on *diakonia*, education, and mission work, both at home and in overseas territories. Their engagement with suffering, underprivileged, and uneducated people, however, seldom was considered revolutionary. Rather, it adapted itself perfectly into the frame of authoritarian state structures. Some efforts were made to influence state legislation in favor of the underprivileged and to promote the construction of decent homes for miserably paid industrial workers, yet the spiritual dimension of aid took priority. Bible reading and interpretation was the backbone of all pietistic movements, and we may consider this type of activity for the poor a hidden way of practicing liberation, which also may bring the fruits of justice and peace in some way. A few theologians went a little step further in trying to influence political and economic decisions directly by organizing a Christian party, for example, Adolf Stöcker (1835–1909), who fought liberalism (labeling it "Jewish" and becoming an anti-Semite) and socialism, and Friedrich Naumann (1860–1919). The latter recognized that the industrial society was undergoing deep transformations that had to be dealt with responsibly in the direction of an impending democratization. The examples given demonstrate how even Christians endowed with a warm dedication to the lowly may remain bound in a traditional conservative world order (occasionally including darkest prejudices) preventing truly liberating breakthroughs.

2.3. Germany: The Twentieth Century

Two World Wars originated in Germany, where a monarchic government gave way to a republican one (1919), which in turn was abolished by Nazi totalitarianism (1933). After its defeat in 1945, a democratic system was installed and slowly took root in Western Germany, while Eastern Germany was organized according to the premises of the Soviet Socialist block. This historical background is important for the emergence of various liberationist strands in modern Protestant and Catholic church history.

2.3.1. General Phenomena

Biblical Criticism. At home in German universities and among intellectuals, biblical criticism had sprung up during the Enlightenment but came to its peak only at the end of the nineteenth and during the first half of the twentieth centuries. Some of the leading names associated with biblical criticism are Julius Wellhausen (1844–1918), Hermann Gunkel (1862–1932), Martin Dibelius (1883–1947), Adolf Jülicher (1857–1938), and Rudolf Bultmann (1884–1976). In this school of thought, the Bible becomes a historical piece of accumulated Hebrew, Aramaic, and Greek literature, to be treated as a human composition like any other ancient tradition. Furthermore, the Bible did take shape in close contact with other ancient Near Eastern cultures and religions. It is not an erratic collection of writings completely isolated from foreign influence (see, e.g., the symptomatic Babel-Bibel-Streit of 1902–1903 between the Assyriologist Friedrich Delitzsch and orthodox churchgoers) but belongs in the religious-historical continuum of Near Eastern cultures. The essence of all this is a loosening of church censorship and dogmatic dominance over scriptural studies, which even applies in an increasing degree to Roman Catholic scriptural studies.

The first encyclical to soften hierarchical supervision, allowing biblical authors to be fully human in personality and individuality, and to grant some freedom of interpretation was *Providentissimus Deus* (1893, by Pope Leo XIII). Full acceptance of historical-critical research in the Catholic realm only occurred at the Second Vatican Council (1962–1965). Thus, a tiny minority of intellectuals throughout Christian mainstream churches freed itself of church tutelage and proclaimed a more open approach to biblical documents under the sole responsibility of the exegete himself or herself. But sometimes, as it were, Bible interpreters overdid their zeal or entered into bondages of different sorts (e.g., F. Delitzsch, who became a fierce opponent of the Old Testament, in consequence of his unenlightened anti-Semitism). On the whole, however, Bible criticism proved to have a liberating effect on faith, church life, and ethos. It remains a basic presupposition for necessary reforms and new ventures of the Christian community.

Outreach to Working Class. State churches had noticeably lost contact with the lower classes because of their alliance with social elites in the nineteenth century. During the Weimar Republic, only slight efforts were made to meet the alienated working population and defend their interests. This task had been taken over by trade unions and left-wing political parties, all quite hostile to the alleged ecclesiastic "superstition," "capitalism," and "exploitism." After a phase of trying to squeeze Protestant churches into their political system, the Nazi government started to curb church activities as much as possible, thereby occupying all accesses to young and working-class people. Only after the Second World War did the Protestant churches recognize the problem and try to cope with it by founding outreach institutions, such as the *Evangelische Akademien* (in analogy to Catholic Academies).

2.3.2. The Nazi Dictatorship

Confessing Congregations. The most important movement for church autonomy evolved between 1933 and 1945. When the nature and political goals of Hitler's party became obvious in 1933–1934, after it had come to power in Berlin, quite a few Christians (but still a very small minority!) resented the projected "Germanization" of Christian faith. Limitations of church rights and falsification of church doctrine were too much to digest for pastors basically very loyal to state organs. The majority of Christians remained submissive to Nazi rule, but a significant number of Protestant laity and clergy broke off from the official state churches and established free, "confessing" communities on their own—which meant, of course, that they lost all state privileges. There were focuses of resistance corresponding to regional traditions. East Prussia, Berlin, Silesia, Bavaria, Rhineland, and Westfalia became centers of church dissidence and opposition. Interestingly, "confessing" Christians complained most of all about infringements on church rights and church doctrines. There was much less readiness to fight for the rights of persecuted and endangered people, such as Jews, Sinti and Roma, Jehovah's Witnesses, the mentally ill, the handicapped, communists, and foreign nationals (especially from Eastern countries).

Soon after the Nazis came to power they started to built up an overarching Protestant *Reichskirche* (church of the empire) under the leadership of national socialist-minded *Deutsche Christen* (Teutonic Christians). In the fall of 1933 and the beginning of 1934, Bible-oriented ministers organized a defense alliance (*Pfarrernotbund*) against this demolition. Martin Niemöller (1892–1984), a survivor of the Dachau concentration camp, was prominent in early opposition in spite of his own nationalist background. Regular congregations and regional church bodies also declared themselves autonomous and formed free-church parliaments and confessing communities, especially in the Prussian territories. On an all-German level, a *Bekenntnisgemeinschaft* (confessional community) convened free synods. The one gathered at Wuppertal-Barmen in May 1934 formulated, under the leadership of Karl Barth (then professor at Bonn University, though he would be dismissed 1935) the famous *Barmer Erklärung* (Declaration of Barmen), a staunch confession to the lordship of Christ in contradistinction to all political powers. Each of the six statements of faith is followed by a poignant condemnation of actual "false" doctrine, the rejection of "other" deities, especially political ones, over against the one God in Christ.

This Confession of Barmen, in fact, used, along with religious discourses of forgiveness, obedience, and allegiance to Christ, the rhetoric of liberation: The second thesis states: "As Jesus Christ is the comforting address of God communicating forgiveness of all our sins, just the same and with equal seriousness he also represents God's firm claim on our whole life; through him we experience merry liberation [*frohe Befreiung*] from the godless ties of this (awkward) world in favor of a free, grateful service to his creatures." For the first time in German church history, a creedal statement of a confessionally mixed group of Protestant Christians drew a sharp dividing line between church and government, rejecting state tutelage and declaring themselves free entities responsible to God alone. The position thus taken proved to be very important for confessing communities and individuals until the end of the Hitler era. More than that, the Barmen Declaration proved to be a powerful heritage in the postwar period, and a number of Protestant churches have incorporated it into their standard confessional documents to this day.

The struggle between confessing communities and the traditional ecclesiastical bodies, now dominated by "Teutonic Christians," went on through 1945, although the sufferings of the war soon would push internal church strife more or less into oblivion. Essentially, strong affinity to biblical teaching inflamed their dissenting attitudes on the Protestant side. Scores of confessing Christians went to prison for their opposition to religious state rule, and many were put into concentration camps and murdered, such as the lonely fighter in a village parish of the Hunsrück mountains, pastor Paul Schneider (1897–1939). Martyred "confessing" Protestants count by the dozens if not hundreds, and on the Catholic side there have been equal numbers of victims.[2]

Defense of the Marginalized. Destruction of "unworthy life" (Nazi jargon denoting physically and mentally handicapped persons) became an issue when the state began to implement a program of "euthanasia" in 1939. This measure, which cost several hundreds of thousands of innocent lives, met some resistance by Christians (e.g., the bishops Graf von Galen and Theophil Wurm; pastor Friedrich von Bodelschwingh Jr.). Protection of Jewish people facing total extermination since 1942, however, occurred only on a still more reduced and individual level, apparently because there had been fostered a pervasive animosity against Jews throughout ecclesiastical history (starting with Matt 27:15–26; John 19:6–16), which prevented significant solidarity with the Jews by Christians. Thus the horrible Holocaust became possible in spite of the confessing church and in spite of some Roman Catholic warnings against inhuman treatment of handicapped persons. That there has been some bad conscience among Germans in general about mass deportations of Jews to the gas chambers (the existence of which was whispered about, although not many persons did know the full facts before 1945), taking place in most neighborhoods, may be seen in isolated acts of protest and concrete help for endangered individuals. In this fashion the Marburg faculty of theology in 1934 issued a statement against racist legislation depriving Jews of public jobs. The clandestine Berlin "Grüber-office" (named for Heinrich Grüber, 1891–1975; imprisoned 1941–1945; his associate pastor Werner Sylten, 1893–1942, himself of Jewish descent, was murdered in a concen-

---

2. Joachim Mehlhausen (1977–2004, 24:65) reports 169 murdered Catholic priests until 1941, and Frank Stoeßel (1977–2004, 8:49) tells of 805 imprisoned Protestant ministers after 1937. Stoeßel also mentions a total of about 4,000 Catholics, mostly clergy, murdered by the Nazi regime (1977–2004, 8:51).

tration camp) as well as a similar institution led by Catholic *Dompropst* Bernhard Lichtenberg (murdered in 1943) helped several thousands to escape the annihilation machine. The pogrom of 1938 (*Reichskristallnacht*) and the final decision of 1942 to eradicate European Jewry (*Endlösung der Judenfrage*; conference of SS-echelons at a Grunewald Villa) drew little response from Protestant or Catholic churches. Katharina Staritz (1903–1953) on the Protestant side and Margarethe Sommer (1993–1965) on the Catholic side are examples of more or less "private" rescue workers. The general attitude of Christians over against the sufferings of Jews (and other minorities) was rather passive due to those age-old (Christian!) prejudices that seriously hampered the evangelical liberation ethos.

Political Resistance. Christians in Germany have been very reluctant to oppose state authorities violently. Especially Luther's doctrine of the two kingdoms proved a very effective barrier to forceful intervention in government affairs. However, Calvin's social political ethics, allowing for the killing of tyrants in extreme cases of inhuman and godless governance, opened up some possibilities to resist even with arms. Most notable, however, became the example of Dietrich Bonhoeffer, a Lutheran, who followed his Christian conscience and joined political circles of resistance eventually leading (after frustrated tentative plans in 1943) to the attempt of a military coup on 20 July 1944. His theological justification of violent resistance aimed at eliminating Hitler himself can be found in his sporadic writings, especially after his imprisonment on 5 April 1943. Bonhoeffer founded his decision basically on Scripture teaching a free conscience before God and a deep-seated responsibility for Christ's rule and justice in this corrupt world. The individual Christian had to stand up to this call for the divine order to the point of joining active conspiracy against the ordained government, which means using and condoning camouflage and treason and ultimately murdering the tyrant. Bonhoeffer was accused of treason, transferred to the concentration camp of Buchenwald, and finally executed, together with five other companions, by special order of Hitler, on 9 April 1945 at Flossenbürg, Bavaria (see Bethge 1967, 811–1038). Bonhoeffer truly was a highly sensitive Christian who understood his own time in the light of biblical tradition, being able to come to radical new conclusions as to the course of action that had to be taken in responsibility to the living and acting God in the disturbing course of actual history. Many other insurgents of that period, also among the military activists, were moved by their Christian conscience and lost their lives (e.g., Helmut James Graf von Moltke and Claus Schenk Graf von Stauffenberg; in all, two hundred persons involved in the coup were executed).

Roman Catholic Opposition. While focusing on Protestant confessing churches, we should not forget that Roman Catholic Christians, both laypeople and clergy as well as nuns and monks, also found themselves obliged to oppose the extremely brutal and criminal doings of Hitler's party and government. Of course, the spiritual basis was slightly different from that of the Protestants. Roman Catholics deeply resented the absolutistic air of Nazi ideology, its war against ecclesiastic doctrines and structures, and its degradation of all humans not corresponding to the idealized blue-eyed and blond-haired, healthy and strong Germanic types destined to rule the whole world. Many Roman Catholics instinctively (given the age-old teachings of justice and good governance within their own church traditions) felt from the beginning of Nazism's rise in the early 1920s that this human-centered, fanatic ideology could by no means be harmonized with the doctrines and practices of the apostolic faith. Strangely (or understandably?) enough, a large majority of Catholic believers still were carried away by nationalistic and socialist pathos of Nazi propaganda, just as it happened on the Protestant side.

Differences of Catholic experiences with Nazism arose out of the church structure. The Vatican soon tried to fortify existing congregations and diocesan structures as well as spiritual and educational institutions in Germany by signing a church-state treaty with the new government (the *Reichskonkordat* of 20 July 1933). The government guaranteed protection and noninterference in ecclesiastical matters to an astonishing degree, as long as Catholic clergy did not deal with state politics and Nazi activities. Thus, a neat demarcation had been achieved between church and state which, *de modo grosso*, left intact all ecclesiastical organizations including confessional schools and preserved, in fact, the body of the traditional church. There was no need for dissenters to split off; they could be sheltered, in a way, by regular hierarchical structures. Of course, the police would not respect too much the precincts of monasteries and cathedrals in case a real or alleged offense against Nazi rules had taken place, and it so happened that many dissenters and outspoken opponents were imprisoned and sometimes sentenced or murdered by the *Gestapo* (secret police) or in concentration camps. However, the high-ranking clergy who dared to contradict Nazi ideology or deeds would not be harmed, such as the bishops Cardinal Faulhaber of Munich, Graf von Galen of Münster, and Konrad von Preysing of Berlin, in spite of their public criticism.

Then again, especially between 1935 and 1937 the state authorities actively tried to curtail Catholic autonomy and discredit the church, its clergy, and its monastic orders. Youth organizations were prohibited, monasteries were sued for tax and monetary irregularities, and priests were charged with sexual misbehavior as well as other improprieties. Many people were put into prison. Throughout the years, more and more Catholic opponents to the regime also were martyred, such as Erich Klausener, chairman of the *Katholische Aktion* (a lay organization) in the wake of the Röhm massacres of 1934; Father Rupert

Mayer, S.J., who ardently preached against Nazi denunciations (1945); Father Alfred Delp, S.J. (1945); prelate Otto Müller (1944), whose firm guide was Roman Catholic social doctrine; and vicar Hermann Wehrle (1944), who had served the parish of Bogenhausen since 1942, in contact with Alfred Delp. They all were involved in planning the *coups d'état* of 1943 and 1944, just like Bonhoeffer. All these followers of a Christian ethos received their prime motivation through Scriptures and official doctrines, even in the face of much political leniency exercised by the Vatican. Bishop von Galen's denunciation of the euthanasia program already has been mentioned.

General Situation of Churches. What we see, therefore, during the years of Nazi dominance has been an awakening of Christian consciences in the face of a brutal, absolutistic ideology that was identified by many Christians as strictly anti-Christian. Resistance sprang up in parish communities among laypeople and practicing theologians because Nazism was, indeed, an existential threat to the survival of traditional church communities and their biblical teachings. Alfred Rosenberg's *Mythos des 20. Jahrhunderts* (Myth of the Twentieth Century) became a literary weapon against Christian churches, a sort of belligerent tool to dismantle that "anachronistic" and "Jewish" faith. Active propagation of ancient Germanic religion and mores, starting early in public schools and party education everywhere, was to conquer the minds and hearts of all Germans and make Christianity obsolete. The new creed centered on *Führer, Volk, und Vaterland* (leader, nation, and homeland). The battle for the minds of all Germans was waged by the authorities with all available means of modern mass communication (radio, film, journals) and supported by the powerful machinery of state and party organizations, such as kindergarten, schools, police, legal courts, welfare groupings (e.g., *Kraft durch Freude* [strength through diversion]). Opposing church bodies and individuals, conversely, were observed, hindered, and threatened. Their meetings, communications, and projects had to take place clandestinely. Spies and denunciators were everywhere. Even in Sunday worship services preachers of the confessing church or Catholic resistance had to be wary of being denounced to the secret police. Material resources of all kinds were scarce, and spiritual support came from the biblical message and the courage and clear-sightedness of participants. There was virtually no help to be expected from abroad, although some personal contacts over borderlines did exist even during the war. The most powerful "weapon" of dissenting Christians was, in fact, the Bible itself. Preachers would read passages from the Scriptures, the actualized and revolutionary content of which became immediately clear to the audience, sometimes including even Nazi spies. Thus, a reading of Isa 14, a taunt on the tumbling king of Babylon going down to hell, could only be understood as aiming at the downfall of the dictator Hitler. The Gospels and

Prophets would take on sharp-edged meanings in daily affairs. The rights of others, solidarity with the weak and disabled, the futility of arrogance and power: these and other biblical insights collided with Nazi ideals. Apocalyptic texts foreshadowed the doom of the Third German Empire. The Bible proved to be a treasure of humane values that did not fit into the chauvinistic and racist worldview of the governing party.

University Life. A special look at the places of theological learning during the Nazi period may be in order, because it was exactly there where—according to common belief and cherished church tradition—the hermeneutics of freedom should have been cultivated. The overall picture of German Protestant theological faculties, nearly all of them incorporated into the state universities since Reformation times, is a sad one. The majority of professors teaching at these theological schools of higher learning either yielded more or less to the nationalist seduction of the Nazis, because the churches had been faithful to the state authorities all along in their millenarian history, or were dismissed and substituted by loyal "brown" teachers (see Karl Barth). A few examples of active proclamation of dissenting Christian viewpoints can be enumerated. I already mentioned the 1934 Marburg statement against dismissing Christians with Jewish background from office. The confessing church, realizing that it did not have a chance to compete with state faculties, very soon tried to establish their own places of theological studies and created several clandestine seminaries. There had been one free seminary of the Protestant main church already at Bethel, near Bielefeld, founded in 1905 by Friedrich von Bodelschwingh. It was to prepare students for the ministry removed from state supervision. The national council of confessing theologians started two more free theological schools in 1935 with this same purpose in mind. Both seminaries, located in Wuppertal-Elberfeld and Berlin, were closed by the secret police on the day of their inauguration. They had to go underground. The Wuppertal institution survived first in a neighboring reformed school, later on in the private homes of its professors. Berlin, likewise, had to hide all its activities carefully. German state universities, meanwhile, including their (state-run!) schools of theology were pretty much under the sway of Nazi rule. Dissenting personnel (and all Jewish staff) were dismissed as early as 1933. Only a few opposing professors maintained their chairs.

What is quite remarkable under these circumstances is the fact that here and there student opposition against Nazism and warmongering rose from a Christian conscience. Most famous is the small group around Hans and Sophie Scholl at Munich University, called the White Rose (*Weiße Rose*). These students distributed six leaflets between June 1942 and February 1943 calling for passive resistance to frustrate all Nazi activities and to work for the overthrow of the "criminal" government. In leaflet 2 they explicitly denounce the murder of 300,000 Jews by Germans in Poland, an abhorrent crime against humanity. Their Christian (Catholic) conviction shines through: "everywhere and at all times of utmost suffering there rose human individuals, prophets, saints, who had preserved their freedom of thought. They pointed to the exclusive God admonishing the people with God's help to repent. Humans are certainly free, but they are helpless without the true God to resist evil" (leaflet 2, July 1942). *Weiße Rose* was denounced by a university maintenance person on 18 February 1943. The nucleus of the group was immediately imprisoned, interrogated for several days, and sentenced to death on 22 February by the *Volksgerichtshof* (people's court), a special court for offenses of high treason under Roland Freisler. The same night both Sophie and Hans Scholl, together with Christoph Probst, were executed without a chance of appeal. Three more members of the group were put to death several months later.

2.3.3. Postwar Reconstruction

After the war the "confessing Christians" became a leading force in German Protestant churches, while on the Catholic side those persons who had resisted Nazism or abstained from active participation also increased their prestige. A prominent example is the first chancellor (since 1949) of the Federal Republic of Germany, Konrad Adenauer (1876–1967), who had withdrawn from politics and "hibernated" during the Third Reich in a small town on the Rhine River. Among the presidents of large Protestant churches were Heinrich Held and Joachim Beckmann in the Rhine country and Martin Niemöller in Hessen, all of them ardent fighters for a church free from state tutelage. Lutheran bishops with resistance background included Otto Dibelius in Brandenburg (1880–1967) and Theophil Wurm in Württemberg (1868–1953). Others were partially compromised by their performance during the Hitler regime. Very important on the whole, however, was the division of Germany into two spheres of influence: the eastern part under Soviet rule and the western part in tight union with the occidental powers. In Soviet-occupied Germany the communist party gained complete control. Their leading figures had survived unrelenting persecution by the Nazis, mostly in Russian exile, such as Walter Ulbricht (1893–1973), who became general secretary of the *Sozialistische Einheitspartei Deutschlands* (SED) and Adenauer's counterpart. The development of the churches took a notably different direction in both parts. The party programs represented by Adenauer and Ulbricht drew the contempt of many Christians wanting a true liberation.

2.3.3.1. East Germany (German Democratic Republic). The communist party, which determined the destinies of about one third of the German population under direct control of Soviet Russia, claimed to have brought freedom to an enslaved people. From the experience of Christians (and other minorities), things looked differently. Ideologically, the political regime was openly committed to atheism, but the socialist constitution only pushed religion and organized churches into the private sphere, guaranteeing freedom of religious faith. The dire reality, however, was one of repression, alternating in intensity according to political opportunities. As a matter of fact, it is noteworthy that churches and individuals were strictly under the surveillance of the state authorities, including the secret service, who also used spies and collaborators within the church groups themselves. Still, there were quite a number of loopholes in this system of control, which parishes and Christians in East Germany could use to cultivate their ties to West Germany and elsewhere. Thus it was certainly the churches during this period (1945–1989) that enjoyed the largest niches of freedom in this absolutistic state. The general situation of repression and denial of constitutional rights did produce a spirit of resistance in many Christians and church communities. Roughly, one might distinguish among three kinds of reaction.

(1) There was a small segment of Protestants who would side with communist party doctrine in considering traditional Christianity as an ally of capitalist interest. This group is not of interest in our context, even if it claimed to renew the church in alliance with communist worldviews. The two others are quite interesting. (2) The adherents of staunch anticommunist beliefs understood themselves as liberators and reformers of the church. They tried to ignore the regime. Bishop O. Dibelius, who was denied entrance into the DDR and who therefore had to perform his job from his West Berlin residence, was reported to have voiced his disdain for communist rule as follows: "I do not even obey communist traffic lights. The reds will not stop me!" The total opposition of Christians against communist structuring of public life was understood as a kind of liberation or emancipation from state supremacy. (3) The third group of Christians tried in varying degrees to exercise a critical cooperation with the state authorities. Apparently, this one was feared the most by party ideologists. Such Christians, as a rule, would be quite knowledgeable in classical Marxism, and they were eager to debate the fundamentals of Marxism even with their persecutors.

After a short period of little-hampered communication between eastern and western churches (about 1945–1949), the "bad influence" from the West was to be quenched. The DDR government enforced a legal separation of both church groups. Further restrictions of contacts across the Iron Wall did not prevent, however, a quite intense interchange of Christians by phone, letter, and (illegal!) visits of westerners in the east. Traveling in the opposite direction was interrupted almost completely. However, many partnerships between congregations and institutions continued, for example, under the pretext of visiting (faked) family members. This subterfuge often was ridiculously obvious. The STASI (*Staatssicherheitsdienst*; i.e., secret police) normally had full information about those western relatives coming in droves to visit a given parish. The DDR police probably collected these data in order to use them whenever necessary in legal suits. Liberationist tactics included cheating the state authorities.

One central issue for state and church was the work with young people. The communist party soon promoted the *Sozialistische Jugendweihe* (Youngster's Socialist Initiation), an ideological rite intended to replace church confirmation. The churches first reacted stubbornly: a youngster of twelve to fourteen years would go either for church membership or for the state-supported dedication. The acts were declared to be exclusive. Waging a losing battle, the church had to give in after a few years: Teenagers who already had gone through the rites of "Youngster's Initiation" (which they hardly could avoid) and thus had been sworn in to their socialist fatherland could apply for confirmation one year after the first ceremony had taken place. Even that strategy failed. Very few and increasingly fewer citizens of the DDR wanted to return to the church. The dire fact is that church membership in those eastern provinces of Germany dwindled to perhaps 20 to 30 percent of the population, with a further diminishing tendency, until the present time. The trend was not reversed by German reunification in 1990.

In seeming contradiction to this general picture, the socialist state authorities, as long as they lasted, all along considered the (Protestant) church as a powerful residue of antiquated, yet alluring superstitious beliefs and thus as a potent threat to their own system. The battle was especially in regard to the young generation growing up in that socialist world heading for complete communism or "consummated justice and happiness." Therefore, the party would create and make obligatory, besides kindergarten and elementary schools, all kinds of youth organizations, sportive and cultural associations, and suppress or hinder as much as possible all parallel church institutions. Youth groups of parish communities experienced severe restrictions. Christian student communities at universities or church seminaries were under surveillance and often threatened by police action. The uprising of workers against the regime, to mention the broader context, was brewing in 1952; it broke out in bloody clashes with the army on 17 June 1953. The church in one way or another was involved in the political upheaval. In this crisis seventy-two pastors and youth leaders of the church were imprisoned for shorter or longer periods. Three hundred young Christians were relegated from high schools.

One case in point was the situation of the Christian Student Association at the University of Halle, seat of pietist movements of old. Student chaplain

Johannes Hamel preached resistance against the state's totalitarianism. He was put into jail on 12 February 1953, denied all outside contacts and legal aid, and relentlessly questioned because of his seemingly conspiratorial activities. Released from prison on 10 July 1953, after the bloody revolt had been smashed, he continued his open, Bible-inspired critique of all kinds of repressions and violations of human rights. Hundreds of students attended his Bible study groups and sought his advice in private conversations. Hamel moved to the church seminary at Naumburg in 1955, where he taught practical theology until his retirement in 1976. He always felt himself to be a member of the confessing church of the Nazi period, which he had joined as early as 1934, while studying theology at Halle. His aim was, comparably to virtually all the surviving members of the confessing church, not to let dictatorial force again take over church and society. Resistance was the path to take. But he also suggested cooperation with the socialist leadership in humanitarian concerns and became one of the leading thinkers in this matter of Bible-centered relations between church and state, asking for a kind of "constructive opposition." His little study "Christ in der DDR" was widely spread, read, and debated, especially in student circles also in West Germany. Some members of the church wanted to create a type of "socialist Christian faith" in intimate relationship with the communist party.

With the economic situation deteriorating since 1982 and the DDR government trying to ease a little growing popular discontent, the churches (although being a minority group) gained some free space of action. Increasingly critics of the regime gathered on relatively safe church grounds. The communities, most of all in Bible-study groups, rallied their spiritual and humanitarian power. By the end of the period they dared to raise their voice in public, as in the "prayers for peace" led by the Leipzig congregation of St. Nikolai church and its pastor, Christian Führer. Every Monday, after the prayer, a public demonstration took place. Christians thus took the lead in fighting peacefully for freedom. These demonstrations united thousands every week and did exercise a decisive pressure on the communist government to give in. Reunification, valued by East Germans as a release from forty years of imprisonment, was achieved, among others, by a Christian grass-roots movement.

2.3.3.2. West Germany (Federal Republic of Germany)

West Germany, occupied by American, English, and French troops, started a new life from quite a different position. Democratic forms of government were introduced, and there was a (not too successful in the beginning) wave of de-Nazification of the older generation and reorientation of school and university students. Most important for our subject, the churches were given full freedom to reorganize and gain influence in public affairs. With the past experience of state persecution in their minds, church bodies to a large extent constituted themselves out of and elected into offices those persons who had suffered from the Nazi regime. Survivors of the confessing church in many regions now became the ruling group in church communities, synods, and theological faculties (e.g., Gerhard von Rad, Hans-Walter Wolff, Hans Joachim Iwand, and Helmut Gollwitzer). A new situation developed, reflected also in freshly designed constitutions and church legislation, that never had existed in Germany before. Regional (former state) churches, on the one hand, retained certain privileges from the past, such as subsidiary taxation of members by state ministries of finances, upkeep of theological faculties in state universities, official status of church pastors, membership of churches in state boards of supervision (e.g., public media), military chaplaincies paid by the state, and confessional courses of religion paid by the state in all public schools. On the other hand, many of those now taking responsibility in church life wanted to continue in their prophetic roles, warning against and resisting any moves into "unbiblical" ways of conducting political, military, and economic affairs. In order not to oversimplify the description of postwar West Germany, I have to admit that the first period after the war (1945–1949) was heavily influenced by the struggle for physical survival and did not—inside religious communities—stimulate much critical thought about the future. Furthermore, the process of adapting themselves to positions of leadership and public prominence (in contrast to bygone suppression and persecution) took hold of an increasing part of Christians in all walks of life.

To ride the high waves of success tends to obscure or eliminate the shadows and valleys of danger and death, lulling in the spirit of countertestimony against entrenched injustice. But all along there have been Christian minorities in Germany since the end of the Second World War, especially those with "confessing" backgrounds, who stayed alert to the discrepancies between the realities of life and the messages of prophets, the Gospels, and inherited teachings. It is on these minority movements inside (and outside!) the churches that we want to focus. They partly reach out beyond the date of German reunification and are still active today.

The first great issue arising after the war, besides reorganizing church structures, was an honest evaluation of the church's role during the Nazi regime. The debates culminated in that famous "Confession of Guilt" formulated in the fall of 1945 at Stuttgart, at the occasion of the first high-level ecumenical visitation and under the decisive leadership of confessing church activists such as Theophil Wurm and Martin Niemöller.[3] No doubt, the new beginning especially in ecumenical relations demanded a statement such as this. It is also safe to say that it was inspired by biblical testimony of how to achieve freedom through absolution. "Through us [referring to the Germans] immeasurable suffering has been brought over many peoples and nations.... We accuse ourselves, that we did not confess our faith more courageously, that we did not pray more loyally, nor believe more merrily, nor love more intensely."

When the division of East and West Germany was formalized by the creation of two separate states, the role of the West German churches became more especially linked with developments in the Occident. Ironically, the first government elected under the chancellorship of Konrad Adenauer was solidly Christian Democratic and geared to "Christian values" throughout. Still, confessing Christians took exception to many government decisions and even opposed the fundamental course that the Bonn government was taking (flat anticommunism, uncritical identification with the West, etc.). Some of the important issues that irritated Christian consciences, provoked reactions from individuals, and concerned church bodies were these: West German rearmament (1956–1957); reconciliation with East European peoples, especially the Polish and Russian (1965); cession of eastern territories to Poland (1971–1972); stationing of atomic weapons on German soil (1981); sexual orientation and acceptance of homosexual partnerships (1971, 1992–1994). These were hot issues at given times. In the long run, problems of justice, peace, preservation of nature, equality of gender, race, and minorities, and world economy, globalization, development of depressed areas, and fair distribution of resources and income have deeply preoccupied Christians in all of Europe. There is much to be argued against the general decisions of society at large, even though it is run by "Christian" Democratic parties. In saying this I am conscious of the biblical roots of much of the agitation displayed by movements and networks of social action within the Christian community. All of this activity is tinged by a spirit of renewal, that is, of a certain juxtaposition and opposition to dominant patterns of life and thought, for example, in West German society. Without meeting liberation terminology in all these points of irritation, we may state: a biblical, prophetic, and Jesuanic wrestling with unjust conditions of life is underway everywhere to bring relief and hope to those who suffer.

---

3. The Stuttgart meeting of the *Rat der Evangelischen Kirche in Deutschland* (Counsel of the Protestant Church in Germany) was to pursue the unification of the regional churches and to establish contacts to the outside world.

To specify a little more the points of challenge felt by Christians of Germany, I would like to sketch some organizational entities or movements that, in fact, are the banner-carriers of "progressive" and liberating goals. A rough purview of the relevant sources of theory and practice of "liberation" demonstrates that official church governments diminished their involvement in hot issues. Main initiatives sprang up more or less as independent lay enterprises.

Popular movements. Feminist interpretation of the Bible and the emancipation of women to take over leadership in the Protestant churches has been the most revolutionary development after the war. Another very influential movement is called the German *Kirchentag* (church rally), an assembly of thousands of (mostly young) people aiming at celebration of Christian (also ecumenical!) communion, discussion of the major problems of faith and world order and of necessary ecclesiastical reforms, and digging up biblical and traditional dynamics of Christian tradition in order to gain force and plausibility in today's issues. The founders of the movement, in the first place Reinold von Thadden-Trieglaff (1891–1976), a leading figure in one-time Pommerania's confessing synod, tried to carry over lay (wo)men's involvement from the past. Although the initial idea and realization were pushed forward by members of the church elite, participants always came from the grass-roots level, and the organization remained strictly antihierarchical and remarkably free from official church influence. This democratic feature also is a distinctive one over against earlier *Kirchentage* in the nineteenth and early twentieth centuries, which had been organized and executed exclusively by higher echelons in the church structure. The first great rally after the Second World War occurred in Hannover (1949); it continued as a yearly affair in other cities (Essen, Berlin, Stuttgart, Hamburg, and Leipzig) until 1954, when it began taking place once every two years. In spite of the Cold War going on, the *Kirchentag* tried to be an all-German meeting of Christians. The first full East German veto came in 1961, when participants from the East were hindered from attending the West Berlin rally. Then the dividing wall was built that interrupted virtually all communication between the concurring states. From 1963 to 1989 the big reunion, drawing increasing numbers of participants (155,000 persons in Berlin in 1989), was a West German affair only, with East German churches having their regional counterparts. After reunification, the *Kirchentag* returned to be all-German again (the twenty-fourth rally, in 1991, took place in the area of the *Ruhr*; the thirtieth rally, in 2005, was in Hannover). The basic structure of the events has remained the same, even if many modifications of themes, aims, and set-ups took place over the years. A preparation committee with intensive contacts to communities and all sorts of organizations and movements sets up a three-day study and cultural program to be realized in hundreds of working groups. The variety of topics coming to the fore is overwhelming. Culture, spiritual life, art and literature, theater, films, political debates, and a big final worship service usually in the largest sports arena of the respective city make the convention a high point of the ecclesiastical year.

Permeating these assemblies is a spirit of brotherhood and sisterhood, of joyful existence, music and dancing, but above all the consciousness of living in a disturbed (unjust, belligerent, insecure, poisoned) world that needs creative assistance and much renewing, constructive thinking, often against prevailing systems, powers, and fashions. The most discussed topics of the time are hotly but peacefully argued in forums and small groups. Leading politicians, church officials, and economic advisors are called to critical questionings. Public media take part and report the proceedings. The documentary editions of speeches and discussions are a source of further inspiration. The hosting city during the days of the rally experiences a profound spiritual, social, cultural upheaval, even if some people disdain overcrowded public transportation, roads and places, and music on the streets. The waves of fresh thinking are felt beyond city borders in the whole country and German-speaking parts of Europe.

A Catholic Church convention of laypeople (*Kirchentag*) goes back to 1848 and really has set the pattern for such mass meetings. It has increasingly turned critical of the official church and sought cooperation with the Protestant event. A wide variety of ecological and peace movements, Third World and social aids groups have emerged inside (and outside) the churches. Third World (now called "One World") shops realize the idea of fair trade; telephone counselors are available in all big cities; meals for the growing number of homeless are cooked in community houses; demonstrations against racial discrimination and other forms of discrimination and against right-wing violence are supported by Christian groups. Global thinking from a Christian perspective is asked for: equality and justice for all, a world order giving opportunities to every human. The ecumenical conciliary movement for "Peace, Justice, and Preservation of Creation" found much repercussion in Germany. High points of the engagement of church folks were the antiwar demonstrations in Bonn 1981–1983 and the campaign for waiving the debts of the poorest countries, in the last instance inspired by the Old Testament Jubilee (Lev 25), during the years 1999–2000. The ferment of liberating ideas in favor of the captive neighbor is germinating in many places. Special cases in this wide field of political and social involvement of Christians have been *Politisches Nachtgebet* centered in the city of Cologne and inspired, for example, by Dorothee Sölle (1929–2003; an eminent theologian, poet, and writer) and Fulbert Steffensky as well as *Aktion Sühnezeichen*, founded in 1958 by Lothar Kreyssing, a "confessing" veteran. The former movement negotiated peace in the midst of an explosive Cold War (which peaked 1968–1980), while the latter organized work camps of young Germans in countries devastated by the war and in Israel, to overcome hatred and guilt and to construct a common amenable future.[4]

In contradistinction to popular Christian movements, liberating efforts of ecclesiastical governments took place mainly on the level of intellect and knowledge, such as publication of important analyses of contemporary situations (e.g., *Denkschriften* of the EKD treating controversial matters of social ethics and politics) or the continuous dialogue with the small but growing Jewish community in Germany (*Christlich-Jüdischer Dialog*). Special emphasis was placed on establishing contacts between churches, labor unions, and politicians in newly created "academies," institutions of adult education and meeting places for all sorts of social groups. This liberation from old exclusivist tradition by way of rethinking traditional structures is, in fact, an example of "institutional" revolution. Many unionists for the first time in their lives experienced direct contact with church people and were impressed by open dialogues within the *Evangelische Akademien*. Many points of common interest were discovered (e.g., social politics, peace movements, gender issues, German reunification).

Theological schools and faculties, especially adjunct Christian student communities, have often picked up liberation impulses coming from Latin America, Africa, and Asia. They sympathized with the struggle of the marginalized, heroizing even armed resistance, as in the case of Father Camilo Torres (1929–1966), who died in guerrilla combat. Student workshops and individual professors brought the topic "liberation" into the theological agenda. Scores of students took part in exchange programs, especially with Latin America. Academic liberation theology thus ended also in liberationist practice (see C. Boff 1978). Special mention should be given to the broad lay movements within European Catholic churches that are struggling for a thorough reform of their rather conservative institutions, particularly in terms of full recognition of women's rights and a modern redefinition of sexual ethos. The official *Zentralkomitee der deutschen Katholiken*, a lay organization founded in 1952 to counsel German bishops, does so very moderately but visibly. More radical are, among others, the movements *Kirche von unten* (Church from Below; see www.ikvu.de) and *Wir sind Kirche* (We Constitute Church; see www.wirsind-kirche.de). They work for the democratization of the Roman Catholic Church and true ecumenical partnership (sharing the Eucharist with other Christians). A courageous association of Catholic women from Austria and

---

4. *Aktion Sühnezeichen* is still active; see www.asf-ev.de.

Germany has begun to ordain females into the priesthood (see www.virtu-elle-dioezese.de; www.womenpriests.org). There has been a first ordination ceremony for seven women on board a Danube ship (29 June 2002) and a second act on Lake Bodensee (26 June 2006) for three female candidates. The Vatican reacted with excommunications, but apparently this new venture of liberation and reform does enjoy a good amount of support within the Catholic Church. Open rebellion against sacred traditional norms becomes possible. The causes of church reform are supported by a series of publications in paper and on the Internet.

2.3.4. Unified Germany (Since 1989/1990)

"Growing together, what is meant to belong to each other" (Willy Brandt) became a slogan in the process of reunification, but bringing together differing structures and mentalities impressed by forty years of separate developments proved quite difficult. According to the rules of power and wealth, the BRD ecclesiastical bodies basically coerced their sister churches in the East back into the old molds of traditional state-supported organisms. As a result, for example, the DDR-communities had to accept state taxation of their (few) members again and to consent to state-paid military chaplains and state-paid religious public education. Only in Berlin and Brandenburg on 26 April 2009 regular lessons of "ethics" instead of "confessional religion" in public schools have been maintained by popular vote. These efforts have been stiffly combated by the Western-minded church government of the present. Behind the differences one may sense also age-old confessional distinctions and underlying societal differences (agrarian versus urban situations) between East and West Germany. Criticism from the East practically went unheard in the West. Instead, churchgoers and politicians in the West imposed for the most part their concepts of property rights, the status of pastors, public responsibilities, financial management, and the role of church publications. Communion between congregations, kept up before 1989 on the basis of Western subsidies to the suffering Easterners, broke off or was severely diminished. Of course, there also was some common ground in matters of social concern, such as race discrimination, unemployment, peace, and violence, and theological concern. Church governments of the different regional church bodies, roughly coinciding with the federal states, do work together, and the union of Protestant churches (EKD) as well as other national ecclesiastical organizations function well. Popular movements in East and West also have some overlapping concerns. Bondages and efforts to overcome them, however, remain regionally different.

2.4. Twenty-First Century

The new century has hardly begun, but it shows signs of Christianity's downfall. Membership numbers are diminishing, and Christianity's public importance is declining. However, there is some renewed interest in religion. The main issues along the lines of liberation theology seem to be to recognize self-made captivities in traditional structures of worship, church governance, patriarchalism, and the relationship to state and society. Our task is to try to overcome these obstacles in the spirit of love, justice, and peace by fresh thinking about God, humanity and the world and boldly believing in the power of the Spirit. Liberationists should look with sympathy toward and in solidarity with the outside world. There is much need for truthful analyses of ills and opportunities, much urgency in supporting the weak and suffering, much demand for restructuring wretched rules and relationships. All these liberating activities can be undertaken only if Christians leave behind age-old claims to be, they themselves, absolutely right in their faith and chosen to rule the globe as vice-regents of God. Exclusivism is a barrier to liberation. Instead, Christians are allowed to hand over everything they own and know to make possible that breakthrough to freedom that enslaved humanity needs.

3. Evaluation

By reflecting on liberation movements through the centuries, we realize that situations of bondage and breaking bonds vary a great deal. Neither is there just one type of liberation envisioned in biblical testimonies. Mental, intellectual, emotional, and spiritual fetters are as real as economical, political, and legal ones. We should be careful not to concentrate too much on just one variety of bondage and not recognize collateral limitations. Even so, each particular case of enslavement needs to be studied carefully, with attention to its own dimensions and ramifications. Being human, though, we shamefully recognize the insufficiencies of all our liberation attempts. Further, as we study history, it becomes clear enough that successful strategies of liberation very soon may become oppressive themselves. Revolutions do swallow their own protagonists. Therefore, a sober and self-critical hermeneutics of liberation is the presupposition of all liberating praxis.

TEXTS AND CONTEXTS

Releasing the Story of Esau
from the Words of Obadiah

Jione Havea

The identification of Esau with Edom meant that Edom received somewhat unfairly, a label which stuck. (Bartlett 1977, 21).

Obadiah's Vision, a First Hearing

The vision of Obadiah blazes against Edom. YHWH sent an envoy throughout the nations (*gôyīm*) to rise against Edom, to make Edom the least and the most despised among the nations (v. 2). Whereas thieves take only what they want and grape-gatherers leave gleanings, YHWH will wipe Edom clean (vv. 3–5). The demolition of Edom shall be total. Then the gnashing of the vision turns from Edom to Esau: "How Esau has been thoroughly searched out, his hidden things sought after" (v. 6; Raabe 1996, 139).

In this first hearing, "Esau" is an eponym for "Edom," just as "Jacob" and "Judah" refer to "Israel" and "Jerusalem" (see Bartlett 1969; 1977; Ogden 1982). The announced judgment is not against Esau son of Isaac and twin brother of Jacob but against Edom, the nation that was enemy to Judah. YHWH condemned Edom, and its allies deceived it (v. 7) by driving it to the border and luring it with "bread."[1] Rejected by YHWH and by allies and strangers, Edom's slaughter will be total (vv. 8–9).

What did Edom do to merit this fate? Obadiah's vision anchors the explanation for the slaughter of Edom to the "slaughter and violence done to your

---

1. See Nogalski for the possibility that "bread" is used here as a metaphor for covenant. Compare Raabe 1996 and Davies 2004, who propose to emend the text to read "those who ate/eat with you" (so JPS and NRSV) so that it parallels the "allies" and "confederates" in the first part of the verse.

brother Jacob" (v. 10, NRSV).[2] Edom is accused of standing aloof while aliens ransacked Jerusalem (v. 11), of delighting and jeering at what was happening (v. 12), of entering and looting the city (v. 13), and of standing at the passes to cut down survivors and refugees (v. 14). Such behaviors are treacherous to the maximum degree, betrayal at its best, warranting ruthless punishment. The day of reckoning is coming upon Edom; on that day, on behalf of Judah, the conduct of Edom will be requited (v. 15). The day of YHWH will shatter Edom and the oppressive nations (v. 16), but there will be a remnant on mount Zion (v. 17).

> The House of Jacob shall be fire,
> And the House of Joseph flame,
> And the House of Esau shall be straw;
> They shall burn it and devour it,
> And no survivor shall be left of the House of Esau
> —for the LORD has spoken. (v. 18; JPS)

The face of Esau continues to be called up.

The vision of Obadiah is captivating. It lures the hearer's sympathies toward the houses of Jacob and Joseph, and the one who accepts the portrayal of Edom will easily accept YHWH's verdict, for anyone who commits what arrogant and betraying Edom is accused of doing deserves to be annihilated. One does not have to belong to Jacob's house to be disgusted with Edom (so Robinson 1988, 93). Obadiah's vision thus has a splitting focus, igniting the hearer's compassion for the house of Jacob and disgust against Edom.

YHWH's intention, in this first hearing, is to enable justice to roll through the streets of Jerusalem by avenging the deeds of Edom. A reader who is concerned for the welfare of oppressed subjects will easily endorse YHWH's mission, through Obadiah's vision, which seeks to avenge Edom's role in Jerusalem's destruction. It is a vision of deliverance and a message of hope for people who have suffered the kind of cruelty that Jerusalem suffered. In this hearing, the vision of Obadiah is liberating … for the house of Jacob.

---

2. Even though proper names are to be read as eponyms, the judgment continues to draw upon the personal relationship between the two brothers, Jacob and Esau. See Bartlett (1969 and 1977) for more detailed discussions of the "brotherhood of Edom."

Tonight I have an audience again; not
as big as I'd have wished, a little
bigger though than what you had when you
breathed life into the dying words of our
drifting tribe. (Pio Manoa)[3]

LIBERATION HERMENEUTICS AND SOUTH PACIFIC ISLAND CONTEXTS

The disciplines of liberation theologies and liberation hermeneutics have not taken root, for better or for worse, in formalized theological education in the islands of the South Pacific. Islander students are taught and disciplined in Western-nourished theologies and biblical criticisms, with English as the language of instruction in degree programs, and are required to research, think, and write as if they are Europeans.[4] Although some of the native theological lecturers are concerned for cultural awareness and liberation in church thoughts and practices, with budding attention to the contribution and place of women in church mission, we have not seriously taken into account the waves of native imaginations and mannerisms. This is partially because we have not been able to shed the shackles of our Westernized theological trainings.

Liberation theologies and liberation hermeneutics sprout in wretched life situations different from our deprived and impoverishing spaces, among peoples far more numerous and resourceful than ours, and they come to us *through* the West. We learn of liberation theologies and hermeneutics as products of Latin America, Asia, and Africa that serve a Western theological agenda: to make the teachings and stories about the Christian God and community appropriate for local faces and interrelations.[5]

---

3. I sprinkle my reflection with verses from Pio Manoa's "A Letter to My Storyteller" (1992, 17–19). Though I will not use all of the verses of the poem and switch the order of the verses, I pray that I have not violated the integrity of Manoa's powerful locating reflection.

4. I found only one B.D. thesis written in Fijian at the Pacific Regional Seminary (Suva, Fiji); the rest of the theses there and at Pacific Theological College were written in English, with a few in French. This was due to our dependence on European lecturers and the financial support of their sending bodies, to the privileging of English and French ("languages of the empire"), and to the lack of scholars who can examine theses in our native languages. The situation has changed as our theological institutions now have many native lecturers; hopefully this will soon be reflected in the way theological education is offered.

5. This is a reference and a challenge to the traditional practice of contextual theology (see also Havea 2004). Pacific Island natives have not questioned the urgings of contextual

The rays of liberation theologies are beginning to swim our horizons, and we are in the process of navigating and weaving the bodies of theologies that make sense in and to our realities.[6] For instance, the curriculum of Pacific Theological College (PTC, Suva, Fiji), the leading provider of theological education in the region, includes a Bachelor of Divinity course on the methods of contextual theology. This course aims to expose the relativity of traditional Western theology and supplement that with "the new approaches of Liberation theology for the liberation of the exploited and the poor, and some examples from contextual African and Asian theologies."[7] Since most of the native theological instructors are trained at PTC, one expects a stronger presence of liberation theologies around the Pacific in the future.

As we in the Pacific region attempt the moves of contextual theologies, we should also take courage to gauge and supplement the contents of what we are urged to contextualize. Not everything that comes from the West, including Christianity and its Bible, models of theology and exegesis, is island(er)-friendly. This essay is another step in the direction of supplementing a text not often discussed in the islands, the book of Obadiah, with an approach that requires a step away from the confines of formalized (in the Western sense) theological education (see also Havea 2004).

Outside the shadows of theological halls, mainly among the grass-roots, within and beyond church settings, are *currents of island life*[8] that are transformative and liberating. These currents (*lōlenga*) were ostracized when the Christian mission arrived, but they survived the onslaught from the West and, figuratively speaking, are rippling at the shores of theological institutions. This essay steps into the ripples of one of those currents, the *telling story* practices shared in the oral cultures of South Pacific Islands,[9] because they

---

theology because we are eager to embrace the tasks of doing theology and the encouragement to find alternatives to Western formulations. As a consequence, we blindfold ourselves from the foreignness of the theological content we contextualize. In other words, contextual theology invites us to substitute Western forms and content with native ones, and we do so for the sake of extending the reaches of Western values, stories and memories.

6. *Pacific Journal of Theology* (a publication of the South Pacific Association of Theological Schools) now and then carries attempts to name Pacific theologies, and recently the *Vakavuku* (Navigating Knowledge) conference at the University of the South Pacific (http://www.usp.ac.fj/index.php?id=1351) dealt with the issue of Pacific epistemologies, but the hermeneutical elements of these tasks have yet to materialize.

7. See the PTC website (http://www.ptc.ac.fj) for further information on its academic programs.

8. The phrase "currents of island life" refers to a Tongan saying, *Lōlenga fakamotu*, that closely translates as "island habits." It is a derogatory label for small-minded islanders.

9. I use "telling story" instead of "storytelling" in order to draw attention to both the

have strands to weave into the mats of island (liberation or otherwise) hermeneutics (see also Havea 2006).

> There are times when I uphold your stories,
> epiphanies of gods, men and women and moments now
> not merely forgotten, but by many hated, denied;
> though they mingle in the tides of our tamed
> insurrections, and echo in the spaces of our bones. (Pio Manoa)

Telling Story Currents

Stories are purposefully told. Islanders, too, tell stories for multiple reasons: in order to generate laughter and angst, to establish roots and relationships, to explain functions and events, to nourish longings and memories, to protect identities and boundaries, to subvert claims and disputes, to energize and extend other tellings and hidden stories, and so forth. *Telling stories* is a mat of many strands, and we cannot squeeze all tellers under the same personality. Nor would all tellings squat under the same purpose. Telling stories in the Pacific Islands is fluid enough (like our oceanic context) to give a different shape to old stories in ways similar to liberation hermeneutics giving new life to ancient texts, with a preferential option for the poor[10] and the resolve to ignite resistance against abusive power structures.

A practice of telling stories in Tongan circles known as *talanoa fakatatau* is helpful in my cause. *Talanoa fakatatau* happens when someone tells a story *in response* to another story that someone else has shared or when someone retells the story just told *with a different twist*. Of course, the story to which

---

"energies in telling" and the "power of stories," which interweave in oral cultures. A telling of a story has energies when it invites retellings of that story and/or that telling; and a story has power when it takes hold of both tellers and hearers, pushing them to the "energies of telling" (see also Havea 2004).

10. There are two interlocking sides to a "preferential option for the poor": the "preferential option" element suggests that liberation hermeneutics is biased and political, as are all hermeneutical programs; "option for the poor" identifies the interlocutor of liberation hermeneutics as subjects who are marginalized (not just the economic poor but all subjects marginalized because of their gender, race, class, age, sexual orientation, and so forth). We have heard of the "new poor" in Latin and South America who are poor as the consequence of wars of arms and drugs and who are growing in numbers also in Asia, the Middle East, and Africa. We may add here the "Pacific poor," who are poor yet laid back and jovial, living from what they can fish up from earth and ocean, both of which are not always friendly or giving.

a *talanoa fakatatau* responds may be a *talanoa fakatatau* to another story at another telling.

At story circles around *kava* bowls or during village functions and toils, *talanoa fakatatau* is signaled when the teller begins with ʻ*Oku ou manatu ai ...* ("I recall through that ..."). The emphasis falls on the recollection of the teller, and it is not critical whether the story is true or not but that it is recalled and shared, passed on, from one teller to another and from one generation to the next. A *talanoa fakatatau* may respond in a variety of ways to the story to which it gives *faka-tatau* (match-up, equal, counter), and I will briefly identify the four most common ones.

First, a *talanoa fakatatau* tells another story to parallel the one first told. For instance, if the first story tells of a seafood feast at an outer island, the *talanoa fakatatau* may tell of an equally plentiful feast at the village where the stories are exchanged. Local villagers usually relish this form of *talanoa fakatatau*!

Second, a *talanoa fakatatau* expands the first told story. For instance, the *talanoa fakatatau* may tell of a fishing tradition for which the island where the seafood feast took place is known. In response, hearers would say something like, "No wonder they have huge seafood feasts," and more *talanoa fakatatau* follow.

Third, a *talanoa fakatatau* aims to unravel the first story. For instance, the *talanoa fakatatau* may tell of how most of the seafood at the feast in question was brought by friends and relatives from other islands. Hence the praise for the seafood feast is stripped from the islanders who hosted the feast.

Fourth, a *talanoa fakatatau* may retell the same story but pick up elements neglected or ignored in the first telling. For instance, the *talanoa fakatatau* may explain that the seafood feast was to celebrate the life of a central figure in the island, which explains why people from neighboring islands came with their contributions of food. The feast is secondary to the celebration it marks, which is anchored to the life of a particular islander who draws affection from other islands.

Craftier tellers will weave a number of these elements into the *talanoa fakatatau* they offer, and in a circle of crafty tellers the listeners will feel as if they are swept in waves of *talanoa fakatatau*. At the end of a telling story sitting, if it is not stopped short by someone acting as an adjudicator, each listener will decide which story or telling to accept and share at other sittings. Through the practice of *talanoa fakatatau*, a story lives among other stories and other recollections; *talanoa fakatatau* is a current in an ocean of stories and tellings, a strand in the streams of island life.

In the remainder of this essay, I shall dip the vision of Obadiah into the waves of *talanoa fakatatau*. I gave a first hearing in the opening section, which is already a *talanoa fakatatau* (according to the first reason given above) of the text. I will give two other tellings to expand, unravel, and curb both Obadiah's vision and my first hearing.

> But I stray from your art and tale.
> When first I sought you out the young said
> you were ash-tongued, arch-fabulist, fibber, not
> knowing that there lay your gift and burden.
> You had to tie in things with things; weave ends
> to means, call forth action from misty landscapes,
> trying always to connect bird and river and egg
> and flood, life, death. All your words
> were of things known, which figured things
> in our active universe, powers felt, seen or unseen.
> Mere myth to those who worship at the shrine
> of the great god Arithmos whose one commandment
> is to measure all and always to count the cost. (Pio Manoa)

Obadiah's Vision, Another Telling

Obadiah's vision opens with tidings from Yhwh concerning Edom being sent among the nations, calling them to "rise against *her* for battle" (v. 1). I retain the feminine pronoun to draw attention to a tension in the gendering of Edom. Edom is feminine in verse 1 but identified with Esau in verse 6, as if Edom is both female and male. What may be the reasons behind the feminization of Edom?

The text does not specify the nations to which Yhwh appeals or how they relate to Edom and Judah, only that they are *gôyīm* ("nations," "Gentiles"), the grouping within which Edom sits in the minds of most Israelites. Yhwh's call to battle appeals for support from *gôyīm* who are not necessarily allies to Judah or foes to Edom. There are therefore no reasons to imagine that the *gôyīm* are enemies of Edom or devotees of Yhwh who would jump at Yhwh's bidding. In other words, the call to battle must be enticing if the *gôyīm* are to respond.

Accordingly, gender biases seem both to promote and camouflage the condemnation of Edom. First of all, referring to Edom as a feminine subject is a sublime way to draw the nations into the task at hand.[11] Nations over-

---

11. I imagine war cries similar to those often heard in the backstreets, such as "kill 'em bitches," which are not always against women. The adversaries are at once feminized and demonized. Note in this connection Ogden's intertextual reading: "In Ps. 137:8 the significance of describing Babylon as having been destroyed is to fortify the petition that Edom its 'daughter' meet the same fate" (1982, 92).

flowing with pride and machismo would find it difficult to refuse the call to rise against *her* in battle; to refuse might give the impression that they are afraid of or weaker than *her*. Whether they are for YHWH and against Edom is not imperative; that they have the courage to *rise against her* in battle is the arrogance to which YHWH appeals.

Moreover, the feminization of Edom can blindfold the nations from the excessive violence to which they are lulled. The intended destruction of Edom will be total and disgracing, and the participation of the nations in YHWH's campaign, and its aggressive brutality, do not require justification because YHWH is calling them to battle a "she-*gôy*."

At the crossroads of interpretation, the double gendering of Edom is an opening for misogynist critics to accept the condemnation of Edom not just because Edom may be bad or because YHWH says that Edom is responsible for the violation of Judah but also because Edom is a feminine subject.[12] The NRSV conceals this by rendering YHWH's appeal with the neuter pronoun: "Rise up! Let us rise against *it* for battle!" This is a more inclusive translation, but it runs the risk of dehumanizing Edom. Such are the limits of language and translation. Edom is condemnable as a feminine subject and degradable ("neutered") in English inclusive language translations.

Edom is not only feminized but also linked to an individual, Esau, who is outside of the sphere of Judah's preferred memories. The identities of a collective (Edom) and of an individual (Esau) intersect, becoming interlocked with references to Mount Esau (vv. 8, 9, 19, 21) and the brother of Jacob (see vv. 10, 12). A vision calling other *gôyîm* to rise against a particular nation (Edom) in battle (v. 1) appeals to feelings toward a particular figure (Esau) as if to justify its violent and violating agenda. These, one may argue, are "naturalization" (see Robinson 1988) acts through which the poet attempts to make the condemnation of Edom acceptable.

Subversive currents ripple under YHWH's campaign. YHWH's intention is to avenge the slaughter of Judah, in which some of the summoned *gôyîm* may have participated.[13] On the one hand, YHWH's call gives those *gôyîm* an opportunity to atone for and/or to cover up their participation in the slaugh-

---

12. Bearing in mind that the conventional practice is to use feminine pronominal suffixes when referring to nations, I am here addressing the consequences of the gender specificity of the language.

13. I do not assume that the events (both the slaughter of Judah and the campaign to avenge it) to which Obadiah appeals are historical. Whether the events occurred (in the way Obadiah's vision portrays them) or not does not affect my telling. I tell Obadiah, like other biblical texts, as a text that "naturalizes" (makes natural, realistic and "history-like") the events it presents (see also Robinson 1988).

ter of Judah. Yʜwʜ gives them a chance to cease being enemies to Judah. On the other hand, Yʜwʜ's call to battle carries a threat to those nations as well, especially the enemies of Judah. Edom (who is a "brother") is the enemy targeted this time, and the other nations/enemies should expect worse treatment when it is their turn. Surely, a battle against a sibling will not be as severe as a war against one who is not a kin!

The foregoing recalls two interlocking inclinations: the inclination to transfer craze from one subject (individual and/or collective) to another; and the inclination to overwrite the story of an individual (e.g., Esau) with the (hi)story of a collective (e.g., Edom, as a nation).

The first inclination points back to Freud, who as a psychotherapist noticed that some patients showed feelings and fantasies about him that were unfounded. He concluded that he must have struck a nerve that reminded his patients of something in their past. Like biological time machines in emotional time warp, patients transfer their past and what they want to see or what they fear onto their therapist in the present, though they know little about him. This process of *transference* is related to *projection*, the process through which one projects one's feelings, emotions, or motivations onto another person without realizing that what one is reacting to has to do more with oneself than the other person. When one feels disgust for or fear of another person, one projects disgust for or fear of oneself. This happens without one knowing why one feels and reacts as one does.

Transference and projection happen in life and in texts, too. A lover might remind one of a parent, especially the irritating things that that parent did while one was growing up. In the story of Moses, for example, his initial refusals to return and lead Israel out of Egypt (Exod 3) have more to do with his fear of Pharaoh, his "father" in Egypt, and of himself than with Yʜwʜ and Israel.

Transference and projection are involved in the telling of stories also. There are many opportunities for tellers to project their own fears onto characters in the story and/or to transfer feelings toward one character onto others. The vision of Obadiah profits from these tendencies. The aggressive words against Edom beg its tellers to project their own rage and fears upon Edom, even though they do not know anything about it. Further, the association of Edom with Esau encourages tellers to transfer their craze toward one onto the other. As Bartlett puts it, "The identification of Esau with Edom meant that Edom received somewhat unfairly, a label which stuck" (1977, 21).

Bartlett interprets from a position where Esau is already *diselected* (Heard 2001). From the other side of the table, the identification of Edom with Esau contributes to the charring of Esau in the eyes of readers and storytellers. I receive Obadiah's vision at a place close to where Elie Wiesel laments, "At the risk of shocking my reader, I feel compelled to reveal my sympathy for a character that the Bible seems to treat rather badly. I am talking about Esau, the elder brother of Jacob. I feel sorry for him" (1998, 26). Wiesel goes on to conclude his reflection in, understandably, painful fidelity: "And with all of that, we are the descendants and heirs of Jacob. / And not of Esau" (1998, 27).

I, too, am sorry for Esau, but I am several steps removed from where Wiesel is. In the next section, I will recall and tell the story of Esau away from the condemnation of Edom in Obadiah's vision.

The second inclination noted above can be seen with respect to parts of the Hebrew Bible where the memories of Israel are established and guarded, especially when read with linear historiographical lenses. Mieke Bal addresses this propensity in her *Death and Dissymmetry*, in which she counters the dominant view that Judges is theologically and historically coherent. The *politics of coherence* intertwines theology with national history in response "to a need so deeply rooted in the interaction between the book and its modern, committed readers" (1988, 5). They read biblical texts "not as sources for knowledge that lie outside them, but as the materialization of a social reality that they do not simply and passively reflect, but of which they are a part and to which they respond" (1988, 6). The upshot is the repression of the ideo-stories of individuals,[14] mostly women, in the interest of a coherent identity and memory of the people and the nation (Israel). To enable the recovery of repressed ideo-stories from under the politics of coherence, Bal applies a process of *countercoherence* on ideo-stories of three murdered and three lethal women, highlighting the intersections of the personal and the political and how political violence gives way to domestic violence (see also Havea 2003, 99–101).

My retelling of Obadiah's vision has thus far tracked on the countercoherence path, and this will continue in the next section. I am sympathetic to Esau, older brother of Jacob, and I hope that he can be released from Obadiah's vision. Toward this hope, I re-call the hold of "prophetic vision" and the contribution of the canonical status of the Bible toward establishing the fears and desires of Obadiah and YHWH against Esau.[15]

---

14. "An ideo-story is a narrative whose structure lends itself to be the receptacle of different ideologies. Its representational makeup promotes concreteness and visualization. Its characters are strongly opposed so that dichotomies can be established. And its fabula is open enough to allow for any ideological position to be projected onto it. Ideo-stories, then, are not closed but extremely open; however, they seem to be closed, and this appearance of closure encourages the illusion of stability of meaning" (Bal 1988, 11).

15. In linking Obadiah to YHWH, I draw attention to Obadiah's Hebrew name, which

Even if Edom was guilty of Obadiah's charges, why was it necessary to draw Esau under his readers' gavel? I raise this question because Obadiah's vision blames Edom for more than can be historically verified (so Wolff 1986, 22). There was enmity between Judah and Edom, since Edom occupied part of southern Judah, but there is no evidence that Edom participated in the destruction of the First Temple or that of Jerusalem (Freedman 1995, 112–13; Raabe 1996, 52–54). Obadiah joins Jeremiah and several latter prophets in griping against Edom (see Raabe 1996, 22–47; Wolff 1986, 17, 21–22), thereby tarnishing the image of Edom in the eyes of readers. By transference, the tarnishing of Edom contributes to the vilification of Esau in rabbinical polemics even though the midrashic impression that Esau was intrinsically wicked and violent "was directly related to the Roman occupation and destruction of Palestine" (Freedman 1995, 108). This was unfair to both Edom and Esau.

Readers tend not to challenge the canonized misrepresentations of people with whom they cannot identify, partially because of ideological blind spots but mainly out of respect for those canonized texts. Such texts, as are all great works, assume mythological status in terms of both power as well as understandability. As Ricoeur explained, "Myths have a horizon of universality which allows them to be understood by other cultures.... The horizon of any genuine myth always exceeds the political and geographical boundaries of a specific national or tribal community" (1991, 488). The vision of Obadiah has crossed several cultures and gained mythological eminence both because it is said to come from YHWH and because of the canonical awe of the Bible. But this does not mean that the defamation of Esau in Obadiah's vision should go unchallenged.

> Can you believe that the learned among them
> say the white man created us anew? that the tradition
> we uphold, or assert, are nothing but this new being
> much like those of tribes that have crossed oceans
> and frontiers, and can call any piece of earth home? (Pio Manoa)

'OKU OU MANATU AI KI HE MATA 'O ISOA![16]

I wish to recall the face of Esau because he does not have a story. In the line of stories that *muli* (nonnative) storytellers read to our people, Esau appears

---

derives from the participle *'ōbēd*, as if to suggest that he is "one who serves/worships YHWH" (see Raabe 1996, 96).

16. Tongan for "I recall through that the face of Esau!"

in the stories of others but does not have a story of his own. He is the first and loved son of Isaac, the graying old man who had a taste for game, and a rival for his twin brother Jacob, whom their mother Rebekah loved more. The brothers struggle against each other since the womb of their mother, and they grow up each with the love of one parent, in a broken home.

Esau grows up into a skillful hunter, a man of the outdoors. In nomadic cultures, he shows the stuff of a desired chief. But around the tents of Isaac's descendants, he would be a regular pointer to his uncle Ishmael, who was a wild ass of a man. Insofar as Esau was not a homebody, he stands not a chance in the setting of patriarchal stories. Like the way things are in our Pacific islands, the one loved by a mother is the one who succeeds. This is because mothers are chiefs of the private (I speak of private instead of domestic) space, as are stories. Esau may have been quite a catch in the public eyes, but he is a loser at home, the place where blessings are received and taken and where stories form and pass on.

In this recalling, I walk on a land where I am a *muli* (nonnative) longing for our native sea of stories that flow a long way back and the *fakataʻane* (sitting crossed-legs) of storytellers who breathe life into the dying words of drifting tribes. I recall with hope of falling into the billabongs of memory in my new home, Australia, and the rebirthing of storytelling.

I "recall" the face of Esau also because his image has been scarred. I call back the scarred face of Esau from the disfiguring memories of visionaries, such as Obadiah. We all know that stories grow in their retellings, and as stories grow taller, branches shoot up and break off, leaves spring to shadow then dry up and fall off. Thus, I sit not to uproot the branches that visionaries replant. They recall Esau for their own purposes, which I cannot adopt. They link Esau to Edom, whose name explains Esau's preference for red (Hebrew: *ʼādōm*) stuff. I have said enough about Obadiah and Edom already.

I recall the face of Esau because he is not a bad guy, really. Others take advantage of him, especially his younger brother Jacob, who behaves as one would expect from a younger sibling. Like the time when Esau came home famished and Jacob bought his birthright with bread and lentil stew (Gen 25:29–34). A hungry man, for honor and power, Jacob robs his hungry brother. Can one be as ravenous?

Many storytellers retell that exchange in ways that give the impression that Jacob gained the upper hand. Jacob won! But those storytellers most likely own properties and birthrights, so they focus on the property that Jacob gained. But put yourself in the place of Esau: he was very hungry, provoked by his brother with his steaming bowl of stew, at the home of his loving father. The birthright would not feed Esau or silence his irritating twin brother, so why not play along? "You want the birthright? Take it. It's really not mine yet, but you can have it. Just give me some red stuff." Was Esau serious? Did he mean what he said? Was he being sarcastic?

It is interesting when storytellers, addressing this stew-birthright exchange, say that "Esau spurned the birthright," because that is a very fluid expression. To spurn a birthright can mean many things. It can mean that Esau took his birthright lightly, which can mean that he was neglecting his duties and responsibilities to his family; it can also mean that Esau found the whole business of birthrights ridiculous, especially for a hungry person; it can also mean that Esau thought that one's birthright should be shared rather than possessed; and so forth. You must have your own explanations. What do you say?

> You knew when you were making up stories
> in the intersecting streams of memory how
> there was always a tradition that gave your tale
> both matter and judgement that sealed approval.
> And your audience knew; it laughed and marvelled
> or grew sad and wept, sharing our common tradition,
> the gods, the heroes, the demons, who inhabit us still.
> And I know we have this heritage that many
> full of other traditions (borrowed, swallowed
> whole or freely negotiated), deny. (Pio Manoa)

While he was young, Esau was dragged along to Gerar when a famine fell on the land that YHWH had promised to his family. There his parents pretended not to be a couple. Isaac told the men of the place that Rebekah was his sister. It was only when King Abimelech of Gerar looked out his window and saw Isaac fondling Rebekah that they figured out that the two were married. This business of saying that a wife is a sister was a well-known family strategy for survival in a foreign land. Grandfather Abraham twice said that Sarah was his sister, so that it might go well for him, and so the kings of Egypt and Gerar, also named Abimelech, took her. Bizarre things happen in the stories of Esau's family. The elders discipline the men not to marry foreign women but allow foreign men to take their wives. If foreign men can take their wives, why can't they take foreign women? In order to expose the conflict between family teachings and family practice, Esau took two wives from Hittite fathers. That's right, two foreign women. Double the pleasure, double the trouble!

Esau was rebelling, and it worked, because his wives became a source of bitterness to Isaac and Rebekah. I am sorry for saying that Esau married as part of his rebellion, for that means that he was using foreign women for his personal campaign. That is a cruel stance, and I apologize. But let me continue recalling the face of Esau. Esau was forty years old when he took his wives. He knew what he was doing, and storytellers remember how his parents did not approve of his wives. But those storytellers do not explain why, or realize that Isaac and Rebekah did not approve for different reasons. I do not know for certain myself, but I say this time that Isaac was bitter because Esau violated the family teachings against marrying foreign women and drew attention to his mistreatment of Rebekah that echoed the mistreatment of Sarah by Abraham. Rebekah was bitter for different reasons. Maybe she was bitter because she could not fully understand her daughters-in-law, who were different both in language and in culture, or maybe because her daughters-in-law reminded her of something else in her past (she was brought into a family where she felt like a foreigner). That is what I say, but you can say something different if you wish.

> My audience at times walks well-trodden ways
> sharing those images or visions that help
> us understand the different spheres we traverse;
> at times it trembles at the edge, not knowing
> which way the stars (or demons?) beckon. These
> are times when our many worlds collapse,
> our trivial fancies dislodge as we resequence time,
> and all our known events
> and backwards is not always the negative step
> for a tale that we can all acknowledge, that we
> must all grow into. (Pio Manoa)

Later on, Isaac calls Esau to his tent. Isaac is closing to the end of his days. Before his sun sets and he is committed to his ancestors, Isaac wants to give Esau his blessing. To formalize the giving of the blessing, Isaac asks Esau to prepare his preferred meal. Something about gamey food stories causes me to pause. Earlier, Esau sold his birthright for food. This time, someone might think that Isaac's blessing is on sale for the price of a gamey, a meaty, meal. As Esau exits to go on the hunt, my heart goes out to him. The old man is going blind so he does not see who else is in the area to hear his instructions to Esau. We all know how loudly old people talk! And being an outdoors kind of person, Esau is not aware that a body can blend into the folds of the text, I mean the folds of the tent, to hear what is said and wished. Esau is not naïve, but in the confines of the tent of his father, he is vulnerable to the ears of the private.

Isaac's family has a flock at home, for they returned a wealthy family from Gerar, so Esau could have picked a kid from the family lot for his father's meal. He was, after all, a member of the family, even though he had two foreign spouses in his tent. We, too, should take note of this. As our people bring *muli* (nonnative) men and women into our tents and into our stories, we should be aware of when we project our own fears unto the *muli*. So my heart goes out to Esau, for I suspect that some members of his family are still bitter and thus go to great lengths to dislocate him from his father's tent.

Esau does not pick a kid from just outside his father's tent but takes his gear, his quiver and his bow, and goes hunting. He goes to hunt both because of the blessing that awaits him in his father's tent and because of his father's dying wishes. Even though he rebelled against family teachings earlier, he is still a man of the family. He is still his father's son. Many storytellers do not realize that it is possible to rebel against family without rejecting responsibilities and relationships. Isaac sees this good quality in his eldest son and allocates a portion for Esau in his fatherly blessing.

Isaac heard how Jacob took advantage of his hungry brother, forcing Esau to sell him his birthright for a bowl of stew. Throughout this time, Isaac had not heard Esau murmur a complaint against Jacob or the special privileges their mother gave him. In the wakeful heart of the blinding and dying Isaac, he realizes that Esau is the one to carry forward his blessing, which he received from his father before him. This makes good sense to me, if I may say so myself, not because Esau was the firstborn but because he was out in the open welcoming the people and cultures around them. Esau was a person of the open space, where blessings flourish.

While Esau is hunting in the open, events happen at the closure of home, but the details of those do not concern me in this telling. The bottom line is that Rebekah ganged up with her favored son to stand over Isaac, squeezing the blessing intended for Esau unto Jacob. I am not surprised. Isaac was in his tent, at home, the realm of the private, which Rebekah and Jacob have come to control.

> Ex nihilo—out of nothing matter and method,
> and time is not river but periods, truth
> only because it's our sacred artifice. (Pio Manoa)

When Esau returns from the hunt, Rebekah and Jacob have just finished their business. Isaac is surprised when Esau enters, and when he realizes that Esau is not the one he blessed, he wails, "Who did I just bless? He must remain blessed!" Esau is upset and bursts into wild and bitter sobbing, then gives a response that intimates his character. He does not speculate about who the person whom Isaac blessed might be. He knows that it must be his younger brother. Who else would deceive his dying father? Esau does not ask Isaac to take the blessing back from Jacob. Jacob can keep his blessing. Esau asks, on the other hand, for another blessing.

At first, Isaac refuses to give Esau another blessing, saying that Jacob has taken the blessing he was to receive. In response, after many years, Esau laments against the way his brother behaved: "Was he, then, named Jacob that he might supplant me these two times? First he took away my birthright, and now he has taken away my blessing. Have you not reserved a blessing for me?" He does not ask for a better blessing, only that his father give him a blessing. In this regard, Esau is a man of another kind of *open space:* he imagines that it is possible for several people to receive different blessings.

Esau was not being unreasonable. The sons of Abraham, he once heard, are supposed to bring blessings to many people, among many nations. YHWH said so. So Esau's request was not out of bounds. He did not come looking for a blessing in the first place. It was Isaac who called and gave him a task. Now that Esau has fulfilled his part, he expects his father to keep his part of the deal. Why can't Isaac bless Esau also? Can't Isaac, the son of delayed blessings, fake a blessing for his firstborn son Esau? If I were Isaac, I would fake a blessing in order to be nice to my son and to show appreciation for his effort. I would fake a blessing because I will soon be gone, and I trust that my son will assure that my blessing happens. That is how things work. One does not succeed because one has received a blessing. Rather, one will succeed because one has a blessing to uphold and materialize. That is how things have been for many generations of our people. The promises of the ancestors will not work if the current generation does not strive to make those promises real. I imagine that this was how promises and blessings worked in the time of Esau also. So if Isaac would just fake a blessing for Esau, Esau would do his utmost best to make it real.

Esau gives Isaac an opportunity to be a giver of multiple blessings. What a gift that is for a dying man. It proves that Isaac is not yet dead. He can be a giver, a source of blessings in his blinding last days, rather than a beggar. Esau is something! Even after hearing that Isaac's blessing makes Jacob master over him and all his brothers, Esau insists that Isaac bless him, too: "Have you but one blessing, my father? Bless me, too, my father!" Only then, twice reminded of his fatherhood, does Isaac give Esau a blessing: "See, your abode shall enjoy the fat of the earth and the dew of heaven above. Yet by your sword you shall live, and you shall serve your brother; but when you grow restive, you shall break his yoke from your neck."

Thereupon Esau harbored a grudge against Jacob. He really wanted to kill Jacob, but he could not act on that while his father was alive. Why do you think this was so? As I said earlier, the responsibility to make the promises and blessings of the ancestors come true falls on the current generation. If Esau killed Jacob during Isaac's lifetime, Isaac would know that the blessing upon Jacob was ineffective. That would be insulting to the dying old man. It might even kill him, and that might bring a curse on Esau. So Esau harbored his grudge, but he could not act upon it.

From that day forward, Esau was intentional about gratifying his father. But what he decided to do was also irritating. There, is for example, the time when he learned that Isaac had sent Jacob to Paddam-aram to get a wife from the house of Laban, Rebekah's brother. This makes good sense, since Jacob grew up under his mother's love. In the case of Esau, he went to the house of Isaac's brother and brought Ishmael's daughter to be his wife. Isaac sent Jacob to his mother's family, and Esau picked from his father's family. This makes good sense, too, since Esau grew up under his father's love. But in patriarchal memory, as I suggested earlier, Jacob's story was destined to flourish. Stories assemble and grow in the private realm, the space of mothers, before they become history in public. That is why we do not hear much about Esau.

> And I want an earnest return to our tale
> to bring me home.... (Pio Manoa)

Later on, after many years, Esau unexpectedly receives messengers from Jacob, with many gifts, announcing that Jacob is returning from living as a *muli* (nonnative) with uncle Laban and that he expects to find favor in Esau's eyes. How infuriating! Esau is still angry about what Jacob did while they were younger, robbing him of his birthright and blessing, and Esau might have calmed down had Jacob acknowledged and apologized for those deeds. Jacob's attempt to buy favor angers Esau more, so he brings four hundred of his men to confront Jacob.

Before meeting Jacob, Esau runs into drove after drove of Jacob's servants bringing more gifts, each drove declaring that Jacob is coming up next. Jacob, however, is at the end of the procession. He sends the gifts in order to soften his lord Esau. In all, Jacob sends Esau two hundred female goats and twenty male goats, two hundred ewes and twenty rams, thirty lactating camels with their young, forty cows and ten bulls, twenty female donkeys and ten male donkeys. Jacob sends Esau more animals than the number of men Esau has brought. While it did not require many men to keep the animals under control, they were a distraction for Esau's men.

As the brothers approach each other, Jacob bows to the ground seven times, and Esau runs to greet him, embraces him, hugs his neck, kisses him, and weeps. I am not sure why the sudden change of heart, but I suspect that Jacob's remorseful stance and the sight of his women and children melted Esau. These were the children with whom God favored Jacob, as were the gifts he sent ahead of himself. Esau does not want those gifts, but Jacob urges him to accept them. Esau then offers to walk alongside Jacob, who gives an excuse and lingers behind to turn away from where Esau is going. Esau goes on to Seir, but Jacob turns to Succoth. The brothers separate again.

The next time the brothers face each other is after the death of their father, at a ripe old age, having lived a full life. Esau and Jacob come together one more time to bury their father, to commit him to his people, his ancestors. The brothers come together to honor the passing of their father, similar to the way we do rituals so that the departed may rest in peace. It is an honorable responsibility to farewell the dead. Failure to do so can cause restlessness for both the departed and the survivors.

After the burial of Isaac, everyone expects Esau to finish off Jacob as he said earlier, when Jacob robbed the blessing of his father. But Esau does not. Rage may die slowly, but death and mourning contribute toward sorting out hatred. Death and mourning are therapeutic. They unravel animosity and give one a chance to live in peace. In mourning the death of Isaac, Esau is able to live with his brother.

> Here tonight I have no enemies, no aliens
> for we entertain the twin gods that we both know,
> and my audience seeks. (Pio Manoa)

What strikes me most about the story of Esau is that he, like his uncle Ishmael, lacks a burial memory, as did his father and brother. Esau had many sons and daughters, but no one acknowledged his death. Without a mourning ritual, Esau continues to haunt the memories of Jacob's son. Esau started the people of Edom, and there is no doubt to that. But there is no denying also that Esau moved away from his father's land in order to give room for Jacob and his growing family. Esau moved away in order to be in peace with his twin brother.

Without mourning and remembering the death of Esau, his face haunts us, too. So, my children, let us perform a ritual of mourning so that Esau may rest in peace. To give Esau rest, we need to give him a burial memory that will release him from the Edom of Obadiah's vision.

How to Hide an Elephant on Fifth Avenue: Universality of Sin and Class Sin in the Hebrew Scriptures

Alejandro F. Botta

The Hebrew Bible does not present us with a homogeneous and uniform view on the subject of sin. My intent is, therefore, to call attention to a widely supported perspective within the Scriptures that has not found the proper place among the systematic treatment provided by theologians or biblical scholars: the class sin.

I will explicitly approach the problem from a Latino/Latin American *Sitz im Leben*. The reading of the Bible from a Latin American perspective within U.S. soil is faced with the challenge of the distorting picture of U.S. social dynamics represented by the racialization of social struggles and the emphasis on diversity instead of equality (see Michael 2006, 21–49). The lack of natural (i.e., existing in or caused by nature) foundations for U.S. racial classification has been emphasized by social scientists[1] and is evident in the particular cases of some of the people who later became Hispanics. "Initially categorized as white by virtue of the class standing of the Mexican landowning elite during the XIX century, Mexicans became non-white after becoming the main labor force for the intensive sugar beet, lima bean, and citrus agribusiness that developed after 1880 and in the 1930 census, they were to be classified as nonwhite" (Brodkin 1988, 72). Latin American liberationist interpretations of the Bible, on the other hand, are specifically rooted in a dialectical socio-analytical mediation that "centers around the idea of conflict, tension, and struggle" (C. Boff 1987, 57) in the Marxist tradition (i.e., class struggle). From this perspective, the origin of racial classification in the United States should be looked for in the economic structure of U.S. society and in the history of the development of class struggles within the United States. A general survey

---

1. See Steinberg 1989 and the bibliography cited there.

of this problem suggests that "work, especially the performance of work that was at once important to the economy of the nation and that was defined as menial and unskilled, was key to their nonwhite racial assignment" (Brodkin 1988, 55).

Looking at the Hebrew Scriptures from this class-conscious perspective does not imply the negation of the possibility of other approaches but recognizes that from this social location we are able to illuminate aspects of the Scriptures that are hidden to other viewers. Our class-conscious approach to biblical texts implies both the awareness of our own class situation and class interests and the class situation and class interests of the biblical author. When we deal with the topic of sin, this approach leads us to ask: Who might be in a class position of committing that sin? Who benefits from it? Who is a victim of that sin? Who suffers the consequence of that sin?

The doctrine of the universality of sin finds different expressions within the Christian churches, but most churches support some version of the belief that humankind "is inclined to evil, and that continually" (United Methodist Church 2004, §103, art. 7, "Of Original Sin or Birth Sin"), and that sin is universal. Similar statements are found in most Christian systematic theologies. To simplify the discussion, I follow the argumentation of one of the most widely used textbooks of systematic theology in the U.S. evangelical context, Millard J. Erickson's *Christian Theology*. Erickson begins his discussion about the extent of sin by stating: "To the question of who sins, the answer is apparent: sin is universal" (1998, 638). This is certainly no surprise, considering the long history of Christian churches and theologians that have supported the religious dogma of the universality of sin and no exception to the treatment of the subject in other similar works.

In the Christian tradition, the doctrine of the universality of sin is closely related to the doctrine of original sin[2] already defined by Ambrosius and Augustine: *in quo, id est, Adam omnes paccaverunt*. This doctrine was reaffirmed during the Augustine-Pelagius controversy in which the following possibilities were discussed: humans are (a) able to sin or able not to sin (*posse peccare, posse non peccare*); (b) not able not to sin (*non posse non peccare*); (c) able not to sin (*posse non peccare*); and (d) unable to sin (*non posse peccare*). The first state corresponds to the state of humanity in innocence, before the so-called fall, the second to the state of the natural human after the fall, the third to the state of the regenerate human, and the fourth to the glorified human.

---

2. See Boureux and Theobald 2004. For the stories of transgression in Genesis, see Westermann 1994, 178–278; and Croatto 1986.

The position of *non posse non peccare* was later confirmed by the Roman Catholic Church at the Council of Trent in 1546. The situation is different within the Jewish tradition, where "Adam's sin was blamed for the death of all generations but not for the sins of his offspring" (Urbach 1979, 425). The human being is therefore free to choose the path of good or the path of evil.[3]

The biblical support for such a Christian position is quite evident, according to Erickson. Citing Gen 6:5 and 11, he writes, "in the time of Noah, the sin of the race was so great and so extensive that God resolved to destroy everything" (1998, 639). But, as Erickson immediately notes, "Noah appears to be an exception ... being described as a 'righteous man, blameless among the people of his time' (Gen 6:9)" (639). Erickson could have immediately concluded that, if there is room for an exception, then we should be talking about the *extension* of sin, not about its *universality*. Erickson deals with this problem by mentioning in passing that Noah was afterward guilty of "the sin of drunkenness (Gen 9:21)" (639), which, according to Erickson, is condemned elsewhere in Scripture (Hab 2:15; Eph 5:18) but not in the story of Noah (639). Erickson concludes that the story of Noah thereby confirms his opinion about the universality of sin. One could add, from a purely logical perspective, on the other hand, that the fact that most people will at some point or another in their lives commit a sin does not make sin a necessity or universal in the same way that the fact that most people sooner or later in their lives will do a good deed does not make virtue universal or necessary.

Erickson's approach, like Christian theology in general, heavily relies on this subject on Paul's statement in Rom 3:9: γὰρ Ἰουδαίους τε καὶ Ἕλληνας πάντας ὑφ' ἁμαρτίαν εἶναι, "for ... all, both Jews and Greeks, are under the power of sin," followed by the prooftexts assembled by Paul in Rom 3:10–18:[4]

> (10) as it is written: "There is no one who is righteous, not even one; (11) there is no one who has understanding, there is no one who seeks God. (12) All have turned aside, together they have become worthless; there is no one who shows kindness, there is not even one." (13) "Their throats are opened graves; they use their tongues to deceive." "The venom of vipers is under their lips." (14) "Their mouths are full of cursing and bitterness." (15) "Their

---

3. The consequences of the first transgression was object of debate in Second Temple Judaism. See the Syriac Apocalypse of Baruch (54:15–19) and 4 Ezra 3:7–23.

4. Paul cites mostly from the LXX: Rom 3:10 = Eccl 7:20; Rom 3:11–12 = Ps 14:2–3; Rom 3:12 = Pss 5:9 and 140:3; Rom 3:14 = Ps 10:7; Rom 3:15–17 = Isa 59:7–8; Rom 3:18 = Ps 36:1. He does, however, modify some texts ad hoc. See Kuss 1963, 106–8; Wilckens 1978, 171. See also Schmithals 1988, 102–15. Leander E. Keck (1977, 142) proposed that this catena was not composed by Paul but was a piece of apocalyptically shaped tradition that Paul appropriated. This position has been accepted by many commentaries on Romans.

feet are swift to shed blood; (16) ruin and misery are in their paths, (17) and the way of peace they have not known." (18) "There is no fear of God before their eyes."

Erickson therefore continues by dealing with some of these additional proof-texts: "In Ps 14 and 53, which are almost identical, human corruption is pictured as universal: 'They are corrupt, their deeds are vile, there is no one who does good.... All have turned aside, they have together become corrupt; there is no one who does good, not even one (Ps 14:1, 3)" (1998, 639) But is it really about "everyone" that Ps 14 speaks?

Taking a less superficial look at the text shows that the psalm presents a contrast between two well-defined groups.[5] The text can be divided into two sections: 14:1–3 and 14:4–6. Commentators agree that verse 7 is a late addition. The parallel of Ps 14 (Ps 53) has been classified as a prophetic rebuke speech against the ruling religious class.[6] Erhard Gerstenberger, on the other hand, understands the first part of the text (vv. 1–3 in NRSV, 1–4 in MT) as a "didactic-liturgical effort to define the godless" and the second part as an exhortation followed by an intercession (1988, 219). The first section can be arranged in the following structure[7] (my translation already reflects my exegetical choices):

Ps 14: To the leader. Of David.
   A 1a The fool [נבל] says in his heart,
     B 1b "There is no God."
       C 1c They are corrupt, they do abominable deeds;
         D 1d there is no one among them[8] who does good.
           X 2a The LORD looks down from heaven on human-kind [בני־אדם]
   A' 2c to see if there is any teacher/religious leader [משכיל]
     B' 2d who seeks after [דרש] God.

---

5. See Jeremias 1970, 114–17; Alonso Schöckel and Carniti 1994, 269–79; Kraus 1988, 220–21; Weissblueth 1983–84, 133–38. Rashi reads this psalm also as a conflict between two groups interpreting a prophecy by David regarding the destruction of the temple by Nebuchadnezzar without one of his troops objecting to his behavior (3a). See Gruber 2004, 222–24.

6. Gunkel 1998, 232–34, referring to Ps 53; also Schmidt 1934, 22; Weiser 1962, 164; Kraus 1988, 220; Jeremias 1970, 114–17.

7. For a detailed structural analysis, see also Girard 1984, 132–37; Auffret 1991.

8. Here the context makes it clear that "no one" in "no one does good" (אין עשׂה־טוב) refers to the fool(s), so the NJB translates "not one of them does right." See also Gerstenberger 1988, 219.

C' 3a They have all gone astray,
  3b they are all alike perverse;
 D' 3c there is no one who does good, no, not one.

The text moves from a description of the behavior of the "fool" to a description of the behavior of what is the opposite a fool: a מַשְׂכִּיל. The participle of שׂכל is used in the Hebrew Bible to describe "how a reasonable or successful person acts and fares" (Koenen 1974–2006, 115). In the Psalms, the verb is used with the focus on theological insight, including knowledge of God or of his works and commandments (116). In Daniel, the מַשְׂכִּלִים comprise a group of God loyalists with especial insight (116). Later uses point to the office or rank of a teacher, priest, or prince "but [one] who above all learns and teaches God's mysteries and laws" (128). It is precisely to this class of people or group to which the "they" of verse 3a and the "not one" of verse 3c refer. The center of the passage is the God looking down from heaven to examine humanity.

The second part of the psalm (14:4–6) can be arranged in the following structure.

A 4a Do they not know, all the evildoers
 B 4b who eat up my people as they eat bread,
  C 4c and do not call upon the LORD?
   X 5 There they shall be in great terror!
A' 5b For God is with the company of the righteous.
 B' 6a You would confound the plans of the poor,
  C' 6b but the LORD is their refuge.

The passage contrasts the evildoers who have no knowledge:

 7 O that deliverance for Israel would come from Zion!
   When the LORD restores the fortunes of his people,
   Jacob will rejoice; Israel will be glad.

The evildoers of verse 4 cannot refer to other groups but to those mentioned in the previous section, the "fools" and the religious leaders (see Irvine 1995). The psalm presents a contrast between two groups: the "fools" (14:1) who deny that God can act and thus "do abominable deeds" (14:1); and the religious leaders who do not seek God. For this reason, the psalmist reports of the religious leaders that "they have all gone astray, they are all alike perverse" (14:3). Those are the evildoers who "eat my people as they eat bread" (14:4) and "confound the plans of the poor" (14:6). They are the ones who will suffer the "great terror" (14:5). On the other hand, "my people" are the ones who are "eaten like bread" (14:4)—the poor and the righteous.

The psalm presents a conflict between these two groups: "the fool/the leaders/the evildoers" and "my people/the poor, the righteous." This psalm, therefore, is not proclaiming the universality of sin or the sin of every human being but the specific sin of a certain group. The sin that it describes is clearly related to the oppression of one group by the other. The basic question to understand the social location of such group is: Who could be responsible for this sin or be in a position of committing such sin? Certainly not the powerless and disenfranchised. The sin described in the psalm is a sin of an elite or dominant class.[9] This fact is mostly omitted by most commentators, with the exception of Gerstenberger, who states that the psalm denounces "the godless oppressor, the rich upper class that made big profits under the protection of a foreign administration" (1988, 220).[10] We could add that the psalm proclaims the universality of sin within that group.

Psalm 10 is another example of this contrast between two classes with opposing interests. Paul (Rom 3:14) cites only verse 7: ὧν τὸ στόμα ἀρᾶς καὶ πικρίας γέμει, "Their mouths are full of cursing and bitterness." Who are they? The psalm provides a clear answer: Ps 10 describes a conspiracy; the victimizers are described as רשע "wicked" (10:2) and רשע ורע "wicked and evil" (10:5) and the victims as "the lowly" עני (10:2), יתום ודך "orphan and oppressed" (10:18). A classical expression of the social dynamic of the conflict between the oppressors (external as well as internal tyrants; Keel 1969, 15, 29–30, 118–29; Gerstenberger 1983, 75) and the oppressed, the psalm can be arranged in a chiastic structure:[11]

> A 10:1. Why, O LORD, do you stand aloof, heedless in times of trouble? 10:2. The **wicked** in his arrogance hounds the *lowly*—may they be caught in the schemes they devise!
>> B 10:3. The **wicked** crows about his unbridled lusts; the grasping man reviles and scorns the LORD.
>>> C 10:4. The **wicked**, arrogant as he is, in all his scheming thinks, "He does not call to account; God does not care."

---

9. For a survey of elite's theories, see Parry 1969. For the concept of class, see Vilar 1980, 109–141.

10. According to Gerstenberger, the same situation is evident in Pss 9–10; 12; 37; 49; and 73.

11. I highlight the two groups by marking the wicked in bold and the oppressed in italic. For a different approach, see Girard 1984, 110.

> D 10:5. His ways prosper at all times; your judgments are far beyond him; he snorts at all his foes.
>> E 10:6. He thinks, "I shall not be shaken, through all time never be in trouble."
>> 10:7. His mouth is full of oaths, deceit, and fraud; mischief and evil are under his tongue.
>> 10:8. He lurks in outlying places; from a covert he slays *the innocent*; his eyes spout *the hapless*.
>> 10:9. He waits in a covert like a lion in his lair, waits to seize *the lowly*; he seizes *the lowly* as he pulls his net shut;
>> 10:10. he stoops, he crouches, and *the hapless* fall prey to his might.
>> E' 10:11. He thinks, "God is not mindful, he hides his face, he never looks."
> D' 10:12. Rise, O LORD! Strike at him, O God! Do not forget *the lowly*.

C' 10:13. Why should the **wicked** man scorn God, thinking you do not call to account?

10:14. You do look! You take note of mischief and vexation! To requite is in your power. To you *the hapless* can entrust himself; you have ever been the orphan's help.

B' 10:15. O break the power of the **wicked and evil man**, so that when tou look for his wickedness tou will find it no more.

10:16. LORD is king for ever and ever; the nations will perish from his land.

A' 10:16. You will listen to the entreaty of *the lowly*, O LORD, you will make their hearts firm; you will incline your ear

10:18. to champion *the orphan and the downtrodden*, that men who are of the earth tyrannize no more.

The last text that we will take a look at is Isa 59. Paul cites verses 7–8:

> Their feet run to evil, and they make haste to shed innocent blood: their thoughts are thoughts of iniquity; desolation and destruction are in their paths. The way of peace they do not know; and there is no justice in their paths: they have made them crooked paths; whosoever goes therein does not know peace.

The text forms part of Isa 59:1–8, where the prophet reacts to an objection of his audience that God cannot save (59:1; see Croatto 2001, 150–61).

The text then presents the sins that are preventing God from acting. Verse 3 gives us a clue about the situation: "For your hands are defiled with blood," says the prophet, and in verse 7, "Their feet run to evil, and they rush to shed innocent blood." This accusation occurs in an almost identical form in Prov 1:16 and 6:18 in connection with false testimony (see Blenkinsopp 2003, 188), one of the several ways in which the justice of the judicial process was undermined. The same association appears here: the corruption of the judicial system removes the last resort for victims of social and economic injustice. How universal can this sin be? Who is in the position of being able to corrupt the judicial system: the foreigner, the widow, and the orphan, or the elite who concentrates the political and economic power? The text therefore presents victims and victimizers. It is interesting that Paul, trying to make a stronger case, omits the word "innocent." There are real "innocents" in this process. That sin is, therefore, not universal but within a certain socioeconomic-political class.

When the author of Ecclesiastes claims, "Surely there is no one on earth so righteous as to do good without ever sinning" (7:20), or when Solomon claims "there is no one who does not sin" (1 Kgs 8:46), the question is: Are both characters just reflecting the guilty conscience of the dominant class? Is this "universality of sin" not actually referring to their own social class's sin?

When we take a look at the traditional sequence of increase of sin in the book of Genesis, a class-conscious analysis of the transgressions described there leads us to ask: Who might be more prone to be like God and to take the forbidden fruit, wanting to be like God, as the transgression of Adam and Eve (Gen 2:4b–25): the people in the upper side of the social pyramid or the people at the base of the social class? Who might be more prone to begin a megalomaniac building project to build a city and a tower with its top in the heavens, to make a name for themselves (Gen 11:1–9): the foreigner, the widow and the orphan, or the elite who concentrates the political and economic power?

How could these conclusions, so obvious from the perspective of the marginalized and oppressed, not find a stronger voice within the communities that have read and interpreted these texts for centuries? How is it that the sin of the elite became a universal sin? The answer is similar to that puzzle presented in the title of my essay: you hide an elephant on Fifth Avenue by filling it with elephants, and you hide the sin of the ruling socioeconomic-political class by making sin universal.

TRUE FASTING AND UNWILLING HUNGER (ISAIAH 58)

Mercedes L. García Bachmann

INTRODUCTION

Isaiah 58 belongs to the so-called Third Isaiah, Isa 56–66, which collects oracles from the restoration period, concerned with life in Judea after the return from the exile in the late Persian period. Like many other biblical texts, Isaiah has been the object of heated debates around the issues of historicity, one of whose aspects is the dating of the texts. Here I am not interested in those discussions. I recognize a Third Isaiah in the sense that Isa 56–66 discuss certain issues in a way that is related to, yet different from, Isa 1–39 and 40–55. Chapters 56–66 also are set in a chiastic structure, pointing beyond chance to a well-thought design that deserves admiration.

Nonetheless, primary attention will be given to Isa 58 rather than to the larger context of the book. Even verses 13–14, the final verses of Isa 58, will receive less attention than verses 1–12.[1] After some hesitation, I have decided to include them here, mainly because the whole chapter is a composite, they do not disturb so much that they should be left out, and they fit in the whole structure. The chapter is built in such a way that there are several repetitions,

---

1. Paul A. Smith takes 58:1–59:20 as a single poem divided into five stanzas (1995, 97–127). José Severino Croatto ponders both options and finally takes 58 as a structural unit of its own (2001, 105, 142). Paul D. Hanson considers vv. 1–12 to be a unit (1975, 100–113). On the one hand, vv. 13–14 share some of the vocabulary with 58:1–12: חפץ "delight" (2x in v. 13); the verb קרא "proclaim" (vv. 1, 5, 9, 12, 13); the reference to Jacob (v. 14); and the sequence "if ... then" (vv. 13, 14), which appeared also in 8–9. Furthermore, v. 12 ends with שבת, Qal infinitive of the verb ישב "sit, inhabit, dwell in." The consonantal text is identical to שבת "Sabbath," with which vv. 13–14 deal. On the other hand, vv. 13–14 seem to reopen issues already closed by v. 12 with its promises of blessings, use some terms that do not appear in the earlier part of the chapter (e.g., the noun and verb ענג for "luxury," "luxuriate"), and fit better as a closing statement for the whole section 56–58 than as a closing of the issue of fasting in chapter 58.

many of which form internal chiasmi. Terms such as קרא "call, proclaim, cry," דרך "way," חפץ "delight, take delight in," נפש "living being, person, oneself," אור "light," יום "day," and several others appear throughout the chapter.

In this essay I want to explore how Isa 58's structure and images work in order to condemn ineffectual fasting and assert Yhwh's preference for the most deprived in society. My context is one of poverty, oppression, corruption, and a growing gap between the few very rich people and most of the population, which is becoming increasingly impoverished. Bodies show these differences in concrete signs of health, leisure, and overindulgence or in disease, malnutrition, and all sorts of deprivation. The popular saying for facing socioeconomic crises is "you will have to tighten your belt" out of increasing hunger. Bodies also show concrete signs of having been fettered, oppressed, bound, tortured, and raped—and sometimes of having also been set free. Unwilling fasting, that is, hunger and starvation, is unfortunately far more common than ritual fasting on this continent and globally. With this reality in mind, Isa 58 challenged me to look beyond ritual fasting. In the last part, I turn to Zech 7, a text that, while sharing a similar concern, sheds a different light on the issue of fasting, hunger, and satisfaction.

The Text[2]

1 Cry out [קרא] with the (whole) throat, do not withhold,
    like the horn lift up your voice [קולך],
and tell my people their rebellion,
    the house of Jacob their sins.
2 Yet[3] daily they seek [ידרשון] me,
    and in the knowledge of my ways they delight [יחפצון],
like a nation that practiced justice [צדקה],
    and the statutes [משפט] of their God(s) did not forsake;
they ask me [ישאלוני] ordinances of justice [משפטי־צדק],[4]
    in God's nearness they delight [יחפצון].
3 "Why did we fast [צמנו] and you do not see?

---

2. My translation; Isa 58 is a difficult text, and several lines can be translated in quite different ways. In order to help visualize internal connections, I include many Hebrew terms in brackets.

3. Most translations and commentaries understand the particle ו to be concessive. Much disagreement turns around the question whether its intention is ironic or not.

4. As Childs (2001, 474) notes, "The precise meaning of this combination is uncertain." Taking the expression to be negative, he chooses "beneficial judgments," thinking that they are asking for "legal decisions directed against others on their behalf" (477).

We humbled ourselves,
> and you did not acknowledge/paid no heed?"

Look! In the day of your fasting [צמכם] you find delight [חפץ],[5]
> and all your toilers you drive hard.[6]

4 Look! For trial and contention you fast [תצומו]
> and to strike with wicked fist.[7]

You don't fast [תצומו) as on this day
> to make your voice [קולכם) heard in the heights.[8]

5 Is like this the fast [צום) I choose:
> a day when humans humble themselves,[9]

---

5. The idea here seems to be that they take advantage of the fast to foster their own businesses instead of observing the fast for its own sake. Several translations thus translate it as "your own business." It seems to me that in this way the wordplay of using the same root, חפץ, as in verses 2 (2x) and 13, gets lost.

6. The *hapax legomenon* here translated "toilers" is a noun derived from the root עצב "wrest, grieve." One other noun from the same root appears four times in the first chapters of the Bible to speak of the origins of human "toil" (Gen 3:16 [2x], 17; 5:29). The noun could mean "laborers" or "labors/pains"; the verb means "press, drive, oppress, exact" (*BDB*, 620). Supposing "laborers" is a correct translation, it is unclear to what type of men (and women?) the noun refers: workers? slaves? debtors?

7. Several translations understand אגרף as in an absolute state and רשע as the object of the verb, i.e., "strike the wicked with the fist" and then choose to translate "the poor" instead of "the wicked." Other translations take both nouns as in a construct chain: "fist of wickedness," thus, wicked fist.

8. This is another instance where several translations of the verse are possible. It literally states, "not you [masc. pl.] will/do fast as/like today to-make-heard in the highs your [masc. pl.] voice." It is not clear whether the imperfect should be translated as a future, an imperative, or a present continuous; neither is it clear whether the action described means a human act of boasting or the intention to approach YHWH with their prayers. Smith (1995, 104) notes the wordplay between הרם קולך "lift up your voice" in v. 1 and במרום קולכם "(make heard) your voice in the heights" in v. 4: "The terms במרום and קולכם in v. 4 seem to refer back to the terms הרם and קולך in v.1. While in v. 1 the poet is told to lift his voice up on high, in v. 4 the people are informed that their style of fasting will not make their voice heard on high."

9. It is hard to translate אדם נפשו into inclusive language that is not "otherworldly." In Hebrew, אדם, a generic term for humans, humanity, human being, is masculine (and singular). Having נפש with a concrete meaning of "throat" and also that which goes through it, indicating and sustaining life, "breath," and thus the person's self, "his life, his soul, himself, themselves," would be possible yet very different from each other. Skinner (1917, 182) understands that ענות אדם נפשו "to afflict his soul" in his translation "is the virtual subject of the preceding, being explanatory of the 'such' at the beginning (and so with the sequel of the verse. The prophet thus repudiates the ascetic idea of fasting entirely and finds the essence of it in the self-denial imposed by moral obligation (v. 6)."

to bow down like a rush his or her head,
    and spread sackcloth and ashes?
Is it for this that you proclaim a fast [תקרא־צום],
    a day of pleasure to YHWH?
6 Is this not the fast [צום] that I choose:
    to loosen the fetters of wickedness,
to unfasten the thongs of the yoke,
    to send the oppressed free,
that every yoke you tear apart?
7 Is it not to split with the hungry your bread
    and bring the poor wanderer to (your) house,
when you see the naked, clothe him or her,
    (and) from your own flesh not to conceal yourself?
8 Then [אז] your light will break forth like the dawn,
    and your healing quickly will spring up,
your righteousness [צדקך] will go ahead of you,
    the glory of YHWH will gather you.[10]
9 Then [אז] you will call [תקרא], and YHWH will answer
    you will cry for help and he [sic] shall say, "Here I am!"
If you put away from your midst the yoke,
    the pointing of the finger, and the speaking of sorrow [ודבר־און],
10 and you bring yourself to the hungry[11]
    and the afflicted you satisfy,
(then) your light will raise in the darkness
    and your gloominess as noonday.
11 And YHWH will lead you continually,
    and he [sic] will satisfy your throat in drought,
and your fingers he [sic] will prepare for war,[12]
    and you will be like a well-watered garden,
like a spring of water whose waters do not deceive.
12 And ageless wastes they will build from you,
    age-old foundations will you raise up,
and you will be called [קרא] "Repairer of the breach"
    and "Restorer [משבב] of pathways for dwelling/inhabiting [לשבת]."

---

10. Another possible reading, "will guard you from your behind."

11. The root פוק means "bring out, furnish, promote." Again, a difficult word to translate.

12. The verb, causative of חלץ, has two meanings: "draw off, strip off" (unlikely here in a promise of blessing); and "make strong, prepare for war." My preference for the latter translation is based on the image of the "Divine Warrior" in Isa 59.

13 If you turn [תשׁיב] your foot from the Sabbath [שׁבת],
  (from) doing your pleasures [חפציך] on my holy day,
and call [קראת] the Sabbath [שׁבת] "pleasure" [ענג],
  YHWH's holy (day) "honored,"
and honor/ponder[13] it (by keeping from) going your ways,
  finding your delight [חפצך], and
  speaking a word [of business? ודבר דבר],
14 then [אז] you will luxuriate [תתענג][14] in YHWH,
  and I will cause you to ride on the heights of the earth,
  and I will feed you the inheritance of Jacob your father.
For YHWH's mouth speaks [דבר].

In terms of its genre, the text has been considered "a prophetic reply to a lamentation on the part of Jews" (Whybray 1975, 212), "a prophetic interpretation of fasting" (Jones 1964, 51), an "admonition" (Westermann 1969, 333), and a liturgical poem, a "response to the plea of the cultic community" (Muilenburg 1956, 677). There is scholarly consensus that this piece of poetry reflects a prophetic approach very much in line with the "great" prophets Amos, Isaiah of Jerusalem, Hosea, and Jeremiah. There is less consensus on the particular meaning of the passage: the text could be a prophet's indictment to the people, a prophet's reply to their inquiry/complaint, YHWH's command to the prophet to go and speak and the prophet's reply to such command, and so on. Similarities to Isa 40:1, with YHWH's injunction to "proclaim," even though in Isa 40 it is plural, enhance this impression. In my view, the text contains a command to speak, a set of three questions and answers, and the affirmation of God's word closing the whole statement. While it is not always clear who the speakers are—especially where God is talking and where a prophet speaks in God's name—the meaning of the text is rather clear.

THE STRUCTURE

The Hebrew text presents several difficulties, some of which have been solved by ancient translations and versions. Other difficulties have been dealt with by several scholars through more or less successful explanations and/or emendations. Despite these difficulties, the text is well-organized in a chiastic

---

13. Croatto (2001, 135) chooses "ponderar," which, like "ponder" in English, means "weigh mentally, consider." I like this translation for the root כבד (2x here), for it makes the whole subject less abstract than "honor."

14. I choose "luxuriate" to distinguish in the translation the root ענג, which appears in vv. 13–14 as a Qal participle and an imperfect Hitpael, from חפץ (in vv. 2, 3, 13).

structure and thus, except for some words, may well be kept as is.[15] Here I will refrain from attempting to draw its structure on paper, because it would look like a spider's web with too many connecting lines. What I present is only a sketch of what I see as the main line of thought of the chapter.

The chapter is structured through two enveloping affirmations (A: 58:1a; A': 58:14c). The first one (58:1a) is a command to call out aloud, with the whole strength of the throat, in order to proclaim a word from YHWH to the whole community. Two names are used to describe this community: "my people" and "house of Jacob." A' (58:14c) is the affirmation "For YHWH's mouth speaks," which both parallels the command to speak (although using another verb, דבר) and affirms God's power to fulfill the promises just made. In this sense, it is more than a linguistic parallel to verse 1; it is the crown to the whole passage. While "people" does not appear again in the chapter, "house" is used in verse 7 and "Jacob" in 14, where the addressees are promised by YHWH to be fed "Jacob's inheritance."

Between A and A', I understand the text as comprised of three main questions and their answers. The questions are: (1) Why does YHWH not "see" or "acknowledge"/"pay no heed" to (ritually proper) fast? (2) What kind of fast is *not* acceptable to YHWH? (3) What kind of ritual observances are acceptable to YHWH?

The first question is indirectly asked through a direct quotation of the fasters' complaint to God. God answers by providing three reasons: "Because while you fast: [a] you oppress your toilers; [b] you contend with others (probably while doing business); and [c] you fast in order to make your voice heard on high." Three strong reasons why ritually proper fasting is not enough! The expression "you fast in order to make your voice heard on high" can be understood in two different ways, both of them reflecting the religious hubris of the oppressors. First, as boasting: "You fast and pray aloud where you can be seen and heard—by your peer and/or the people" (see also Matt 6:1–16). Second, as an intended pressure on God: "You think your fast will make your voice heard by me 'up here.'"

The answer to the question, Why is (ritually proper) fast not answered? could be summarized in these terms: ritually proper fasting is not enough when accompanied by oppressive practices. The oppressors' detailed attention to religious rituals and public displays of religious piety should not mislead the oppressed. Those who follow oppressive practices and policies, no matter how orthodox their beliefs and rituals, are under YHWH's judgment.

---

15. I follow Croatto (2001, 140–41), who takes and slightly modifies Polan's structure (Polan 1986, 233).

To the second question, What kind of fast is *not* acceptable to YHWH? (v. 5a), the answer is: a fast with ritual signals of mourning or repentance such as lowering the head, spreading ashes, and sackcloth that are performed for their own sake, as cited in the text, "Is it for this that you proclaim a fast?" (v. 5b) or in order to draw YHWH to forgive them. Those external expressions of religious piety do not impress Israel's liberating God.

The third question, What kind of ritual observances *are* acceptable to YHWH? receives three answers in this chapter. All of them are presented by a protasis introduced in different ways (vv. 6–7, 9b–10, 13) and an apodosis (vv. 8–9a, 11, 14). Note that this question is not directly concerned with fasting. Graphically, it would appear as follows:

OUTLINE OF THE "ARGUMENT"	OUTLINE OF THE STRUCTURE
1 Call out aloud unto my people (and tell them this):	A Command: speak in YHWH's name
2 They seek to be close to me	
3 (They say) "Why do we fast and you do not answer!?"	first question (indirectly through introductory statement and quotation)
(It is because) you fast for your own sake, (while) you oppress your oppressed 4 you fast for fight you fast to raise your voice on high	first answer
5 Is this the fast I want?	second question
(No), you fast for humbling yourselves	second answer
Is this a day acceptable to YHWH?	third question
6–7 (No) The "fast" I want is this:	third answer as protasis: (When you do so)
to loosen the fetters of wickedness, to send the oppressed free, to feed the hungry, to clothe the naked, etc. 8 then, you will be blessed	third answer as apodosis: then
9 YHWH will answer you;	

If you stop doing and speaking evil to others,	third answer as protasis: if
10a and (if) you give yourself to the needy,	
10b–12 then you will be blessed.	third answer as apodosis: then
13 If you ponder the Sabbath and if you do not keep it for your own sake,	third answer as protasis: if
14 then, you will be blessed.	third answer as apodosis: then
For Yhwh's mouth speaks.	A' Affirmation: Yhwh has spoken

A true fast is, according to these words, one that is performed for the sake of the poor, the needy, the homeless, the workers, a fast that makes straight the paths of justice, peace, and righteousness, made crooked by dealings and ordinances that are lawful yet unjust.

Therefore, a true fast, according to Yhwh, is not a ritual fast or any kind of refraining from eating. A true fast, according to Yhwh (v. 6), is, first, "to loosen the fetters of wickedness," "to unfasten the thongs of the yoke," "to send the oppressed free," "that every yoke you tear apart." True fast, therefore, should be understood as concrete acts of liberation. Second, a true fast, according to Yhwh (v. 7), is "to split with the hungry your bread," "to bring the poor wanderer to (your) house," "when you see the naked, to clothe him or her," and "from your own flesh not to conceal yourself." True fast, therefore, should be also understood as concrete acts of hospitality, of providing for the poor, and of being available for the one who needs you.

Notable Features of the Chapter

Polemical Tone

Several facts are remarkable in this chapter. One is the polemical tone of the group represented by the writer against those addressed, referenced, and even mocked in the text. It is a direct attack on the religious ideology that supports an oppressive system. Hanson notes that "implied is a dichotomy within the nation whereby one element is threatened with judgment while the other is promised salvation" (1975, 107).[16] Those who are threatened with judgment

---

16. Hanson (1975:107). He also infers that the oracle we are discussing is to be

are those who considered themselves "religious"; those who are promised salvation are those who were suffering the religiously sanctioned oppression.

INTRATEXTUAL CONNECTIONS

Another remarkable characteristic of this chapter is the amount of inner connections, many accomplished through chiastic structures. For example (see Croatto 2001, 112):

A (v. 2a) *me* they *seek* [אותי ... ידרשון]
   B (v. 2b) in the knowledge of my ways they delight [יחפצון]
      X a (2c) like a nation that practiced justice [צדקה]
         b (2d) and the statutes [משפט] of their God(s) did not forsake
A' (v. 2e) they *ask me* [ישאלוני] ordinances of justice [משפטי־צדק]
   B' (v. 2f) in God's nearness they delight [יחפצון]

They seek God daily (A: v. 2a), and they delight in their knowledge of God's way (B: v. 2b); they even keep asking for "ordinances of justice" (A': v. 2e). Their knowledge of God is not denied in the text. The problem is not their knowledge but their behavior: they are not practicing justice//they have forsaken God's statutes (X: 2c–d), and these two actions cannot be separated. Those who do not practice justice have indeed forsaken God's statutes.

Also in verse 13 Croatto notes how refraining from trafficking (your foot) is parallel to refraining from speaking (business or idle talk), and "doing your pleasure" is parallel to "finding your delight," while at the center remains YHWH's Sabbath as "luxury" and "YHWH's holy (= day)" (Croatto 2001, 134).

There are noteworthy connections between Isa 58 and 59, to the point that several scholars group them together (Smith 1995, 97). Most notable are those related to body images, cries against social injustice, and divine intervention if these do not cease. There are also several other intratextual and intertextual connections, some of which are explored below.

RITUAL PREOCCUPATION

Several scholars have noted the ritual connotations of this passage. The expressions "seek [דרש] YHWH" and "(God's or YHWH's) nearness" (in our

---

deemed as "transitional, since that dichotomy is not yet complete." Most commentaries, noting after Muilenburg that there is no mention of the temple or sacrifices, understand v. 12 to refer to Jerusalem's walls (to be reconstructed) and date the oracle in Nehemiah's times.

text, קרבת אלהים) are technical terms related to the cult.[17] Scholars hold divergent opinions on whether "they ask of me משפטי־צדק" has a positive or a negative connotation. To take it positively would mean that the fasters are well-intentioned in their search for God's will; that is, they lack actions according to their good intentions, but they are well-meant. To take it negatively would mean that those fasters ask God and God's representatives for ordinances that privilege them over those they oppress. It should be remembered that, despite its polemical tone, the text is not against ritual per se but against rituals unaccompanied by ethical actions. Thus, the issue is not between ritual or not ritual but how one lives his or her whole life in the presence of God, from the first day of the week to the Sabbath.

Use of Images

This chapter uses a rich variety of images to convey its message. In the remaining pages I will explore some of them.[18]

Comparison

Some of the images are presented through comparisons, most of them introduced by the preposition כ. The elements introduced by this particle are a horn sound (v. 1), a people (v. 2), this day (v. 4), a bulrush (v. 5), dawn (v. 8), noonday (v. 10), a watered garden, and a spring of drinkable waters (v. 11). In some instances it is hard to decide whether an object brought up is to be taken literally or whether it is meant as a comparison.[19] In verse 2, for instance, the text reads literally:

---

17. According to McKenzie (1968, 165), "2. inquire. A formal ritual petition." Westermann (1969, 334–35): "The whole of this relates to acts of worship, denoting a variety of attempts to hold fast to God." Skinner (1917, 181) states, "they seek me, i.e. inquire of me,—the word used of consulting an oracle." The root קרב, on the other hand, often has the technical meaning of an offering brought to God or a related verb (approach the altar, etc.).

18. Since Miscall has worked on the semantic field of "light," I will not go into it here. He states (1991, 117), "The Lord makes and creates opposites: good and evil, light and darkness. Light, both the specific Hebrew words for it and the extensive imagery involved with it, can be positive, beneficial, life-giving. Darkness, on the other hand, is usually negative, maleficent, death-dealing. However, light can be the blazing and desiccating sun, and then darkness is shade and refuge. Opposites are held together in this imagery." Throughout the article he also traces some of the recurrences of water and fire in Isaiah.

19. A third comparison appears in v. 4: כ + "this day" or "today." Many scholars do not take it as a comparison; for instance, Skinner (1917, 182): "ye fast not this day so as to make your voice to be heard"; Childs (2001, 473): "You cannot fail as you do today//and

as a people [כגוי] that righteousness practiced
and their God(s)' [אלהיו] justice/statutes did not forsake.

Since it is an image introduced by the comparative particle, "a people" could be interpreted as referring either to Israel and Elohim or to any people and their God(s).[20] Thus, several translations, in order to avoid the ambiguity, add "as if they were" a people.[21]

The second ambiguous comparison to deal with here is the chiasmus between the first and fourth cola of verse 7:

Is it not [לא] to split with the hungry your bread [לחם],
and the poor wanderer bring to (your) house,
when you see the naked, clothe him (or her),
and from your own flesh not [לא] to conceal yourself [ומבשרך]?

Dahood understands these cola as the breaking-up of the composite phrase לחם ובשר "bread and meat" and thus takes "meat" literally as food. Brueggemann, on the other hand, understands this sentence as a summary of the three previous ones, in the sense of Israel's "neighborly affirmation," that is not to be taken literally as a fourth requirement or example (1998, 189).[22] It is also possible that both images are used as double entendres and thus their meaning should be kept, as much as possible, open to multiple interpretations.

---

expect your voice to be heard on high"; Westermann (1969, 332): "Fasting like yours is no fasting//to make your voice to be heard on high." (I use // to indicate separation of cola in the original.)

20. There are only two occurrences of the (proper) name אלהים in this chapter. The first is in the comparison just mentioned above. The second, also in this verse, refers to the group criticized in v. 1, who seek אלהים's nearness with no right ethics (קרבת אלהים). It seems to me that this second use of אלהים instead of YHWH plays with ambiguity, thus allowing for two different readings. One reading is conveyed in the translation; the other possible reading is "like a nation that [כגוי working as double-duty modifier] delights in God's/the Gods' nearness."

21. Brueggemann (1998, 186); Hanson (1975, 100); Childs (2001, 473): "as if they were a nation." See also Westermann (1969, 331) and McKenzie (1968, 163): "like a nation"; Skinner (1917, 181): "as a nation"; Croatto (2001, 107): "Como pueblo que practica la justicia."

22. Brueggemann 1998, 189. There are, of course, several positions in between; these two are just extremes. Brueggemann points out also that these are the three concerns against which Jesus speaks in Matt 6:25.

Bodily imagery

With chapter 59, Isa 58 shares an unusual amount of bodily imagery and per-sonification. Body parts include: throat (58:1); fist (58:4); head (58:5); finger (58:9); throat and fingers (58:11); foot (58:12); mouth (58:13); hand and ear (59:1); face (59:2); hands, fingers, lips, and tongue (59:3); palms of the hand (59:6); feet and blood (59:7); eyes (59:10); heart (59:13); arm (59:16); head (59:17); and mouth (4x, 59:21).

Together with these body members, in both chapters there are several physical actions performed through one of these body parts. There is also the semantic field related to "nonphysical" processes such as feelings, which I am not considering here. In Isa 58 alone, physical actions include: shouting (with the throat); raising the voice as a horn (58:1); calling upon God and crying for help (58:2, 9); oppressing the oppressed/workers (58:3); fasting (58:3–4); fighting with fists (58:4); giving physical signs of mourning (= lowering the head, spreading ashes) (58:5); loosening the fetters, unfastening the thongs, sending free, and tearing apart the yokes (58:6); being hungry, naked, and homeless/wonderer (58:7); splitting bread and giving shelter and clothing (58:7); pointing of the finger (accusing?) (58:9); speaking evil (58:9); and (re-)building breaches, walls, and pathways (58:12).[23]

Contrasting Oppression and Liberation

Together with body images, there are several sets of oppositions. Most notable are those related to oppression-liberation. The semantic field of "oppression" is presented through several words.

Among the nouns, (1) several refer to social groups or people who suffer some kind of oppression and who, according to the kind of "fast" that God wants, should be protected: toilers (58:3); oppressed (58:6); hungry (58:7, 10); poor (58:7); homeless/wanderer (58:7); naked (58:7); afflicted (58:10); freed (58:6). (2) Several refer to literal and figurative instruments of oppres-sion and bondage: fetters (58:6); thongs (58:6); and yoke (58:6 [2x], 9); slavery or indentured labor is implied in the use of the technical term "send free" (58:6). (3) Several refer to social behaviors that, seen by themselves, could be deemed simply as rude or impolite, yet, in fact, are added social mechanisms of oppression: one's own pleasure or interests over against those of the larger community (58:3, 5, 13 [2x]); trial and contention (58:4); raised or evil fists

---

23. I leave out other images such as "riding on the highs of the earth," which could have a literal referent from Israel's past but may very well be metaphorical.

(58:4); pointing of the finger (58:9); evil speaking (58:9); and idle words/bad word/discussion of commercial issues on the Sabbath (58:13).

Among the verbs, (1) those with a negative connotation are: exact (58:3); strike (58:4); seek one's own interests (over and against those of the larger community, especially those of "your own kin," 58:4, 7, 13); afflict, that is, self-humiliation before God but in its plain meaning oppression, hostile action (58:3). (2) Those with a positive connotation, which are *not* performed, are: loosen fetters (58:6); unfasten thongs (58:6); give freedom to the enslaved (58:6); tear apart the yoke (58:6); split bread and feed the hungry (58:7, 10); clothe the naked (58:7); give shelter to the homeless/wanderer (58:7); give oneself to the "kin"/give your meat (58:7); give oneself to the hungry (58:10); satisfy the afflicted (58:10); and ponder the Sabbath (58:13).

While we recognize that the use of oppositions is a helpful literary device, we should not lose sight of the fact that these behaviors, whether the negative performed ones or the positive denied ones, are related to, and impinge on, *bodies*: hands, stomachs, ears, eyes, backs, legs, skin, throats, wombs, and breasts of oppressed bodies, to be more precise; oppressed gendered bodies; bodies on whom shame and suffering are inflicted in particular ways, depending on their being men or women, young or aged, fertile or past menopause, and so on.

This is one reason why I think that "not to conceal yourself from your own flesh" (Isa 58:7) is the best summary statement on what YHWH wants from YHWH's people. I take "and from your בשׂר [flesh, meat] not to conceal yourself" in its broadest possible sense. When you conceal yourself from your own body, you cannot see your kin's needs; when you conceal yourself from your own flesh, for instance, by hiding into an "unfleshed" spirituality, you cannot see there is no meat on another member's table; when you conceal yourself from your own kin, you cannot see the social needs that go beyond them and you. As Croatto states, "In Isaiah 58 the problem is extreme. Fasting has lost its meaning because it has been deprived of its balancing element, *justice*, which prevents existence of poor, and solidarity with these, when the system has already created them" (2001, 117).

Conversely, when people get out of their own בשׂר and are open to see what is happening around them, they cannot fail to notice wanderers, poor, hungry, oppressed, about whom, according to our chapter, God cares enough to reject fasting that does not include justice toward them. Then, God's salvation is poured on. This is the logic of Isa 58. As I see it, a hermeneutics of liberation requires a commitment with the underprivileged that would not avoid embodiment and prophetic confrontation with death-blowing powers, be they political, economic, cultural, or even religious. In other words, God's salvation in Isa 58 is brought about by political actions of restoration, freeing, and sharing one's flesh on the part of YHWH's true followers.

Healing

One of the nicest images used to speak of God's acts of salvation in this chapter is that of healing (58:8). Healing (אֲרוּכָה) will spring up. The root צמח literally means "grow, spring forth" and, as a noun, "bud." In Isaiah, it is often used in parallel to instauration of justice and righteousness, as the following examples show:

> And they shall *spring up* [צמח] (as) from among the grass, as willows by the water courses. (Isa 44:4)

> Drip down, heavens, from above, and the clouds pour down righteousness; let the earth open and fructify [וְיִפְרוּ־יֶשַׁע] salvation, and let righteousness *spring forth* [צמח] together; I, YHWH, have created it. (Isa 45:8)

> For as the rain comes down, and the snow from heaven, and they do not return (there), but they water the earth and make it bring forth and *spring forth* [צמח], and give seed to the sower, and bread to the eater, so shall my word, which comes out of my mouth. (Isa 55:10–11)

> For as the earth brings forth her *bud* [צמח], and as the garden makes the things sown in it to *spring forth* [צמח], so the Lord YHWH shall cause righteousness and praise to *spring forth* before all the nations. (Isa 61:11).

What "springs forth" in Isa 58:8, אֲרוּכָה, has the literal meaning of restoration in two texts (Neh 4:1; 2 Chr 24:13), while in three other texts in Jeremiah it refers to growth of skin in a wound (8:22; 30:17; 33:6.).[24] Again, a bodily (physical) image is used to speak of God's acts of deliverance and blessings! It is true that every human action requires some part of the body to work; indeed, there is no human life without a human body. Yet what I stress here is the *embodied* relationship Israel is to have with its God.

The Horn

The horn or trumpet (שׁוֹפָר) was originally used to gather men for war (Josh 6:5) or to gather the population for protection from invaders (Jer 4:5, 19); later it became a musical instrument gathering people for worship. While most occurrences of the word do not shed much light on the use of this image in our chapter, the following texts seem to be particularly relevant:

---

24. Hillers (1964, 66) includes Isa 58:8 as one example of the reversal of the curse of incurable wounds.

Blow a horn in Zion, and make a sound (of alarm) in my holy mountain; may all the inhabitants of the land tremble. For Yʜwʜ's day has come; for (it is) near. (Joel 2:1)

Blow a horn in Zion, sanctify a fast, call a solemn assembly. (Joel 2:15)

And it happened on the third day, being morning, that thunders and light-ning, and a thick cloud upon the mountain and the voice of the horn, very loud; and all the people who were in the camp trembled. (Exod 19:16)

And the voice of the horn grew louder and louder, and Moses spoke and God answered him by a voice/thunder. (Exod 19:19)

Note the words that these texts have in common with Isa 58. In Joel 2:1, the adverb "near" is קרוב, from the same root as "God's nearness" in 58:2; "holy" (mountain, הר קדשי) is the same noun as in 58:13, where the Sabbath is called "the day of my holiness" (יום קדשי; incidentally, "day" is another common term); and "inhabitants (of the land)," ישבי, is the same root as in 58:12, "(pathways for) sitting/dwelling," לשבת. Again, in Joel 2:15 there are nouns and verbs common to our text: the horn (שופר), the fast (צום), make holy (קדשו), and call/proclaim (קראו).

Noteworthy in Exod 19 are the word קול, used for thunder, for the sound of the horn, and for God's answer to Moses, and the adjective "thick" (cloud), כבד, which comes from the same root as "ponder/honor" and "honorable" in reference to the Sabbath in Isa 58:13.

While in Joel 2:1 the horn is to announce Yʜwʜ's day of judgment, in 2:15 it is to announce a holy gathering of the people, which includes a fast. In Exod 19 the horn announces God's nearness, which is again one of the themes in the text, prior to giving the people God's Torah.

It should be pointed out that, while Joel identifies explicitly the events to happen with Zion, Isa 58 does not identify the ruins to be rebuilt with any particular location. It is, of course, easy to make such an identification; in fact, several commentaries do identify the promise in verse 12 with Jerusalem's reconstruction in Nehemiah's times and date the chapter from this identifi-cation. Yet even without an explicit mention of Zion, the stock of common imagery and vocabulary is noteworthy between these texts.

INTERTEXTUALITY

If we ask for the importance of the images used in Isa 58 in order to condemn ineffectual fasting and assert Yʜwʜ's preference for the most deprived in society, there are a few texts besides Joel 2 that seem to be of particular interest. Although we cannot afford a detailed study of them here, I would like at least to call attention to them. By addressing the same issue(s) in a different context and manner, they shed light on our quest.

Leviticus 25:9–10

The context here is that of legislation related to land, particularly the Jubilee year.

> Then you shall have the trumpet sounded loud; on the tenth day of the seventh month—on the Day of Atonement—you shall have the trumpet sounded throughout all your land. And you shall hallow the fiftieth year, and you shall proclaim liberty throughout the land to all its inhabitants. It shall be a jubilee for you: you shall return, every one of you, to your property and every one of you to your family. (Lev 25:9–10)

Here again the noun "horn" appears twice (first in construct with "shouting, alarm"), establishing the solemn occasion on which it will be blown: when and where. More important, it is a time, no longer a day but a whole year, made holy (קדש). The horn is to be blown to proclaim (קרא again!) release of debtors and return of indentured workers, enslaved Israelites, to their families!

Finally, the verb שׁוב "return, turn" appears in this text in reference to coming back to their possessions and families. The same verb is employed twice in our chapter. In 58:12 the people are promised they will be called "Restorer [Polel of שׁוב] of pathways." In 58:13 it is used in the conditional "If you turn your foot...." It is true that this is a very common verb, yet, together with the other instances of common vocabulary, it adds to its force.

Zechariah 7

Here a question brought up by the people of Bethel to entreat the favor of YHWH makes YHWH review the immediate past: the seventy years since the temple's destruction and the deportation of the leaders, and the people's responsibility in it. Some of the tensions (fasting and lack of the expected answer from YHWH; fasting and lack of social justice) are quite similar to those in our text:

> Say to all the people of the land and the priests: When you fasted and lamented in the fifth month and in the seventh, for these seventy years, was it for me that you fasted? And when you eat and when you drink, do you not eat and drink only for yourselves? Were not these the words that the YHWH proclaimed by the former prophets, when Jerusalem was inhabited and in

prosperity, along with the towns around it, and when the Negev and the Shephelah were inhabited? (Zech 7:5–7)

The verb צוֹם "fast" appears twice in the first verse to denote the ritual actions performed by the people and the priests and those who come seeking to appease God's wrath and move God to further action. Then the opposite action is described, also supposedly performed for Yhwh but in reality for the performers themselves: eating and drinking. Again, קרא is used here. In verse 7, the root ישׁב is used twice in an explicit reference to Jerusalem and its cities around her, the Negev and the Shephelah. This same root, it will be recalled, made a wordplay in Isa 58:12–13 between dwelling places and the Sabbath (לשׁבת־לשׁבת).

Again, while one could explain some of these recurrences as common words and common prophetic stock, to me it is noteworthy that Isa 58 shares so much with so many "prophetic" texts such as Isa 59, Zech 7–8, and Lev 25. Here I am not using "prophetic" as a technical term but as an adjectival description for the prophetic call to cry against social evil, lack of justice and truth, and lack of care for the weaker members of society. While in Isa 58 much of those invectives are presented as rhetorical questions, in Zechariah they are direct statements. Zechariah 7:9–10 mentions some particular groups: "Thus says Yhwh Sebaot: Render true judgments, show kindness and mercy to one another; do not oppress the widow, the orphan, the alien, or the poor; and do not devise evil in your hearts against one another." The widow, the fatherless, and the foreigner are three, though not the only, concrete expressions of groups especially oppressed and humiliated when there is lack of social justice. When the provider died, families were in serious economic and social hardship. Even with explicit legislation aimed to protect the rights of the weaker members of society, they would find themselves in a very vulnerable position, as they had little chance of defending their rights.

The fourth term used in Zech 7:10, "afflicted" (from the same root as "afflict" in Isa 58:3, 5, 10, ענה) is rather vague in terms of identification. From what we know in biblical Israel, these would range from the three groups just discussed to indentured slaves, impoverished farmers, dayworkers, despised guilds, slaves, unprotected elderly, physically and mentally challenged people, the sick and impure, and others. One can name them in each society.

Zechariah 7 is especially helpful as an intertext, as it makes explicit some of the elements that are only hinted at in Isa 58. These include prophetic words of judgment against Israel/Judah in relation to ineffectual fasting, the people of the land and the priests as the message's addressees, and four particular groups—widows, orphans, foreigners, and oppressed—as those whom the powerful, who are also the religiously observant, should not oppress.

Because they were indeed oppressed, there is need to mention them! Thus, while Isa 58 dwells on body imagery and ineffectual fasting, Zech 7 dwells on naming specific social groups as those who cry out to Yhwh.

Why Fasting?

Why is fasting the ritual practice chosen by the prophet to speak about the wrong approach to Yhwh? Why not prayer, worship, sacrifice or others? One could answer this question with a historical reason, such as the postexilic milieu, lack of a temple for sacrifices, and so on. While those could very well be weighty reasons, I suggest another reading. I do not claim it was in the poet's mind, since I do not have any access to his or her mind; I only think it adds an ironic touch to the serious charges being made.

Considering that these fasters are charged with accusations of injustice, lack of solidarity, oppression, and violence, they belonged to the social class that could and ought to change society for the better: the ruling class. These, then, are powerful men (and some women), ruling men—including priests, since there are so many allusions to ritual practice in verse 2. For them, fasting is a ritual. Yes, they could be hungry for some hours if they were not used to fasting, but they knew a good meal awaited them after half a day or so. Such fasting is self-serving. I am not challenging their intentions, although the prophet does, crediting it as self-serving because it seeks to manipulate God.

What the text speaks of is not a private, individual decision to fast, as many individuals do today.[25] Rather, those with the power to do so, that is, politically and religiously powerful men, proclaimed a fast that was to be observed by every healthy person in order to get what they, the powerful, wanted from God. This is a self-serving fast. The way these powerful people are fasting brings hunger—not the hunger caused by fasting but the hunger imposed on those oppressed and deprived by the oppressive practices of those who order the fast. It is self-serving also because the oppressed are ordered to fast in order that the oppressors can receive God's favors, which, from their perspective do not include justice toward the poor and oppressed. Such a proclamation of a fast is an affront to those who fast every day out of lack of bread on their table. It is insulting to them and to Yhwh as well.

The way that images of eating-not eating alternate produces a nice literary effect. Starting from a horn that proclaims not a fast, but Yhwh's words,

---

25. Only a few notable men fast alone in the Hebrew Bible: David (2 Sam 12:16); Ahab (1 Kgs 21:27); and Nehemiah (Neh 1:4). All other instances are communal events.

it continues with the proclamation of a fast by the powerful, to no avail. Why? The hunger in the oppressed is caused by those proclaiming the fast. The text continues with the need to feed the hungry, so that God will answer and bestow all kinds of blessings, including vigorous bones. Finally, the Sabbath, not a fast but a feast around a family meal, is mentioned, again not for oppression but in honor of YHWH. When this is carried on, YHWH will feed the people.

Concluding Remarks

Isaiah 58, like many other chapters of this superb book, is a nourishing fountain. I have tried to show that both the structure of the chapter with its three questions and the imagery related to the semantic field of justice-oppression, including the horn and the rituals, work to produce a strong accusation against those who feel very secure socially and politically but who do not manage to twist God's arm according to their own projects. The very same action, fasting, acquires a wholly different meaning when performed by the powerful or the oppressed, willingly or imposed, with true hearts or hypocritically.

Talitha Cum Hermeneutics of Liberation: Some African Women's Ways of Reading the Bible

Musa W. Dube

The Legacy of Kimpa Vita/Dona Beatrice (1682–1706)

Sub-Saharan African women's academic biblical readings are possibly less than thirty years old. However Sub-Saharan African women's biblical interpretations go as far back as the time when the Bible came to co-exist with Sub-Saharan African cultures, people, and lands.[1] I particularly want to recall the story of Kimpa Vita, a Congolese woman who was renamed Dona Beatrice after her Christian baptism (Thornton 1998). Kimpa Vita was an African Christian woman in colonial times, when biblical readers of that time and place operated within the colonial ideology and practice of domination of other cultures, lands, people and minds (Mudimbe 1988). Kimpa Vita was therefore a colonized African Christian woman who together with the rest of her people was subjugated to foreign rule, religion, culture, and economics and was taught to despise all that represented the cosmology of her people.[2]

Through her faith, Kimpa Vita crossed cultural boundaries and the power worlds of the colonized and the colonizer (see Brah 1994; Anzandula 1987; Blunt and Rose 1994). This was highly dramatized by the fact that she was renamed Dona Beatrice. She had embraced the agenda of the colonizer by accepting Christianization, allowing herself to enter another cultural world, one that bid her to despise her Congolese being. By renaming her, the colonial church symbolized that she had accepted the gospel of conversion,

---

1. North African Christianity is as old as Christianity itself. Perhaps the birth narrative of Matthew captures this by underlining that at his birth Jesus fled and sought political asylum in Egypt until such a time when Herod was no longer alive.

2. See Barbara Kingsolver's *The Poisonwood Bible* (1998), a recent narrativization of the colonization of Congo. Joseph Conrad's *Heart of Darkness* (1899) is the classical colonial narrative construction of the same.

"civilization," and rejection of her Congolese identity. Baptism is a Christian ritual that symbolizes dying and rising with Christ. In African colonial contexts, however, it took on further meaning. It also symbolized dying to one's African culture and rising to Western civilization. Assuming a new Christian name and discarding one's so-called "pagan" name came to underline that one had been buried to one's African cosmology and had now risen with Christ to live a Christianized and civilized/European lifestyle.

This missionary assumption was, perhaps, not the experience of Kimpa Vita/Dona Beatrice. Despite this border crossing, this seeming betrayal of her culture, the selling out to the colonizer, we do well *not* to think of Kimpa Vita as one who had bought "a one-way ticket" into the colonizer's agenda. As the story of her revolt will highlight, Kimpa Vita is perhaps better seen as one who had "bought a lifetime round ticket." That is, she had a ticket that allowed her to keep crossing boundaries, going to and from one world to another (Guardiola 1997; 2002). Each time the footprints of her crisscrossing painted the other world with the colors of another world, until the paint of her crisscrossing could not go unnoticed. One can very well say that the Christianized and "civilized" Kimpa Vita answered to the name Dona Beatrice when she was in her Congolese African world and to the name Kimpa Vita when she was in the colonial church space. With all this crisscrossing, one can say she began to mix up her old and new names—at times becoming Kimpa Dona, and other times becoming Vita Beatrice, on others, becoming Vita Dona, and still in other times becoming Kimpa Beatrice. In so doing, she was mixing the supposedly separated and opposed worlds of the colonized and the colonizer. Kimpa Vita was bound to lose any sense of these boundaries. It was not long before Kimpa Vita/Dona Beatrice's true colors were discovered. That is, while she was supposedly dead to her Congolese world, she was discovered to be wearing and weaving a new multicolored coat of boundary crossing—in that highly unequal world of the colonized and the colonizer of her time.

To use Leticia Guardiola's words (1997, 73), Kimpa Vita had played a "chameleon, … trick[ing] the system," but somewhere she must have forgotten to wear the right colors in the right place. Thus Kimpa Vita/Dona Beatrice began to talk her walk. She began to prophesy, calling into being a new world.

Kimpa Vita proclaimed that the spirit of Saint Anthony, a popular Catholic saint and miracle worker, had taken possession of her. Empowered by the spirit, Kimpa Vita's preaching became a powerful protest against the Catholic Church and the colonial government. She wanted all the crosses, crucifixes, and images of Christ to be destroyed because, as she said, they were just as good as the old fetishes. She proclaimed that God would restore the subjugated kingdom of Kongo. Vita held that Christ came into the world as an African in São Salvador, which was by then the colonial capital of Congo, which she apparently renamed Bethlehem, and that he had black apostles. She is held to have told her followers that Jesus, Mary, and other Christian saints were really Kongolese. With this radically subversive proclamation for both the colonial church and government, Kimpa Vita was recognized as a dangerous thinker. She was thus condemned to death and was burned at the stake in 1706 (Dube 1996, 113).

Through her proclamation Kimpa Vita was rewriting and retelling the Christian script in a colonial space. To the colonial missionaries, Kimpa Vita's proclamation was a shocking revelation for one who had supposedly bought a one-way ticket into the world of colonial conversion and civilization. Colonial missionaries were shocked to discover that she had a dangerous lifetime return ticket that brought back black paint into a white colonial church space—one that was filled with a white, blue-eyed, blonde Jesus; Mary the mother of Jesus; male disciples and apostles. Worse, Kimpa Vita was not only journeying to and fro and mixing colors; she also refused to embrace the unequal inclusion that was served to her Congolese people. She realized that the divine images of power were as white as the colonizers themselves—legitimating and feeding each other and serving to suppress the colonized black people of Congo. Kimpa Vita/Dona Beatrice, with her lifetime round ticket, her crisscrossing footprints, had brought black paint into the white colonial church, repainting Jesus, his disciples, and his mother as black and reasserting that this black Jesus would restore the kingdom of Congo. Clearly, Kimpa Vita had not died to her Congolese world when she accepted colonial Christian conversion, "civilization," and a new name, Dona Beatrice.

By assuming this position in her proclamation, Kimpa Vita/Dona Beatrice accomplished four things. (1) She revealed herself not as a dead and buried colonized African Christian woman who was now renamed Dona Beatrice. Rather, she was Kimpa Vita of the resurrection power, who rises and returns with her suppressed African and black identity. Resurrection is the power to come back against powers of annihilation and the powers of colonial domination. It is the art of insisting on the right to be alive and to live freely.

(2) Through her proclamation, she was calling for the redefinition of the colors of power, in the divine and political space of the colonial Congo. By repainting Jesus with black colors and insisting on the restoration of the kingdom of Congo, Kimpa Vita was insisting on the empowerment of the black colonized people of Congo. She was calling for decolonization. It is notable that she claimed that Jesus and his apostles/disciples were black Congolese and called for the pulling down of all the white images in the church. This would create a situation where the black Christ would be embodied by the black people of Congo. A black Christ would identify with

the colonized Congolese and their struggle for liberation. Kimpa Vita's talk challenged whiteness and its colonizing ideology both at the spiritual and political levels.

(3) By painting Jesus and his disciples/apostles black, Kimpa Vita articulated an African Christology of resistance. The Jewish Jesus and his apostles were now black Congolese Africans. Moreover, the black Jesus, unlike the white one, supported the restoration of the colonized kingdom of Congo. This new Jesus, much like her, was a "border crosser" who did not endorse the colonization of the other. The baptized Dona Beatrice had emerged with a new body—the black body of Jesus. She was, according to African theological thinking, inculturated, a term that means that one simultaneously inhabits the biblical and Africa cultural world but without privileging one world over the other. Her blackening of Jesus is a postcolonial African Christology that seeks liberating interdependence of cultures rather than exclusiveness or the domination of one by the other, and certainly not the unequal inclusion of colonial conversion.

(4) By claiming that the spirit that moved her was the spirit of Saint Anthony, not that of Jesus or that of the Trinity, in many ways Kimpa Vita/Dona Beatrice did three important things. First, she shifted and neutralized the focus away from Jesus, who in the colonial space was one of the outstanding instruments of colonization. The status of Jesus as single intermediary rendered the African community of ancestors, who are considered the intermediaries between God and the living, as irrelevant. Claiming the spirit of Saint Anthony was thus a way of revaluing the many living voices of the dead who continue to inspire and inform the living, according to African cosmology. Second, by claiming to be informed by the "spirit," Kimpa Vita was opening an oral canon that would become a subversive text that refused to be tied to the written biblical text. This spirit canon would be an asset to African women's empowerment in the highly male Christian church and canon (Dube 1996). As many researchers of African Independent Churches (AICs) indicate, African women have risen to become church founders, prophets, bishops, faith-healers, and the like, often claiming that the spirit has authorized them to assume these positions of authority in the society. The spirit canon subverts the patriarchal biblical texts, becoming an oral canon that empowers women and men. Third, as a woman, Kimpa Vita/Dona Beatrice is empowered by a spirit that allows her to speak and to challenge colonial church ideology and colonial state. In so doing, she transgresses the gender divide that relegated most women to the periphery of power. She at once embodies the oppositional space of crisscrossing genders, races, religions, class, cultures, and texts. In this crisscrossing Kimpa Vita calls into being the space of multiple boundary crossing, a state of a lifetime round ticket of traveling to and from the

guarded boundaries of the colonized and the colonizer and other guarded social boundaries.

As the story tells us, Kimpa Vita of the resurrection morning and her subversive text did not escape the colonial missionaries policing of boundaries—for the challenge it was positing to the highly unequal world of that time. It did not escape the missionaries' ears that she was challenging both the colonial church and state and calling into being a highly inculturated space, a hybrid space of cultural intimacy. She was quickly marked as a heretic and was martyred on the stake in 1706. Her martyrdom was the second death, given that the first attempt was made through burial by baptism and renaming her in order to eliminate her African identity. But what would happen now, would the spirit of Kimpa Vita arise again? Would she keep on rising against the oppressive structures of colonialism and colonizing Christianity? Would she continue to rise and cultivate a new inculturated space of cultural kissing, which empowers men and women, white and blacks, Christians and non-Christian—all people? Historically, Kimpa Vita is held to be the founder of AICs.[3] These are churches that sought to resist colonization of their countries and colonizing Christian practices.[4] As I have said elsewhere,

> The centrality of women in AICs could not be ended with the crucifixion of Kimpa Vita. A line of other women have ever since heard and responded to the word of the Spirit of God to serve as church founders, leaders, prophets, and faith healers. Outstanding among these are Ma Nku, Grace Tshabalala, Alice Lenshina, and Mai Chaza, who became founders and leaders of massive AICs movements in this [last] century. (Dube 1996, 113)

In other words, it is my contention that Kimpa Vita's spirit and vision is repeatedly resurrected. It is my contention that her spirit dwells not only among the AICs' women and men leaders but also among many African academic biblical readers of today. I therefore want to highlight what I call the *talitha cum* African women's biblical hermeneutics of reading by briefly highlighting the practices of four African women: Mercy A. Oduyoye; Madipoane Masenya; Musa W. Dube; and Teresa Okure. *Talitha cum* hermeneutics refers to the art of living in the resurrection space. It refers to the art of continually

---

3. Following closely in the identity of their founder, AICs are well-documented for what has been termed, in colonial language, "syncretistic." For the history of AICs, see Sundkler 1961; Daneel 1987.

4. According to Norbert C. Brockman (1994), "The Antonian movement, which Kimpa started outlasted her.... Her ideas remained among the peasants, appearing in various messianic cults until, two centuries later, it took new form in the preaching of Simon Kimbangu."

rising against the powers of death—the powers of patriarchy, the powers of colonial oppression and exploitation, the powers that produce and perpetuate poverty, disease, and all forms of exclusion and dehumanization. Walking in the legacy of Kimpa Vita, African women's *talitha cum* hermeneutics are ways of living and insisting on staying alive; even where one confronts oppressive powers that crush, one dares to rise. Before I turn to discuss the four women identified above, I need briefly to elaborate on the source of naming, that is, *talitha cum* African women's (biblical) hermeneutics of life.

Resurrection Power: *Talitha Cum* Hermeneutics of Life

As used here, the term *talitha cum* is drawn from the Markan story of Mark 5:21–43. In the story, Jesus is thronged by a huge crowd when a synagogue leader, Jairus, comes pleading: "my daughter is at the point of death, come lay hands on her so that she may be healed and live." Jesus begins to walk with Jairus to his house to attend to the dying child. His emergency journey gets hijacked by a bleeding woman seeking healing from her twelve-year bleeding. Meanwhile, the daughter dies. Jesus insists on walking with Jairus to attend to the dead girl. He arrives at the house of Jairus, goes to the place where she is sleeping, and says to her, "*talitha cum*," which means, "Little girl, I say wake up." She wakes up and starts walking around, to the utter amazement of the mourning crowd. In this essay I use the term *talitha cum*, drawn from Mark 5:21–43, to frame African women's practice for several reasons.

First, it is a story that has captured the imaginations of African women theologians, inspiring a number of articles (Okure 1992; Dube 2003b; 2004a), books (Oduyoye and Kanyoro 1990; 1992; Dube and Njoroge 2001, performances (Dube 2000; 2004b), and practices. (I am particularly addicted to the story and find my way to the story many times.) Its centrality became evident at the launching of the Circle of Concerned African Women Theologians in 1989, when the two books from this historical meeting were named after this story: *The Will to Arise: Women, Tradition, and the Church in Africa*; and *Talitha, Qumi!*

Second, the story is popular because it represents the struggles of African women against colonial powers and patriarchal oppression—with the highly desired results of liberation and life. In the story, the discourse of colonial resistance is underlined by assigning the number twelve to both the dying daughter and the bleeding woman, thereby suggesting that Israel is a sick, dying daughter, a bleeding woman who has endlessly sought for healing, which is finally delivered by Jesus. This reading for national liberation is further underlined by the beginning of the chapter, where Jesus meets a man who is heavily possessed by demons and lives among the tombs. The demons that possess the man are apparently a "Legion," that is, a term evocative of the Roman imperial guard assigned to this region. The guard is representative of the Roman Empire. Legion trembles before Jesus, suggesting that he is confronted by a different and decolonizing power. Jesus casts out Legion into a herd of pigs, which then run and get drowned in the sea. In all the stories of the demon-possessed man, the bleeding woman, and the dying daughter, Jesus is presented as liberator from colonial occupation, which, according to the story, is a situation of living in deadly ill health, so much so that one basically comes to dwell with the dead, hurting oneself. For African women, the story thus highlights the impact of colonial domination, affirms their struggles against international exploitation, from colonial times to neocolonial times and the global village era.

Third, the story provides for gender empowerment. First, by using women's bodies to symbolize the state of a colonized nation, the story perhaps also succeeds in communicating that in colonized settings women are likely to suffer more, given their prevailing gender oppression (Dube 2004a). The story, however, not only exposes exacerbated gender oppression; it also provides for gender empowerment. That is, a bleeding woman whose health status makes her further distanced from the public space and empowerment within patriarchal system takes it upon herself to seek and to get empowerment. She reaches for the garment of Jesus with the full intention of getting healing and she does so without asking any permission from Jesus. In so doing, she appropriates for herself the right to healing. (Healing here refers to healing from colonial, patriarchal, physical oppression—basically all that is oppressive.) Jesus only gets to know when power leaves his body. When Jesus discovers it, he searches and finds her. Without rebuke, he pronounces, "Daughter, your faith has healed you; go in peace." The story, therefore, provides a framework for women's agency, insisting that oppressed women (and nations) have the right to search and reach for their own empowerment against all that oppresses and exploits them—and there is no need to ask permission from those in power. That is, disempowered women and nations must make it their duty to seek for healing. Gladly, in this story, Jesus is characterized as one who supports their search for liberation and healing from all forms of oppression.

Lastly, this story is magnetic to African women because it seems to embody the arts of hope, healing, resurrection, and liberation. Where one walks too close to death and cohabits with the dead (the demon-possessed man/the young girl), where one lives for too long in ill health and suffering (the bleeding woman), one can actually be healed. One can resurrect from death and return to life. Hope is sustained for those who are internationally oppressed, those who are oppressed due to gender and physical ill health.

According to this story, liberation is a divine right that is in fact attainable. Death is denied its power, as one can actually resurrect, just as the demon-possessed man and the dead girl were liberated from the clutches of death. Jesus also stands in contrast to the colonizing employment of his figure as the single intermediary by the colonizers.

Talitha cum African women's hermeneutics is therefore the practice of living daily in confrontation with international oppression of the past and present, gender oppression of the past and present, physical wounds of the past and present—a confrontation of sickness and death, which must give way to healing. Healing here is a concept that includes the healing of international relations, class, race, ethnic, age, spiritual, environmental, gender relations, national relations, and physical bodies of individuals and communities that get sickened when relations are not well (Dube 2001b). The stories of the bleeding woman, the sick daughter, and Kimpa Vita thus embody that liberating energy and vision that empowers African women to live in the resurrection power from the ever-unending death-dealing oppressive forces that invade the continent and their lives. Let us now look at the individual examples of the women mentioned above in their given order and how they articulate their *talitha cum* hermeneutics.

Mercy A. Oduyoye: Inculturated Feminist Hermeneutics

Mercy A. Oduyoye is not trained as a biblical scholar, yet she is the most illustrious African theologian on the continent. Her star lies not only in her publications; above all, it lies in her historical effort to establish the Circle of Concerned African Women Theologians, which is now a vibrant Pan-African association of academic women in religion and theology. The Circle has a membership of about six hundred women who mobilize each other regionally, nationally, and continentally to research, think, write, and publish theological material in search of the resurrection space of life from international exploitation, gender, class, ethnic, national, environmental, and age oppression—all that keeps Africa and the African people as a whole suppressed. Oduyoye has published a number of books, including *Introducing African Women's Theology* (2001); *Daughters of Anowa: African Women and Patriarchy* (1995); *Beads and Strands: Reflections of an African Woman Christianity in Africa* (2004).

How, then, does Oduyoye embody the legacy of Kimpa Vita? How does she articulate *talitha cum* hermeneutics? Oduyoye's work is much too extensive to be adequately and fairly treated within the limits of this essay. I wish to use two brief examples: her acknowledgement of the coexistence of multiple scriptures in the African context and her use of them. In her chapter "Jesus Saves," Oduyoye points out that:

The religious background of these studies is the primal religion of Africa and Judaism. What we in Africa have traditionally believed of God and the transcendent order has shaped our Christianity. But that is only part of the story. Islam strides shoulder to shoulder with Christianity in Africa.... Religious maturity, traditional hospitality to the stranger and the sacredness of blood ties have enabled the adherents of these faiths to accept the other's right to exist and in the family to share each other's festivals. (2004, 18)

In an article co-authored with Elizabeth Amoah, "The Christ for African Women," Oduyoye demonstrates this historical crisscrossing tradition of Kimpa Vita in the service of resurrection. Oduyoye and Amoah hold that "most Christians refer to Scripture as meaning the Hebrew Bible and its Christian supplement, the New Testament, but we would like to start with a reference to the "unwritten Scripture" of the Fante of Ghana" (Amoah and Oduyoye 1988, 35). In their construction of African woman's Christology, Amoah and Oduyoye insist that "all human communities have their stories of persons whose individual acts have lasting effects on the destiny and ethos of the whole group. Such people are remembered in stories" (36). Living between the Hebrew, Christian, Fante, and women's stories/scriptures, Amoah and Oduyoye begin to construct their Fante feminist Christology in this way:

> When the Fante were journeying to their present home in Southern Ghana, they crossed vast tracts of waterless plains and they thirsted. Such an agony of a people on the move, but their leader Eku, the matriarch, did not despair. She spurred them on.... they came to a place they could settle in peace and prosperity. They then came to a pool of water. Having suffered much treachery on their journey, none dared to salve the parched throat with the water, invitingly before them. It could have been poisoned by their enemies. Matriarch Eku took her life into her hands, drank from the pool, and gave to her dog to drink. The people waited. They peered at the woman and her dog with glazed eyes. Neither human nor animal had suffered from drinking water of the pool. All fell to and drank their fill, shouting Eku *Aso* (Eku has tasted).... Eku has tasted on our behalf. We can now drink without fear. (36).

In this article, which begins by recognizing other scriptures and other Christ figures, Amoah and Oduyoye do a number of other things: they return to the Christian Testament; review African male constructions of Christology; assess christological titles of nonacademic women faith leaders; and assess "Africa's business," that is, the existing "life-denying forces." They conclude that "Jesus of Nazareth, by the counter cultural relations he established with women, has become for us the Christ, the anointed one who liberates the companion, friend, teacher, and true Child of Women.... Jesus is Christ—truly woman, yet truly divine, for only God is the truly Compassionate One" (44). Here the story of the matriarch Eku has merged with the story of Jesus as well as the stories of African women in search for liberation. They go on to conclude that "*an African woman perceives and accepts Christ as a woman and as an African*" (44). Here Christology crosses boundaries of texts, cultures, gender, and colonizing Christian perspectives and paints Jesus in many colors and genders in search of *talitha cum*—the resurrection from the "life-denying forces." No doubt the crucified Kimpa Vita of 1706 is alive in the hermeneutics of Oduyoye!

MASENYA MADIPOANE: *BOSADI* HERMENEUTICS

Madipoane Masenya is the first black South African woman Hebrew Bible scholar. She has published numerous articles in journals and books and written a book entitled *How Worthy Is the Woman of Worth*. Her embodiment of Kimpa Vita's legacy and efforts to articulate *talitha cum* hermeneutics in the historically exclusive, exploitative, and oppressive context of apartheid South Africa is best articulated in what she calls *bosadi* hermeneutics. According to Masenya, "a *bosadi* perspective investigates what ideal womanhood should be for an African-South African woman Bible reader" (2001b, 148). Masenya's description of *bosadi* highlights that it is a concept drawn from Northern Sotho tradition, which seeks to look critically at both the Sotho and biblical traditions in search for liberating perspectives (1997).

Her article "Esther and Northern Sotho Stories: African South African Women's Commentary" (2001c) demonstrates her crisscrossing of boundaries by reading both from the biblical stories and Sotho oral stories and proverbs. At times she compares these narratives, while at other times she uses them to illuminate one another, thereby demonstrating a blackened and expanded canon that goes beyond the written biblical text. This expanded canon certainly resists the colonial missionary dismissal of African cultures by revaluing the oratures (oral literature) of Sotho people.

It might be worth pointing out that another black South African woman, Gloria Plaatjie, also demonstrates this tendency to expand what constitutes scripture. In her "Toward a Post-apartheid Black Feminist Reading of the Bible: The Case of Luke 2:36–38" (2001), Plaatjie insists on reading with and from nonacademic women Bible readers, thus upholding the authority of Kimpa Vita's space of discernment and resistance. Plaatjie also insists that what is authoritative, what is redemptive, and what is empowering for black South African women, who were the worst victims of apartheid South Africa, is not just to read the Bible, a book that was instrumental in shaping the apartheid ideology; rather, it is also to read the Bible with and in the light of the current South African constitution. According to Plaatjie,

> The constitution of post-apartheid South Africa is that country's biggest achievement, for it recognizes the racial and gender equality of all South Africans.… for Black South African women who sacrificed all other interests and focused on fighting against apartheid, the constitution of post-apartheid South Africa is in everyway a central and authoritative text. It carries sacred status for it symbolizes what black people fought and struggled for: *justice and dignity for all.* (2001, 116)

MUSA W. DUBE: POSTCOLONIAL FEMINIST BIBLICAL HERMENEUTICS

The present writer also stands within the legacy of Kimpa Vita and *talitha cum* hermeneutics in her work, which is mostly characterized as postcolonial feminist interpretation of the Bible. This perspective is best articulated in her *Postcolonial Feminist Biblical Interpretation* (2000) and other articles. According to Dube,

> Postcolonial readings of the Bible must seek to decolonize the biblical text, its interpretations, its readers, its institutions, as well as seeking ways of reading for liberating interdependence. Liberating dependence here entails a twofold willingness on the part of readers: first, to propound biblical readings that decolonize imperialistic tendencies and other narrative designs; second, to propound readings that seek to highlight the biblical texts and Jesus as undoubtedly important cultures, which are nonetheless, not above all, but among the many important cultures of the world. (1998, 133)

This agenda upholds the Kimpa Vita vision of a round-ticket approach to cultural worlds that resists the colonialist approach of hierarchy and binary oppositions. The elaboration of Dube's work simultaneously seeks to resist gender and all forms of oppression through seeking to cultivate a framework of liberating interdependence.

The *talitha cum* edge of Dube's hermeneutics has recently been highlighted by her focus on the global crisis of HIV/AIDS epidemic, which she describes as an epidemic driven by social injustice (Messer 2004). In this area, Dube has recently edited volumes such as *HIV/AIDS and the Curriculum: Methods of Mainstreaming HIV/AIDS in Theological Programs* (2003a) and *Grant Me Justice: HIV/AIDS and Gender Readings of the Bible* (Dube and Kanyoro 2004). Given that HIV/AIDS is a global crisis that calls for global action, Dube argues, "In a world where 21 million people have died in 21 years and 40 million are infected, we [scholars] have to realize that our highest call is to become prophets of life" (2003a, 43). In her latest reading of the Mark 5: 21–43, from a postcolonial feminist and HIV/AIDS perspective, Dube asks: "How can New Testament readers and Christians stand in the narratives of postcolonial, feminist and HIV/AIDS search for justice and healing the world…?" (2004a, 137). She goes on to say, "while I have no formula to give, what I definitely know is that this is a fitting duty for all of us who live in the HIV/AIDS era to read for healing and liberation" (137). According to Dube, "one must struggle with how they can take the challenging role of calling *talitha cum* to the dying and the dead in the age of HIV/AIDS epidemic" (138).

TERESA OKURE: HERMENEUTICS OF LIFE

The questions posed by Dube are perhaps better addressed by Teresa Okure's biblical hermeneutics of life. Okure, the first New Testament woman scholar in Africa, has written numerous articles and either written or edited a number of books, including *To Cast Fire upon the Earth* (2000b) and *The Johannine Approach to Mission* (1988), and co-edited *Global Bible Commentary* (Patte 2004).

In her article "First Was the Life, Not the Book," Teresa Okure holds that

> Life as the starting point and abiding context of hermeneutics is not only important; it is the reality that imposes itself. Emerging and liberating trends in biblical studies (Third World, women's feminist, womanist, reader-response hermeneutics and inculturation) require that readers address their life situations as part of interpreting scripture. The biblical works themselves are records of people who struggled to understand the meaning of their life in relation to God. (2000a, 196–97)

Okure insists that the whole Bible should be seen as an attestation of people seeking to understand and live their lives in their situation and in relation to God. The writers of Genesis only wrote as they reflected on life itself, just as the rest of the books in the Hebrew Bible were written from their own life situations. Okure insists that "the story of the Bible is therefore about life and life holds the key to comprehending it" (2000a, 194). It is on these bases that she entitled one of her articles "First Was the Life, Not the Book." In an earlier paper, "Reading from This Place: Some Prospects and Problems," Okure is very emphatic about the implications of her proposal for the ethics of reading. Okure holds that with a life-centered hermeneutic, "it becomes possible to discern those interpretations that are in accordance with the one will and intention of God, which is to give and promote life in all its fullness (John 10:10)" (1995, 55). She goes on to say "any interpretation that fails to do this becomes suspect and should be regarded as inauthentic" (1995, 57). The life-centered hermeneutics, in other words, are grounded not only on God as the creator of life but also on God as the author of a good life. The biblical texts are but a fraction of human testimonies of grappling with living the God-given life. For Okure, therefore, the authenticity of any interpretation should be measured by its capacity to promote and support life—qualitative life, life as God meant it to be for all members of the earth communities.

CONCLUSION

The various proposed methods of African women theologians stand in the legacy of Kimpa Vita's resurrection: the power to resist and rise from death-dealing powers of oppression, suppression, and exploitation; the art of insisting on life and quality life. This often entails resisting colonizing and patriarchal ideologies in biblical and African oral canons as well as constructing a space of liberating interdependence between cultures, genders, ethnicities, races, sexualities, religions, nations, cultural worlds, and the environment. Teresa Okure's proposal for a hermeneutics of life, her assertion that "first was the life, not the book" radically extends the canonical boundaries of what we read and why we read. In short, Okure reinscribes *life as the scripture* that we ought to read and therefore to be in the business of maintaining its quality against all the death-dealing forces and the social injustices that often trivialize the lives of many. This seems to me the best summary of the *talitha cum* hermeneutics of reading in the resurrection space for life.

Paul against Empire: Then and Now

Theodore W. Jennings Jr.

The question of a liberative reading of biblical texts has its origin in Latin America and, not infrequently, has been developed in contradistinction to the traditional hermeneutical strategies of Europe and North America. An indispensable aid to the work of a liberative hermeneutics was an appreciation of certain insights of Marxism in so far as this assisted in the illumination of the structures that produced the massive poverty that characterized the Latin American reality within which the Bible was to be read, as well as instantiating a modern prophetic impetus for dramatic transformations in these same structures. Among the early works that signaled the fruitfulness of such a hermeneutical strategy was the seminal work of José Porfirio Miranda (1974), which not only demonstrated the overwhelming biblical testimony to the divine claim of justice against structures of exploitation and marginalization but also pointed to the way in which this theme was present not only in the Synoptic Gospels but also in John and, most importantly for our purposes, in Paul.

There are those who have maintained that, with the collapse of the Soviet Union, the liberative hermeneutical project has been dealt a decisive blow, precisely because of its dependence upon the plausibility of a certain Marxist interpretation of global economic reality. Indeed, it is true that many of the heirs to a liberation theology perspective have adopted alternative or additional hermeneutical strategies such as postcolonial, culturally contextual, as well as adaptations of feminist hermeneutics.

At the same time, however, the global economic hegemony of consumer and financial capital and of a certain mediatized democracy under the umbrella of U.S. military hyper-power status has resulted in the sort of "empire" diagnosed by Hardt and Negri (2000). In this context, the collapse of the Soviet Union notwithstanding, a number of voices, especially in Europe, have emerged that not only take the challenge of developing a Marxist analysis of the current global reality seriously but who also engage, precisely as "atheists" or "materialists," in a rereading of the biblical texts generally and, more especially, of Pauline texts and themes. It is this wedding of post-Marxist thought and biblical interpretation that I want particularly to explore.

Before doing so, however, there is another piece of the hermeneutical puzzle that it is necessary to explore that will help to set the stage for this turn to a radical political interpretation of Paul. It is the work that has been done for some time now in terms of setting the discussion of Paul within the context of first-century imperial reality. It is this that will enable us to see a certain resonance between counterimperial discourse in the first century and a similar discourse today.

First, it is not the case that Paul is the only New Testament writer who has been reread against the background of the imperial reality of the first century. It has long been clear that the Apocalypse of John must be understood within the context of a critique of the Roman Empire (Babylon). For many years the work of Richard Horsley (1987; 1989) has concentrated attention upon the context of the ministry (and birth narratives) of Jesus as intelligible against the background of the effects of imperial rule in Palestine and within the attempts to subvert such rule. More recently, Warren Carter (2000) has shown in a number of interesting studies the significance of this macro-political context for an understanding of the Gospel of Matthew.

However, what has been most surprising is the number of studies that have taken on the task of demonstrating the radical political significance of Paul in relation to Roman imperial authority. This is surprising because of the way in which Paul has traditionally been understood either as a support for the most reactionary political options or as at best taking an utterly apolitical stance toward the gospel, urging instead a purely interior transformation that is disengaged from exterior "works."

The reactionary Paul has been developed through an interpretation of the first few verses of Rom 13. These verses have routinely been read to license the complete subservience of the faithful to whatever form of governmental authority (even if in the course of the American Revolution and even later in the struggle against apartheid there have been those who read these same verses as licensing a certain legitimate rebellion against unjust governmental rule). When these verses were read in connection with what has been supposed to be Paul's unquestioning attitude toward slavery, his enforcement of masculine domination, and his allegedly antihomosexual critique in Romans, one then has the full emergence of Paul as the champion of a reactionary politics. He becomes the hero of those who support such an option and the privileged target of those who seek a more progressive, emancipatory, or even liberative political stance.

The quietist Paul has been the product of a reading that privileges what Krister Stendahl has called the divided conscience of the West. In this case an Augustinian reading of Paul hyperbolized through a Lutheran emphasis on both the bondage of the will and salvation by faith alone has largely withdrawn the reading of Paul from social-political relevance. This pietistic and Protestant reading of Paul has largely been left in place by existentialist perspectives that, beginning with Bultmann, have had a profound influence on the reading of Paul in the twentieth century.

In the United States, the quietist reading of Paul and the reactionary appropriation of Paul have existed side by side and even have reinforced one another, while the existentialist Paul has often been associated with a more "liberal" or even progressive political stance.

However, it is the Barthian reading of Paul as bringing under judgment the whole of culture and civilization that has perhaps actually opened the way to a reading of Paul that is neither quietist nor reactionary. The political significance of such a reading already became evident in the resistance fostered by such a reading of Paul to the Nazification of the German Protestant church in the 1930s. Further, Barth's refusal to give theological sanction to the Western demonization of the Soviet Union in the 1950s opened the space for the Christian Marxist dialogue of the 1960s, a dialogue that may have served as a helpful antecedent for the willingness of Latin American theologians constructively to engage with Marxist insights and analyses in the 1970s.

In the United States, however, it was the work of Krister Stendahl that actually opened the way to a more directly political reading of Paul in his own time. What Stendahl accomplished was to bring into question the Protestant consensus that Paul was to be read as emphasizing a justification by faith alone that addressed itself to what he termed the divided conscience of the West (1976). By breaking the spell of a traditional notion of the doctrine of the justification of the sinner that held sway in both liberal (existentialist) and in conservative (Protestant "orthodox") circles, Stendahl cleared the ground for a rereading of Paul both as a profoundly Jewish thinker and as one who did not fit into the straitjacket of an interiorized piety. Even though Ernst Käsemann strongly protested Stendahl's relativizing of the justification of the sinner (or more precisely of the godless), his own insistence upon reading Paul as an apocalyptic thinker whose vision of transformation was not contained within the individual conscience but had to do with cosmic transformation as well also made a decisive contribution to the reconsideration of Paul.

While there have been a number of attempts to understand Paul in his own, especially religious, context, whether in connection with Hellenistic religion and philosophy or, more recently, in the context of emergent Judaisms, what is decisive for our purposes is the growing attention to the social, economic, and political/imperial context within which Paul worked and wrote. Many of the results of this work have been gathered together in collections of essays and other materials edited by Richard Horsley (1997b; 2000). When Paul is viewed in this light, it becomes clear that he is engaged in a work that delegitimizes the pretensions of Roman imperial rule and that sets up a countersociety exhibiting values subversive of the Greco-Roman economic and political order.

The delegitimizing occurs first through an appropriation of Roman imperial ideology for counterimperial purposes. This has been obscured for us by the association of certain Pauline terms with a specifically religious provenance; terms such as "Son of God" and "world savior" were associated with the emperor. Similarly, terms such as "gospel" and "faith" (*pistis*) had specific and sociopolitical meanings (Brunt 1997). "Gospel" referred to imperial proclamations of weal for the empire (victories at war, for example) while *pistis* was deployed to affirm the cohesion of client and patron in a system of patronage of which the emperor was the chief patron (Garnsey and Saller 1997; J. Chow 1997; Gordon 1997) Terms such as *ekklesia*, regularly translated as "church," had in view the political assemblies of urban centers of the empire (Horsley 1997a), and so on. By restoring Paul's distinctive terminology to its political frame of reference, the political import of his project comes more clearly into view.

Similarly, terms that Paul uses that have been mythologized—"principalities and powers," "rule and authority," even "pillars of the cosmos"—can be returned to their context in imperial ideology in order to see how Paul's project actually competes with and is critical of the existing imperial order. Moreover, terms such as "peace" and "justice" can be understood against the background of imperial ideology that legitimated itself by reference to the alleged provision of these values to the empire. It was precisely because the Roman rulers could claim that they made justice rule through law or brought peace that they could plausibly be designated as world saviors (Elliott 2000, 30).

At the level of what we might term micro-political practices, Paul's establishment of assemblies that include different nationalities and cultures, that abolish the distinction between slave and free at the level of corporate participation, and that erode the privileges of masculine domination contrast sharply with Greco-Roman social values. The unplugging from the legal system (do not take one another to court, 1 Cor 6:1–8), the disruption of the patronage system of relationships (as in the common meals in Corinth, 1 Cor 11:17–34), the intentional erosion of the ethos of competitiveness in favor of solidarity, and so on all point toward the emergence of an alternative sociality.

It is undoubtedly the case that Paul does not develop a fully independent or autonomous social order that fully exemplifies the principles that he articulates. At the micro-political level there appear to be a number of compromises with the existing social order (e.g., with respect to women in Corinth, 1 Cor 14:34) that are, perhaps, intelligible from the standpoint of his expectation that the existing social order was in any case coming to an abrupt and complete end. Further, there is the inevitable danger that appropriating imperial terminology for subversive purposes can be simply reversed at a later stage to become a relegitimation of empire. This danger is unavoidable, since no one can simply invent his or her own language, still less ensure how later generations will interpret what one writes or says. Still, careful attention to Paul's language and practices within the context of Roman imperial ideology and practice makes clear that Paul's project was one that entailed a radical rejection of imperial ideology and the establishment, however tentatively and temporarily, of a sociality that makes concrete a very contrary ethos and sensibility.

How indeed could it be otherwise for one who claimed that one who had been executed as an outlaw by Roman legal and military power was in fact the designated Messiah of God and that God had already acted to overthrow the verdict of the empire through the resurrection of the executed? What was therefore necessary was the emergence of new social forms that took for granted the utter collapse of the existing imperial order and that instead instantiated a wholly new social reality in which there was neither Greek nor Jew, slave nor free, male nor female.

When we turn, as we now do, to a consideration of contemporary radical political thought, we must be clear that what is at stake here is not the suggestion that Paul somehow managed to escape the confines of his own epoch in order to offer timeless truth regarding the political order. Rather, Paul is seen as one who engaged in counterimperial theory and practice who can serve as something of a model or prototype (to use a suggestion of Elisabeth Schüssler Fiorenza 1998, 116) from which contemporary counterimperial theory and practice has much to learn. What is remarkable about this is that these philosophers have apparently little or no awareness of the historical and sociopolitical labors of exegesis in this direction. Moreover, they have no interest in Paul as a religious authority, as one whose religiously sanctioned authority must somehow be salvaged or verified or mitigated. They are, as Derrida said of himself, rightly regarded as atheists. They read Paul in the same way as they read Plato or Aristotle, Cicero, or Seneca, but they find in Paul one who radically subverts the elitist and authoritarian political projects with which these figures are so readily associated.

The specific context within which Paul is read by materialist philosophers today is the hegemony of what Hardt and Negri have termed "Empire." In their discussion of this theme they do not specifically mention Paul, but what they say about early Christianity sets the stage for the perspectives to be discussed.

> Allow us, in conclusion, one final analogy that refers to the birth of Christianity in Europe and its expansion during the decline of the Roman Empire. In this process an enormous potential of subjectivity was constructed and consolidated in terms of the prophecy of a world to come, a chiliastic project. This new subjectivity offered an absolute alternative to the spirit of imperial right—a new ontological basis. From this perspective, Empire was accepted as the "maturity of the times" and the unity of the entire known civilization, but it was challenged in its totality by a completely different ethical and ontological axis. In the same way today, given that the limits and unresolvable problems of the new imperial right are fixed, theory and practice can go beyond them, finding once again an ontological basis of antagonism—within Empire, but also against and beyond Empire, at the same level of totality. (Hardt and Negri 2000, 21)

As we shall see, it is with a similar set of concerns that a number of contemporary radical thinkers have turned to reread Paul.

The Militant Paul (Alain Badiou)

In the last decade or so, it is with the work of Alain Badiou that the political reading of Paul has come to be associated. Badiou is a mathematician turned metaphysician who was shaped by the revolutionary currents of heterodox Marxism in the events of 1968. Like many French intellectuals of that generation, he found an initial attraction to Maoist ideas as a certain counterweight to the still Stalinist postures of official party Marxism in Europe. He became the successor of the controversial Marxist philosopher Louis Althusser at the École Normal Supériure in Paris, and it is in this context that he has shaped his radical post-Marxist political thought (a thinking that also is rooted in the practice of grass-roots political activism).

His principled atheism leads him to deny the reality of any "One" and thus to develop something like an ontology of the multiple (composed of multiples … all the way down) that is treated in accordance with mathematical set theory, which he modifies to maintain that all multiples are infinite. While he has developed elements of his mathematical ontology in a major book on existence and event (Badiou 2005), it is his ethics and politics that is most of interest for us, since it is this that will lead him to write a book on Paul.

Briefly, Badiou's ethico-political perspective is that a situation composed of multiplicities may also be the site of what he calls an "event" that is also a rupture with the situation. This event is the occurring of that which in ordinary or customary perception has been excluded from the situation. Something happens. This happening is taken as an event in that it is a nonempirical occurrence that cannot be "known as such," since knowledge pertains to the situation.

What then happens is that a "someone," a human animal, otherwise simply a member of an animal species, is caught up in this event in such a way that the situation is transformed. In this way the someone becomes a subject or begins to constitute itself as a subject in loyalty or fidelity to the event (2002, 12).

One becomes a subject by becoming the subject of an event, through commitment, perseverance in the event, thinking through/acting through the situation on the basis of the event. This thinking/acting is what Badiou terms a "truth process," and one of the features that he emphasizes most strongly concerning his view is that precisely the category of truth appears here in a decisive way, thereby distinguishing his views, he believes, from those now regnant in philosophy (hermeneutical, positivist or postmodern; 2004, 42–44).

Like Lacan (1992, 170–71), he emphasizes that it is possible and indeed legitimate to read Paul apart from confessional belief: "we may draw upon [these phrases] freely, without devotion or repulsion" (Badiou 2003, 1). In terms of the general ethical perspective that we have outlined, Badiou makes clear why Paul is so necessary:

> For me, Paul is a poet thinker of the event, as well as one who practices and states the invariant traits of what can be called the militant figure. He brings forth the entirely human connection, whose destiny fascinates me, between the general idea of a rupture, an overturning, and that of a thought practice that is this rupture's subjective materiality. (2003, 2)

The specific register in which Badiou will read Paul is that of the political militant. We recall Badiou's own political perspective and commitments. It is thus extraordinary to read his specific justification for taking up Paul at this time: "There is currently a widespread search for a new militant figure ... called upon to succeed the one installed by Lenin and the Bolsheviks at the beginning of this century, which can be said to have been that of the party militant" (2003, 2). Here, of course, Paul is to Lenin as Jesus is to Marx. But a new figure, what will this mean?

It is precisely here that Badiou situates his own reading:

> No we will not allow the rights of true thought to have as their only instance monetarist free exchange and its mediocre political appendage, capitalist-

parliamentarianism, whose squalor is ever more poorly dissimulated behind the fine word "democracy." That is why Paul, himself the contemporary of a monumental figure of the destruction of all politics (the beginnings of that military despotism known as the "Roman Empire"), interests us in the highest degree. (2003, 7)

Thus Badiou asks: "what are the conditions for a universal singularity? It is on this point that we invoke Saint Paul" (2003, 13).

For Paul, as Badiou notes, the resurrection of the crucified is at the heart of his apostolic proclamation. Although Badiou regards this as a "fable" in which it is strictly impossible to believe, he nonetheless offers an intriguing interpretation in terms of his own perspective. "Death is the construction of the eventual site insofar as it brings it about that resurrection (which cannot be inferred from it) will have been addressed to men [that is, of course, to all]" (2003, 70). This means that death simply designates the site of the event. It is not the event as such. The event is resurrection, but resurrection is for all or addressed to all. It designates "newness of life" or true life or life beyond the situation of death. In his *Ethics* (2002), Badiou calls the life of the subject dedicated to the event "immortal," and this is what he seems to mean here.

> The fact that in the end we all die, that only dust remains, in no way alters Man's identity as immortal at the instant in which he affirms himself as someone who runs counter to the temptation of wanting-to-be-an-animal to which circumstances may expose him. And we know that every human being is capable of being this immortal—unpredictably, be it in circumstances great or small, for truths important or secondary. In each case, subjectivation is immortal, and makes Man. Beyond this there is only a biological species, a "biped without feathers," whose charms are not obvious. (2002, 12)

This seems, then, closely to parallel the concern of Heidegger to distinguish authentic from inauthentic existence.

In relation to Paul, Badiou emphasizes three themes that are of particular interest to him in his search for a politically relevant militancy: universality; equality; and what we may term sociality. We will take these in turn.

In Badiou's view, Paul emphasizes universality through his repeated emphasis upon "all." For example, Paul says "all have sinned" and also "all will be made alive." Here he draws in particular from 1 Cor 15, but the Adam/Christ contrast of Rom 5 is also present in his reflection. The important point is that none are in principle excluded from Paul's message; all are called to devote themselves (and so become "singularities") to the event. In this connection Badiou also cites Gal 3:28 to emphasize the breaking down of various divisions of class (slave/free), race or culture (Jew/Gentile), and gender (male/female). Indeed, one of the most controversial aspects of Badiou's thought, not only in connection with his reading of Paul but also in connection with the contemporary political perspective, is that all such communitarian or identitarian distinctions are in Paul and must be in the present, abolished in favor of a form of universal singularity (2003, 14).

Following from this is Badiou's emphasis on equality among these singularities devoted to the event. In the case of Paul he emphasizes, following up on Freud's perspective in *Moses and Monotheism*, that Paul emphasizes the community of sons, which has abolished the rule of the "father" and so of any and all forms of mastery: "One must depose the master and found the equality of sons" (2003, 59).

While this seems to depend on Paul's adoption formulas and his calling all to be fellow workers with him, it may somewhat overstate the case in that Badiou claims that for Paul we are sons and not slaves (2003, 63). We are not told, however, how this is to be squared with Paul calling himself a slave of the Messiah (Rom 1:1) or his calling upon his readers to be slaves of justice or of God (Rom 6:18; 7:25). In my view, it would be possible to understand Paul as calling for a strategy of "downward social mobility" as the way to accomplish equality, but that is not Badiou's argument.

In any case, from the vision of or commitment to the equality of "sons" follows Badiou's insistence that Paul calls into being a new form of sociality in which law is abolished in favor of love. Here again the emphasis falls upon 1 Corinthians, but now chapter 13, as well as Paul's insistence that what matters is faith working by love (Gal 5:6). In this it may be that Badiou is closer to Paul than many who read "faith" as simply opposed to "works," rather than as the way in which love of the neighbor and of all comes into being and practice.

Now the reader of Badiou's Paul may find that several of these themes seem to echo the well-known formula of "liberty, equality, and fraternity" associated with the French Revolution, although they also correspond in fateful ways to what Badiou claims is the true essence of "communism." Badiou asks "What does 'communist' signify in an absolute sense?" and answers: "Egalitarian passion, the Idea of justice, the will to break with the compromises of the service of goods, the deposing of egotism, the intolerance of oppression, the vow of an end of the State ... provides the ontological concept of democracy, or of communism, it's the same thing" (2004, 130). Thus it is not fortuitous that Badiou can associate Paul with the figures of Robespierre as well as Lenin.

It is in this connection that Badiou places great stress upon Paul's confrontation with the law, which he understands to be, on the one hand ,the law of Moses and, on the other, the cosmic law of the Greeks: "Paul's profound idea is that Jewish discourse and Greek discourse are two aspects of the same figure of mastery" (2003, 42). It is remarkable that in this connection Badiou does not place even greater emphasis on the Roman law that was invoked in the execution of the Messiah.

While Badiou correctly understands that the resurrection of the crucified Messiah is the heart of Paul's message, he regards this nonetheless as a fable (perhaps in the specific sense of Nietzsche) in which it is simply impossible to believe. What seems to be at stake, then, is that Badiou finds in Paul the necessary formal characteristics of the thought process that follows from attachment to an event even if the material content of this proclamation is fabulous and thus perhaps not a real or true event after all.

Love Beyond Law: Slavoj Žižek

In this respect Slavoj Žižek may be somewhat more cagey in his assertion that it may be that contemporary thinkers, atheist and Marxist though they may be, may believe more than they are ready to admit. The really surprising thing, he says, is that "People who profess their cynical distance and radical pragmatic opportunism secretly believe much more than they are prepared to admit" (Žižek 2003, 8).

Žižek is the astonishing Slovenian intellectual whose combination of Hegelian philosophy, Lacanian analytical theory, and mastery of pop-culture phenomena (especially movies) has made him something of an academic rock star. His references to Paul are largely determined by his reading of Badiou, which begins in *The Ticklish Subject* (1999) with a somewhat cautious reading of Badiou and continues into *The Fragile Absolute* (2000) and *The Puppet and the Dwarf* (2003). In these last two books Žižek is making a case for taking Christianity seriously and indeed in the last spends considerable time on the remarkable catholic perspective of G. K. Chesterton. It is in this last book that Žižek suggests that what Badiou designated a fable be understood rather as what he calls "the perverse core" of Christianity, perverse in the sense that it is subversive of what is conventionally taken to be reality.

While Žižek's thought is extraordinarily complex, it may be helpful to indicate several ways in which he seems to offer further developments beyond Badiou's reading of Paul. Žižek is certainly prepared to read Paul from a Marxist and so materialist perspective, maintaining that perhaps only a materialist can truly read Paul (2003, 6), in a formula not unlike Ernst Bloch's formula that only an atheist can be a good Christian and only a Christian can be a good atheist. But it is far more clearly in a Lacanian register that his appropriation of Paul takes place.

Two themes are especially important: as Lacan had already pointed out, Paul is right about the dialectic of desire and transgression ("if it had not been for the law, I would not have known sin," Rom 7:7; Lacan 1992) and so the importance of the abolition of the law as the way into deliverance from the sort of repetition compulsion of the pursuit of substitute objects of desire that makes of us all in consumer capitalism simply cogs in "the service of goods"; and the suggestion that Paul, in his reflections on love, opens up a way beyond both the service of goods and the dialectics of law, desire, and transgression (Žižek 2003, 98–116) that may be understood as undermining in principle both the repetitive/compulsive nature of consumption/transgression. Thus Žižek wonders: "Or does Christianity, on the contrary, endeavor to break the very vicious cycle of prohibition that generates the desire to transgress it, the cycle described by Saint Paul in Romans 7:7?" (2000, 135). A few pages later, the question becomes an assertion: "However this superego dialectic of the transgressive desire engendering guilt is not the ultimate horizon of Christianity; as Saint Paul makes clear, the Christian stance, at its most radical, involves precisely the suspension of the vicious cycle of the Law and its transgressive desire" (2000, 143). He then suggests that it is Paul's understanding of love that leads him beyond this dialectic, a beyond he believes also to be signaled in Lacan's last seminar (Lacan 1998).

Thus Pauline thought (and, by extension, certain motifs of orthodox catholic Christianity) may offer us a way both to understand and to actualize an ethos that would counter the global capitalist social order.

PAUL AGAINST EMPIRE

While there is much more in the reflections of Badiou and Žižek to ponder concerning the pertinence of a rereading of Paul within the new context of empire, I think it is also possible to point to ways that they have yet to grapple fully with the radicalism of Paul's insight for our own situation. In order to make this clear, let me refer to the work of Jacob Taubes, the remarkable Jewish philosopher who declares, "I am a Paulinist, not a Christian, but a Paulinist" (Taubes 2004, 88), and who insists that precisely as the message concerning a crucified messiah, Paul's message subverts imperial authority. Indeed Taubes can, with only a touch of hyperbole, regard Romans as a declaration of war on the Roman Empire, "a political declaration of war on the Caesar" (16), and thus make a clearer connection to the undermining of contemporary empire.

The shortcoming of the readings of Badiou and Žižek is not that they overly politicize Paul but that their readings are not political enough. This is already signaled by Badiou's supposition that Paul contests the provenance of the law of Moses and the cosmic law of Hellenistic gnosis but without referring to the contestation of imperial or Roman law. He is misled at this point, I believe, by deflecting attention away from the specific circumstances of Jesus' death. He does this, it seems, in order not to fall into the ways in which attention to this has been misread in Christian tradition as an excuse to blame the Jews for Jesus' execution. But this then has the price of not recognizing the role of imperial authority precisely in terms of crucifixion. That Jesus is crucified rather than stoned must surely point us toward the question of the legitimacy of Roman law and Roman judgment, something actually foregrounded by Paul when he writes that the "rulers of this age" executed "the Lord of glory," as he does in 1 Cor 2, after he has maintained that he has focused his proclamation precisely on the crucified Messiah.

Perhaps it would be helpful to attend a bit more closely to this text. In a situation marked by contention among factions in the Corinthian community, Paul reminds his readers that "I decided to know nothing among you except Jesus Messiah, and him crucified" (2:2). This assertion, that Paul's "knowledge" was limited to the executed Messiah of God, is what he terms his proclamation: "we proclaim Messiah crucified" (1:22). This proclamation, Paul admits, is weakness and folly by the standards of his world. That is, it appears to contradict what passes for wisdom and strength. While Paul will maintain that this proclamation is actually divine wisdom and strength, it is not the sort of wisdom that is understood or possessed by "the rulers of this age." These same rulers, Paul says, "are doomed to perish." (2:6). Oddly, commentators rarely ask themselves who the rulers of Paul's age might be. That they might be the very ones in whose name and whose behalf the penalty of crucifixion was routinely administered by the military forces who pledged vows of personal loyalty to none other than the emperor seems seldom to occur to post-Constantinian readers of Paul. But Paul leaves us in no doubt about the connection, since he expressly states that, if the rulers of this age had possessed true as opposed to merely human wisdom, "they would not have crucified the Lord of glory" (2:8). However, centuries of attempts to depoliticize the reading of Paul have meant that even the most obvious connections get lost in a kind of mythic haze. In Paul's view, moreover, the execution by crucifixion of the Messiah results in a sentence of death upon the empire. What he says is that God chose what is low and despised in the world, things that are not, to reduce to nothing (or nothingness) things that are (1:28). Thus the very instrument (the cross) by which the imperial order terrorized the world into submission becomes the instrument of its undoing.

It is this that makes possible his subsequent argument at the beginning of Romans that subverts the claims of Roman law and judgment by demonstrating the injustice of the Roman social order that "unjustly imprisons the truth." Of course, this depiction of Roman injustice has generally been transformed into simply a list of bad behavior usually understood as individual vices. This is especially true in English, where injustice (*adikia*) is translated as "wickedness." But Paul's frame of reference is made clearer when we read his indictment: "for divine wrath is revealed from heaven against all ungodliness and injustice of those who by their injustice imprison the truth" (1:18). That the truth is jailed is something that may be seen in many (imperial) social orders but was quite sharply focused in the arrest, torture, and execution of the Messiah. Paul's indictment of Roman society will lead him to demonstrate that those who administer Roman law are, as representative of that same social order, condemning themselves when they pass judgment on one they consider to be a criminal (2:1). His indictment then aims at disqualifying Roman "law" and Roman "justice": "They were filled with every kind of injustice: evil, covetousness, malice, full of envy, murder, strife, deceit, craftiness; they are perjurers, slanderers, god-haters, insolent, haughty, boastful … foolish, faithless, heartless, ruthless" (1:29–31). Paul concludes: "They know the divine decree, that those who practice this deserve to die" (1:32). The death sentence passed on Roman social (dis)order is strikingly like what Tacitus will also say a few decades later as he writes about this same period of Roman history. "I have to present in succession the merciless biddings of a tyrant, incessant prosecutions, faithless friendships, the ruin of innocence, the same causes issuing in the same results, and I am everywhere confronted by a wearisome monotony in my subject matter" (*Annals* 4.33). He also reports that "the force of terror had utterly extinguished the sense of human fellowship, and with the growth of cruelty, pity was cast aside" (*Annals* 6.19).

Badiou has oddly diverted attention away from this dimension of Paul's indictment of the Roman legal form of justice and so has emphasized a more general and even "mythic" reference to cosmic law. The result is an oddly depoliticized reading of Paul precisely at that point that Badiou regards as the fable of the resurrection of the crucified. Indeed, when we read Badiou we may get the sense of an oddly Heideggerian move that will take the significance of this theme to be simply that of the fatedness to death of the creature and the "immortality" of the one who is grasped by the radical event.

As it happens I believe that we can go some considerable distance toward remedying this depoliticizing of Paul's central theme by attending to the reflections of one who is himself an assiduous reader of Heidegger yet who specifically engages the most fundamental questions of political thought. I mean, of course, Jacques Derrida.

OUTLAW JUSTICE (JACQUES DERRIDA)

I have argued in another context (Jennings 2005) that what is most interesting from Derrida concerning a reading of Paul is not the series of specific references to Paul that appear in the most diverse texts but precisely the way in which Derrida's reflections on some of the themes most important to his thought in the last fifteen years or so actually illumine Paul's own concerns, especially as these come to expression in Romans. I will not try to repeat the argument of the book here, but I will indicate two areas of Derrida's thought that I think help us to approach the more decisively political insights of Paul as well: the themes of justice and of sovereignty.

The concentration of Badiou on 1 Corinthians results in a privileging of the question of love as that which surpasses and supplants law and thus tends to elide questions of justice that are foregrounded in Romans. Of course, the privileging of the theme of love also helps Žižek make his case for an even more Lacanian reading of Paul, one that seeks to relate Paul on love to Lacan's seminar XX (Lacan 1998). It is not my intent simply to oppose the concentration on the theme of love but rather to "correct" it by reference to justice. Surely Badiou and Žižek are right to suspect that an essential feature of global capitalism is precisely the incitement and deflection of desire and that therefore the question of love and desire is essential to a critique of capitalist empire. But it is odd when this seems utterly to displace the question of justice, and Derrida clearly makes more of the question of justice than he does of the theme of love. (It is surely one of the ironies of the current intellectual scene in Europe that intellectuals who avow their Marxist affiliations seem to be more attracted to the question of love than to the question of justice and that the thinker most concerned with the question of justice is one whose own relation to Marxism is most often questioned, especially by those who think of themselves as the legitimate heirs of a Marxist tradition.)

That Paul is concerned with the question of justice is something often hidden from the Anglophone reader of Paul by the way in which the translators actually erase this theme from the text of Romans, substituting "righteousness" for "justice" or "wickedness" or "unrighteousness" for "injustice" in such phrases as: "For in it [the gospel] is revealed the righteousness of God" (1:17); or "the wrath of God is revealed against all ungodliness and wickedness of those who by their wickedness suppress the truth" (1:18); or "no longer present your members to sin as instruments of unrighteousness but … present your members as instruments of righteousness" (6:13). Who would guess that Paul was speaking of the question of a public justice?

What reading Derrida helps us to think, I have maintained, is that the claim of justice is unconditional but that its very unconditionally places it in a complex relation to law and to the laws. Thus, while in an early essay he can maintain what he will often repeat that justice is indeconstructible (Derrida 1990, 945), he will also from this perspective engage in a deconstruction of law that is always both heterogeneous with respect to law (justice outside or before the law, Paul will say) but also indissociable ("is the law sin? by no means," Rom 7:7; rather, "the law is holy, just and good," 7:21, Paul will also say).

Before going further, I should remark that the notion that justice in contrast to law is "indeconstructible" has been characterized by John Caputo in the question: "is justice another name for God, or is God another name for justice?" (Caputo 1997, 68, 116). This question of the substitutability of justice and God comes pretty close to José Porfirio Miranda's assertion that God is nothing other than this implacable claim of justice (Miranda 1974, 60). That this is actually not far from Derrida's own perspective is suggested by some of his remarks in the posthumously published essay "Justices," in which, pursuant to a reading of Gerard Manley Hopkins's poem that begins "Thou art indeed just, Lord," Derrida himself remarks upon the convertibility of the names "just" and "God" and, in passing, notes that the standard English translation of John 17:25 obscures this point by making Jesus call God righteous rather than just (2005a, 694). In this same text Derrida again underlines the necessity "to think justice in its essential link to law, as well as its irreducibility to law, its resistance, its heterogeneity to law" (2005a, 714).

In a reflection on the "Critique of Violence" by Walter Benjamin, Derrida will begin to make clear that what distinguishes justice from law has to do with the indissociability of law and violence, or what is termed the force of law. It is precisely the force or violence of law that, for Paul, comes to bear upon the execution of the Messiah, who is therefore either an outlaw, sin itself, Paul will suggest (2 Cor 5:21), or the one in whom the law with its force is exposed as opposed to the divine justice inaugurated by the Messiah. Thus what Derrida, following and intensifying Benjamin's critique of violence, sees as the general principle in terms of which law "deconstructs" itself is, in the case of Paul, concentrated in the collision between law and justice in the fate of the crucified Messiah.

But if justice forever remains heterogeneous to law, how is justice to be made effective? Paul suggests that justice comes as a gift, indeed as a free gift, and it is not without significance that it is precisely the theme of gift that Derrida links, indissociably, we may say, to that of justice. But it is precisely here that the standard interpretation of Paul runs aground. For while it is true that gift stands against law and thus against the retributive and distributive economy enshrined in law, gift or grace does not stand in similar contrast to the claim of justice. On the contrary, gift or grace is precisely that which makes good the claim and call of justice that those who are faithful or loyal to the gift are those who are or become or are made just. Justification then would mean precisely doing that which the law aimed at or intended but was unable to accomplish: justice.

It is the failure to see the connection between gift and justice that has made it possible for theologians to suppose that justification means anything but becoming just; rather, it often enough has come to mean that which substitutes for and suspends the claim of justice. Belief becomes simply "make believe," which is what doctrines of imputed justice or forensic justification have come to mean: not that we are actually to be just but merely that God pretends as if we were what we are not and are not intended to be, namely, just. That this is a travesty of Paul's own position is precisely clear when Paul maintains that the life of those who are to be found in the messianic reality to which he attests is that they "fulfill the just requirements of the law," and of course they do this, as he says, through the love of the neighbor, the other, even the enemy or persecutor (Rom 13:8–10; 12:13–14). Derrida's way of speaking of this is to point to a duty beyond debt, one that is not simply reducible to the economy of debt (works, Paul might say) but that "owes no one anything" yet loves and so fulfils what the law requires, that is, justice. This then suggests a way in which the reflections of Badiou and Žižek on love of the neighbor can be brought back into contact with the properly political question of justice.

Derrida himself broaches the question of the force of the question of justice with respect to questions of the political today through meditations on such themes as hospitality and forgiveness, or pardon. To be sure, these themes may be understood as apolitical when their connection to the social is severed, but Derrida takes over, for example, the theme of hospitality that is located in the sphere of the ethical by Levinas to direct it to some of the more pressing issues of national and international politics. On the one hand, the question of cosmopolitan right to refuge as adumbrated by Immanuel Kant is directed to the ways in which hospitality brings into question the political order of the nation-state that protects itself through the limitation placed upon hospitality, going so far actually as to contemplate the making of certain forms of hospitality a crime (subversion of the restrictions upon immigration), and this in turn leads him to point to a certain Paul (the one of Ephesians) as the inspiration for a sense of the cosmopolitan that may be understood as the subversive obverse of what is now called globalization (Derrida 2001). It is not without significance in this regard that Paul can develop his own ethic of sociality in terms of the injunction to "welcome one another as Messiah has welcomed you" in Rom 14:1–15:7.

Similarly with the question of pardon, linked indissociably by Derrida (following Jankélévitch) to the question of gift (French: *don*). For despite the aporias related to a thinking of forgiveness, aporias that closely resemble those that appear in the thinking of gift and of duty beyond debt; for example, it is still an increasingly prominent discourse in the relations among peoples as national and supranational bodies (e.g., the Vatican) that find themselves engaged in the confession of what can only be termed crimes against humanity. Derrida recalls, for example, the confession of the Japanese Asian adventures during the Second World War (especially in Korea), the collaboration of France through the Vichy government with Hitler, and so on (Derrida 2001). Although Krister Stendahl (1976) was quite right, I believe, to contest the supposition that forgiveness as such is a prominent theme in Paul, and Levinas is right to suppose that a certain view of forgiveness attributed to Paul has been deployed throughout the history of the West to excuse injustice rather than to produce justice, Paul's own insistence on the abrogation of condemnation in the messianic reality (Rom 8:1) and the abolition of judgment among those who belong to this reality (14:13) may have rather more radical political pertinence than is often recognized.

These last questions of hospitality and pardon have been the site not only for a reflection on justice in the work of Derrida but have also been the site for the emergent deconstruction of sovereignty as perhaps the decisive issue of political thought today. Initially the question of sovereignty emerges as the question of the apparent complacency of the subject who extends welcome or pardon from out of a certain plenitude of self-possession. But as Derrida makes clear, the extension of hospitality precisely undermines any such self-possession on the part of the host who in fact becomes hostage to the guest, to their being a guest in order to be host. Similarly with respect to forgiveness, which entails the subversion of the borders of selfhood that must find itself in an uncomfortable solidarity with the transgressor. Similarly, the state sovereignty that seems to be the precondition (according to Kant) for the extension of the right of refuge to the alien is itself consistently undermined in its pretensions to sovereignty precisely by the question of welcome. But the deconstruction or auto-deconstruction of state sovereignty is already far advanced as the state apparatus becomes subservient, whether as victim or as agent, to articulations of global capital.

Now what has Paul to do with this question of sovereignty? As we have seen, it is a question that plays on three registers at once: the individual subject; the political sovereign; and the sovereignty of God. That Paul contests the self-possession of the self comes as no great surprise: the "subject" is represented as either the slave of sin or the slave of justice (6:18–19), as under the dominion of death or invaded by an alien life, as overwhelmed by flesh or as invaded by spirit (7:6). This is not merely indicative but also imperative as Paul exhorts his readers to be crucified with Christ (Gal 2:19), to be as if dead to the world and flesh (Rom 6:6; 7:5–6) and so to receive life, not from themselves, but from outside themselves. That is, on virtually every page, Paul contests the ipseity of the self.

In important respects this is true as well for Paul's view of the divine, which he does not hesitate, in 1 Corinthians, to associate with weakness and folly. But it is this same weakness and folly (connected, we may recall, to the theme of the cross) that ultimately displays the stupidity and impotence of the "rulers of this age," who are also known as "weak and beggarly elemental structures of the cosmos" (Gal 4:9). It is often supposed that Paul is here simply making reference to cosmic powers, that his thinking is in that way mythological, but this simply ignores the way in which imperial propaganda of his time was also "mythological," attributing to Rome and its emperors mythic status as that which upholds the cosmos (Elliott 1997, 172–83).

At the conclusion of each of the two essays that make up the book *Rogues* (Derrida 2005b), a book that takes up the charge of Noam Chomsky that the United States is a rogue state, Derrida is led to an invocation of Heidegger's enigmatic assertion in relation to what might be termed the state of the world that "only a god can save us." Derrida makes clear that the appearance of a god who is sovereign can only mean destruction, but what, then, might it mean to await a god without sovereignty? He ends: "to be sure nothing is less sure than a god without sovereignty; nothing is less sure than his coming to be sure" (2005b, 114). In a gesture that repeats and extends the first, he writes at the end of the second essay in pointing to a hope that is not swallowed up in the implacable sovereignty of the omnipotent One: "For whenever the name of God would allow us to think something else, for example a vulnerable non-sovereignty, one that suffers or is divisible, one that is mortal even … it would be a completely different story, perhaps even the story of a god who deconstructs himself in his ipseity" (2005b, 157). Here I make only two remarks. The first is that for Derrida this is the very heart of the political question, since the question of politics has been the question of sovereignty, a sovereignty that models itself upon divine sovereignty. The second remark is that a divine that suffers and dies is the very heart of the Pauline theology of the cross. This only indicates that there is much more to be done in order to grasp the radical political significance, then and now, for Paul's anti-imperial thought.

Messianic End of the Law (Giorgio Agamben)

Before concluding, however, I must briefly indicate something of the relevance of the thought of another of Europe's most important philosophers, who has also devoted himself to a reading of Paul precisely in the context of a reflection of political philosophy today: Giorgio Agamben, whose book on Paul recently appeared in English translation (2005b).

There is much to ponder in Agamben's often enigmatic and allusive references to Paul, including his reference to Rom 8 in a discussion with Heidegger in which Agamben contests the disjunction between the human and the animal as formulated by Heidegger, or Agamben's reflections on the messianic time of an especially Pauline apocalyptic, but here I will only indicate some of the ways in which his perspective may be understood in connection with Derrida's emphasis upon justice and the law.

Especially in *State of Exception* (2005a) but also in the earlier *Homo Sacer* (1998), Agamben is attempting to come to terms with the supposition of Carl Schmitt that the decisive character of political sovereignty is the declaration of "the state of exception" that suspends the law. The extreme case of this is the death camp that establishes and "normalizes" such a state of exception. The obverse of such a catastrophic state of exception, Agamben wants to argue, is the suspension of the law that at the same time abolishes violence. It is this that he finds expressed in Paul's suspension of the law in the name of justice, a justice that may also be associated in Paul with weakness and folly and in Agamben with the figure of the child. Let us see how this works.

Agamben does suggest that the messianic is precisely to be understood as the crisis of the law and that this is true not only for a (Pauline) Christianity but for certain forms of Judaism and Islam as well. Writing in *Means without End: Notes on Politics*, Agamben says:

> the Messiah is the figure in which religion confronts the problem of the law, in which religion and the law come to the decisive day of reckoning. In the Jewish as much as in the Christian and Shiite contexts, in fact, the messianic event marks first of all a crisis and a radical transformation of the properly legal order of religious tradition. (2000, 135)

In a later text, *State of Exception*, Agamben proposes that the key to this crisis of law is precisely the exposure and messianic overturning of the connection between law and violence. "The only truly political action, however, is that which severs the nexus between violence and law" (2005a, 88). What, then, becomes of law? "What becomes of the law after its messianic fulfillment? (This is the controversy that opposes Paul to the Jews of his time)" (2005a, 63). But this is also at the same time a question that he can associate with the Marxist perspective as well: "a problem that can be formulated (and it was effectively formulated for the first time in primitive Christianity and then later in the Marxian tradition)" (2005a, 63).

Nevertheless Agamben does not suppose that the messianic entails the simple abolition of law but rather has something to do with the fulfillment of the law or with the intent of the law. "There is, therefore, still a possible figure of law after its nexus with violence and power has been deposed, but it is a law that no longer has force or application" (2005a, 63).

The character of such a law finally delivered from its connection to force or violence is what opens the way for the image of children at play: "One day humanity will play with law just as children play with disused objects, not in order to restore them to their canonical use but to free them from it for good" (2005a, 64). Yet Agamben will maintain that this separation of law from the violence of the force of law is by no means itself justice but is rather that which in a certain way opens access to justice: "The decisive point here is that the law—no longer practiced but studied—is not justice, but only the gate that leads to it" (2005a, 64).

For Agamben, it is precisely in the meantime of messianic time that a space is opened for a radical politics that contests the closing in of law upon life, that resists therefore the biopolitical confiscation of life, whether in the ever-growing application of law or of an enforced state of exception to bare life. And at many of the decisive points in this argument, Agamben has had recourse to Pauline images and insights.

Conclusion

Some years ago David Harvey, writing in the introduction to his remarkable exposition of Marx's analysis of capital, noted the considerable irony that North American youth had been enamored of Marx in the 1960s, when many of the original Marxist insights seemed to be disproved by developments in capitalism, while more recently, as global capital seemed more and more to lend itself to Marxist analysis, there seemed to be correspondingly little interest on the part of a newer generation of students to study Marx and learn from his analyses (1999, xv). The acceleration over the intervening years of the rule of what some have called turbo capitalism or casino capitalism, together with the military hegemony of the United States and its apparent determination to make the globe subservient to its own interests, or at least the interests of certain classes of Americans, has evoked images of a new global empire. It is in this context that certain analogies have been recognized between our current situation and that of the Roman Empire.

It is in this context that a renewed liberative (and especially counterimperial) reading of the Bible assumes something like global significance, and it is here that the figure of Paul has come to have particular salience.

On the one hand, we have seen that there has been a striking turn in historical-critical approaches to Paul in terms of reading Paul against the background of Roman imperial ideology and micro-political practices and institutions. This is resulting in an appreciation of Paul as inspired by a counterimperial vision in which the collision between the Roman Empire and the messianic hope is concentrated in the image of the resurrection of a crucified messiah resulting in the establishment of communities that contest the values and practices of that imperial order as well as the hegemony of imperial propaganda.

At the same time, and operating almost completely independently, there arises in Europe among thinkers who have been inspired by a Marxist humanism a sense that Paul may provide important insights for ways to grapple with our own situation of global empire. This is, of course, not to say that our situation is the same as Paul's. On the contrary, our situation is far more complex, characterized as it is by a late stage of capitalist development, by a media- and advertising-saturated pseudo-politics, by an emergent social order in which there is no true exteriority, and by a reserve of unimaginable military force.

What is at stake, then, is not a simple equivalence between "then and now" but the discovery of fruitful and suggestive analogies that offer leverage for thought upon the new and in many ways unprecedented global reality in which all contemporary struggles for liberation and life may take place. It is in this context that a rereading of Paul comes to have particular importance not only for those who think of themselves as Christians but also, and perhaps even more importantly, among those who think of themselves as atheists but who are keenly aware of the need to find a language and conceptuality within which to contest the hegemony of global capitalist empire. For what Paul enables us to think is an event and a praxis that anticipate the end of empire and the dawn of a social reality characterized by true or ultimate (or, as Paul would say, divine,) justice.

THE KINGDOM OF GOD IS NOT LIKE YOU WERE MADE TO BELIEVE: READING PARABLES IN THE CONTEXT OF GERMANY AND WESTERN EUROPE

Luise Schottroff

1. LIBERATIONIST READING OF PARABLES: HOW DID IT HAPPEN IN MY CONTEXT?

During the last forty years there were three influential movements inside the Christian churches and beyond them in my context: a movement for social justice worldwide based on a hermeneutics of liberation;[1] the Christian-Jewish dialogue; and the feminist movement. All of them came to broader public relevance in the 1970s. From the beginning, each of these movements was not interested in the focus of the other movements. There was for a long time no dialogue between or among them. In theological education, moreover, these movements were more or less ignored. The situation today, however, is much different.

Illustrative of this difference is the development of the relationship between Jewish and Christian feminists. There was once much animosity between Jewish and Christian feminists.[2] At first Christian feminists refused to hear Jewish complaints about feminist anti-Judaism, but then something remarkable happened—what I call a miracle: feminist theology was further developed in a deep and honest dialogue with Jewish feminists and a critical awareness of Christian anti-Judaism. More and more a new generation of scholars took this hermeneutics to the universities. The situation today can be described best by pointing to a significant project based on women and men who are rooted in dialogues across the lines of the three movements:

---

1. The books by Gutierrez (1973b) and Cardenal (1976–78) were for a long time especially influential for this movement in German-speaking countries.

2. Documented, e.g., in Siegele Wenschkewitz 1988.

the movement for social justice worldwide; the Christian-Jewish dialogue; and the feminist movements. This project is a complete new translation of the Bible into German committed to a hermeneutics of justice. Of course, we love Luther's translation into German, but we have learned to become aware of anti-Judaism as well as the marginalization of women, slaves, poor people, and all the "others" in Bible translations—not only in Luther's translation. We try to be conscious of what it means, for instance, to be a middle-class German woman when we translate the Bible. Our tradition teaches us to understand the gospel of the poor as a gospel for the poor as "others," as in the giving of alms. In my context, many Christians believe that the praxis of Christian faith should not touch or question the status quo. Our tradition teaches us to understand Judaism as a religion of "law" and legalism and Pharisees as hypocrites. The Christian and Western-European middle-class identity depends on feeling superior. Other religions and especially Judaism are seen as of minor value. Middle-class women take part in this network of prejudices but are at the same time its victims: they are more often jobless or paid less than men. Poverty is female—in Germany, too. All these asymmetries in our society have a strong impact on Bible translation. Based on historical research, the new German Bible translation, called *Bibel in gerechter Sprache* (Bail 2006), tries to overcome these traditions of injustice. This Bible documents that liberationist praxis and theology did not die—as many used to proclaim, hoping for the end of liberationist movements. This Bible translation is based on scholarly work but is not integrated into the academic mainstream. It has strong ties to Christian communities and groups.

This is the background to my reading of the parables in a different way. The dualism of traditional theologies taught us not to take the little parable stories as referring to social reality. We learned to read them as pictures for something outside the story, for God and God's kingdom. But if I take the stories at face value and read them from the perspective of a middle-class woman who knows about Christian strategies to silence the poor and show contempt toward Jews, the parables change their character. Many of the stories become horror stories that I have to refuse to read as images of God's kingdom.

2. Parables as Horror Stories

In the parable of the talents (Matt 25:14–30), three slaves receive the task of taking care of a rich man's money while he is traveling. Two slaves earn interest, which doubles the amount of money. Since earning 100 percent interest is unusually high, they had to be extremely clever. They may have loaned the money to small farmers and then afterwards taken the land when the farmers could not pay back, which is a well-documented method to get rich

(Goodman 1983). The third slave refuses to take part in this cruel business. He even criticizes the master, accusing him of "reaping where [he] did not sow," which means that the master is a thief (Matt 25:24). The master calls him worthless and throws him "into the outer darkness, where there will be weeping and gnashing of teeth" (25:30).

For centuries this story was read as a story about a God who punishes his lazy slave, the believer who does not obey God's commandments. That means that the slave owner is understood to represent God and the slaves God's children. A horror story about a violent and extremely wealthy slave owner is by interpretation converted into something declared to be the gospel. This gospel makes people who do not identify with the rich man or the successful slaves—but with the critical slave—feel cold and uneasy. Is not the third slave speaking the truth about his master?

Many parables of the Jesus tradition confront us with this structure and the questions instigated by looking at the victims in the stories. In the ten virgins parable, five young girls forget to bring sufficient oil for their torches and therefore arrive late to the wedding house, but the door is closed, and they cannot get in. The bridegroom speaks a judgment: "Truly I tell you, I do not know you" (Matt 25:12). These poor girls were not as clever as their five companions who had oil and did not want to share. According to the dominant exegetical tradition, I have to hear as gospel that it is important to get oil in a timely manner (for this oil symbolizes good deeds); otherwise, Christ the bridegroom will exclude me from salvation. If I am not seduced by the drug of allegorization, I read that as a story about disciplining young girls for being lazy. To lose eternal life for such a little mistake is by no means the gospel; rather, it is a horror story.

In the parable about the wedding banquet we read a story about royal meal politics in the Roman Empire. A king invites elite men: people who own land or business and people who are the representatives of a city. This is the usual way the emperor or his administrators used to confirm and test the loyalty of important people in the empire. In Mark 6:21 we read about such a feast, a birthday party, that Herod Antipas gave "for his courtiers and officers and for the leaders of Galilee." This birthday party ended in bloody fashion: the head of John the Baptizer is presented to the guests on a plate.

In Matt 22:1–14 the first group of guests refuses to come, an open rebellion against the king. Some even mistreat or kill the slaves of the king. Slaves are the weakest in this society. They suffer violence and death in place of their master. The king takes cruel revenge; he kills not only the murderers but destroys the whole city they represent. Jerusalem in 70 c.e. was not the only city that was destroyed for political reasons by the imperial army. The second invitation for all people in the streets, good and bad, stays also in the usual frame of imperial meal politics. Whole populations of cities were invited: *panem et circenses*, bread and circuses for the masses. The people should express loyalty, and they were controlled by secret police during the meal. In this case the king controls how his guests are dressed. He interprets the everyday cloth of one man as rebellion against his orders. He orders the man bound and thrown into the dark prison of the palace in order to die there. This story is a horror story showing imperial violence and politics. It is a fictive story describing structures and not a single event. It presents an analysis of the Roman Empire. It is a frightening idea to read this story as a story about God, God's punishment of Israel, and the kingdom of God. As soon as I understood that this is a horror story, I was not able to take the king as an image of God any longer.[3] The relation to the kingdom of God and to God must still be found—but the story has to be read as it is and cannot be taken as a chain of metaphors or something like that. When we read the so-called images of the parables as stories and take them at face value, they turn into horror stories. When they are read from the perspective of women, slaves, and day laborers, they *cannot* be understood as stories about God.

3. The Status Quo of Parable Interpretation

Until today these stories have been read by allegorizing, meaning they contain metaphors or allegorical elements. This scholarly consensus emerged from the discussion about the parables after Adolf Jülicher. This discussion brought forth a differentiation between allegory and allegorical element. His book on parables, written at the end of the nineteenth century, was successful in that no one wants to treat these parables as *allegories*, where every detail has to be about something else. No one wants to identify the innkeeper (Luke 10:35) who hosts the victim in the parable of the good Samaritan with the apostle Paul; no, that interpretation is ridiculous. This was the way of reading before the Enlightenment. But Jülicher was not completely successful in so far as scholars came to the conclusion that there are *some* allegorical elements or metaphors in the parables. Let us say, for example, that the oil of the ten virgins is a metaphor for good deeds, but their torches are not to be understood allegorically. So biblical scholarship works until this very day (with few exceptions) with the assumption that there are fixed metaphors in the parables: the king represents God; the bridegroom is Christ; the vineyard is Israel; the oil is the good deeds; and so forth. Further, the outer darkness

---

3. In my book on parables (2006), I give an interpretation of the parables of the Jesus tradition.

is not the prison in the king's palace but hell, the place of God's eternal punishment. This is the tradition of reading parables in Western churches and universities and beyond.

Some exegetes feel uneasy with allegorization in this way and, as heirs of Jülicher, ascribe these allegorical elements in parables not to the historical Jesus but to the writers of the Gospels. So they suppose that Jesus used fewer allegorical elements. Nevertheless, even parables to which nobody ascribes normally allegorical elements are de facto read by allegorizing. Let us take the parable of the prodigal son as an example. The father is read as representing God the Father, the younger son as representing a repenting believer, and the older son as representing Pharisees or Jews in general; this last identification is questioned in the exegesis of the last generation, when Christian anti-Judaism became obsolete, so now the older son is identified with self-righteous Christians. Still, the allegorizing is not questioned.

There is a tradition of critiquing this kind of parable interpretation, but this critique did not reach the ears of the many Christian interpreters in mainline exegesis. The first critique I know goes back to the beginning of the 1930s to the German poet Berthold Brecht (Brecht 1967, 13:1141–65). He criticizes the parable of the talents as being used to justify exploitation. The next critique of which I am aware comes from the Greek poet Nikos Kazantzakis in *The Last Temptation of Christ*. In his narrative of the ten virgins, Jesus asks Nathanael what he would do if he were the bridegroom. Nathanael answers: "I would have opened the door" (1960, 217).

William R. Herzog's 1994 volume was a big step in the same direction by an exegete. His *Parables as Subversive Speech* does not treat the parables as metaphorical but as stories teaching social analysis, using the method of Paulo Freire's *Pedagogy of the Oppressed* (1973). So Herzog does not identify the landowners, rich men, and kings with God. He takes them as representatives of an unjust society where people like them exploit the poor and the small landowners.

In feminist exegesis today, more and more authors are beginning to criticize the parables themselves in this way—not so much the scholarly interpretation. In the book on parables edited by Mary Ann Beavis (2002), for example, Vicky Balabanski (2002) criticizes the parable of the ten virgins (Matt 25:1–13), where at the end the door is closed for five lazy girls and the bridegroom speaks the final judgment, "I do not know you." She reminds readers that in the Gospel of Matthew the closed door does not have the last word. In the narrative about the tomb of Jesus, the door is opened for resurrection. So she criticizes one text in Matthew with another text in the same Gospel.

I conclude this survey of critiques of the assumption of fixed metaphors in parables with a quote from Amy-Jill Levine: "There is no compelling reason to equate the younger son [in the parable of the prodigal son] with Christians or the older son with Jews. Indeed, there is no compelling reason to see the parable as an allegory. Not all fathers, rich men (16:19–31) or judges (see 18:1–8) must represent God" (2002, 96).

This is good news for me, and I repeat: not all fathers, rich men, or judges—and, I would add, kings—must represent God. But I have to face the situation that this good news will perhaps not be heard. I see two reasons for that: the allegorizing is deeply ingrained in our perception of the parables; and Western Christianity has a long tradition of justifying the powers that be. Therefore, there is something like a Christian love for unquestioned authorities. As a consequence, many preachers and exegetes struggle hard finally to justify the king who destroys a city or the bridegroom as the heavenly judge who excludes lazy girls from salvation. Even the only exegesis I found in mainline commentaries where the author sees the problem finally ends by justifying the closed door (Luz 1997, in his interpretation of Matt 25:1–13).

4. Developing a Feminist Theory of Parables in the Jesus Tradition Using a Hermeneutics of Liberation

My own approach starts with the *analysis of the underlying hermeneutics* of the allegorizing reading. Metaphors or allegorical elements are understood as referring to two levels or two worlds. The metaphor "kingdom of God" refers on the first level to the world of kings, imperial rulers, or political realities. On the second level it refers to God's realm, God's world of true life and grace. The relation between these two levels or worlds is normally not explicitly reflected. Parables are taken as pedagogical tools on a neutral field, serving only the purpose of opening the window to transcendence. Parables are treated as fictive stories whose relation to the social world of real people is arbitrary and unimportant. A consequence of this perspective of the images is that there is in many cases no scholarly tradition of doing social-historical analysis of the images of the stories about wealthy men and kings. We have some social-historical analysis for some of the parables, but normally one will not find information in the scholarly exegesis about, for example, the political and social background of the imperial banquets that is the basis for understanding the parable of the wedding banquet. To understand the parable of the ten virgins, we need information about the testing of young girls in a patriarchal society that wants to make sure that they will be diligent and obedient wives.

So I have to conclude that the status quo of parable theory and exegetical praxis is that the images are being treated as unimportant signs pointing to something else beyond them, because only God is important, not what kings may do when they burn a city or kill a guest. That is taken as normal, the way things used to be. The underlying hermeneutics of parable theories is dualistic, separating the world of kings, violence, and human bodies from the world of God, separating "this world" from the "other world." This dualism must be criticized with the tools feminist theory prepared for recognizing and criticizing the dualism that makes the bodies of women, slaves, and poor people unimportant. I want to treat the images as having a message about the real world, the kings and the victims. I have chosen to do social-historical analysis of the images using a hermeneutics of liberation. Even if they are fictive stories, they present a valuable insight into the social history of people under Roman rule.

This nondualistic reading of parables must *interpret* the metaphors contextually—if any are included in the text. An assumption of fixed metaphors must be replaced by interpreting the text with the question: Is there a metaphor at all? If there are reasons to assume a metaphor, what does it say about historical experiences of human beings? *How* does it relate God to the image? I stay with the example of a king metaphor. Matthew 22:1, the beginning of the parable of the wedding banquet, indeed introduces a king. In the light of the First Testament and contemporary Judaism, I have to understand "king" as a metaphor or a referent pointing to God as the king. This king destroys a whole city with his army and kills a guest at his party because the guest is not wearing the proper wedding attire. This interpretation fits into the imperial banquet politics of Rome but not into the tradition of Israel's God. So I must interpret what the story wants to say about the relation of this human story king to God. I cannot assume automatically that the king *represents* God. In this case, I would conclude that we have to read Matt 22:1–14 as an antithetical parable. A human king (*anthropos basileus*, Matt 22:1) is *contrasted* to God. God is only to be seen in a counterimage. In rabbinical parables we hear sometimes: this is a king of flesh and blood; and even: but our God is *not* so. So I must look at this story king contextually. What is the literary document—the Gospel of Matthew—saying as a whole, and what is it saying about kings? How does this message relate to the history of Jews and Christians under the Roman Empire? I understand this parable to be speaking about the deep difference between God and the brutal imperial suppression people experienced under Roman rule. The military violence of Rome is depicted in general. People had good reasons to be afraid when looking at Rome's imperialism before the war of 66–70 C.E. and afterwards. This is the perspective of the text. There is no hint that the text is justifying these imperialistic wars of Rome and the destruction of Jerusalem.

Where do we find the means to interpret the parables? We cannot interpret parables that are stripped from their literary context. In historical criticism, scholars used to cut away the introduction and the conclusions, labeling them secondary additions. A naked parable, the little fictive story, cannot be interpreted historically any longer. The literary context provides the explanation to the parable we need for interpretation. The history of research for the *Urform* (prototype) of a parable, the original parable as told by the historical Jesus, by stripping it from its literary context and later additions has failed. This naked parable, as I call it, is an artificial product of scholarship. The parables have never existed that way. They were retold again and again—always with an explanation for the audience showing which referential in the fictive story could be used to look at God's history with humankind. We can interpret texts only when they themselves give the clues regarding how they want to be interpreted.

This principle can be learned by the work of David Stern (1981; 1991) on rabbinical parables. He makes it clear that the assumption of allegory is not really adequate for rabbinical parables, and he prefers to speak about the "referential" character of the rabbinical parable. Its function is "to bring a certain message to bear upon an ad hoc situation before its audience." The "referential features of the *mashal* exist only for the sake of enabling its audience to grasp for themselves the ulterior message the mashal bears" (1981, 265). We must look at the literary evidence—because that is all we have—to understand the ad hoc situation of the audience. I would add that what he calls the "ad hoc situation," the situation of the audience as a part of the people of Israel in its political, social, and religious dimensions—that situation is the key to the parable. This key allows us to understand the metaphors, if there are any, and the relation between the story and the history and presence of God with God's people.

I give an example from the Gospels: the parable of the wicked tenants (Mark 12:1–12) tells a story about violence, the violence of the landowners of large estates who ask tenants for their share of the production—who often are unable to pay or deliver; the load is too high, which is a typical situation in this time. The tenants try to get rid of this violence by violence, killing the slaves of the landowner sent to collect the share of the landowner. The violence of the tenants is narrated in a moving way: they add violence to violence to murder. At the end it is clear: the landowner has the power to destroy all these tenants. A final bloodbath can thus be expected. This story highlights in a dense way the violence resulting from the loss of land that the small farmers had to suffer during the first century c.e. in Palestine (as well as in other parts of the Roman Empire). The vineyard metaphor can be recognized by the allusion to Isa 5 at the beginning. So we can know that the parable speaks about Israel, because in Isa 5 the image of the vineyard is used for Israel. But we should hesitate to identify the landowner with God, because the image

of God in Isa 5 and of the landowner in this parable are absolutely different. I read this parable as speaking about bloody social conflicts over land in
Israel during the first century c.e. The parable wants its hearers to look at the
bloody and desperate situation that is Israel's fate in this time.

At the end we have an explanation of the parable referring to a source of
hope in a situation like that: the stone that the builders rejected has become a
"cornerstone" (Mark 12:10f; Ps 118:22–23). The ad hoc situation is described
only indirectly in this fictive story with its allusions to the struggle for the
land. Its explanation refers to Ps 118, which has a long tradition of giving
promise of a better life to the suffering people of God. I refer the cornerstone
to the Jewish people, not only to Jesus Christ. The owner of the vineyard does
not represent God but owners of land, of large estates that leave the small-
holders in a desperate situation. Some of these small-holders may try to avoid
being driven away by killing innocent people. We have to reconstruct the ad
hoc situation, the social situation of the audience, and learn to imagine the
implied answers from the audience.

Parables in the Jesus tradition consist of three parts: (1) a fictive story; (2)
an explanation preceding and/or following the fictive story, the "frame" or,
better, literary context; and (3) unwritten words of people hearing or reading
these parables, which can be imagined sometimes from the rhetoric of the
text. Instead of working with the assumption of fixed metaphors, we must
contextualize the metaphors. The main task is to overcome that underlying
dualism in parable interpretation that denies the importance of human experiences, of the history of real people, of their bodies. Since one generation
of feminists worked hard to unveil the dualistic contempt of human life, of
woman's life of real bodies in Western philosophy and theology, it is possible
to gain a new nondualistic approach to the parables.

5. THE KINGDOM OF GOD

What about the kingdom of God? The answer to this question is to be found
in the literary context and in the social context: many parables have an introduction and a conclusion; all of them have their whole respective Gospel as
their literary context. In the case of Luke 19:11–27, the parable of the ten
pounds, we have an introduction saying that Jesus told this story about the
pounds to wake up people who followed him, to rob them of their illusions
that God's kingdom would appear immediately when Jesus enters Jerusalem.
The story confronts them directly with the cruel reality of the Roman Empire,
which is about to crucify Jesus. A vassal king is approved by Rome, uses slaves
to exploit people, and kills the opposition. The parable has no formal conclusion but is followed by a narrative about Jesus as Messiah. The plot develops

as follows: Jesus comes as the poor king of the poor into Jerusalem—sitting on a young donkey, as prophesied in Zech 9:9—a poor, nonviolent king without a military army. He anticipates the destruction of Jerusalem and weeps over it. A compassionate poor man, going to die, whose message was that only the people could change their fate and suffering by listening to the word of God in the Torah. But even with this poor, nonviolent Messiah losing his life, God would not forget God's people: hope in God's kingdom would awaken after his death with even more power, the power of resurrection. Already in *this* life, Jesus' nearness—God's nearness—turns them, the people who follow God's word, into "children of the resurrection" (Luke 20:36).

In Luke, or the other Gospels for that matter, the kingdom of God is never defined in the way Western theological thinking would prefer to have abstract definitions. Instead, the texts speak about the kingdom of God by telling parables and stories about Jesus and other people.

When God will be king, the life of the people will be renewed; justice, compassion, and nonviolence will emerge as soon as people hear the voice of Jesus or other prophets' voices as the voice of God. The parables are told to evoke the question: In light of the fact that the kingdom of Rome is like this, brutal and unjust, how will God's kingdom be? The hearers can respond by speaking words to each other and to God, and these words always must include a new praxis.

Many parables invite their hearers to compare God's kingdom with what is told in the parable story. I quote one example: "The kingdom of heaven is to be compared…" (Matt 22:2, my translation). But in many Bible translations we find here "is like." "Das Himmelreich gleicht einem Koenig, der seinem Sohn die Hochzeit ausrichtete" (Luther translation, 1984revision: "the kingdom of heaven is like a king who…"). In this case the NRSV has: "The kingdom of heaven may be compared to a king who gave a wedding banquet for his son" (Matt 22:1). Here in NRSV *homoiothe* is translated as "to be compared," but in other parables we find "is like." "Then the kingdom of heaven will be like this" (NRSV for *homoiothesetai* in Matt 25:1). The problem with this latter translation is that it implies a whole parable theory where parables are read as likening God to a king. By this parable theory, the stories about kings, slave owners, rich men, and so forth are read as images of God, and this parable theory implies a theological justification of violent and suppressive power structures.

How are the parables to be linked to the kingdom of God? I read the invitation in parables to *compare* the kingdom of God to the story and *not to liken* it to it. Rather, it is just to be read as an invitation to realize the *difference* of God's kingdom to this kingdom of Rome with its military and violence on all levels of society. The kingdom of God is *not* like this; the parable stories are not images but *counterimages* when they speak about structures of power in societies.

In the Bible, the kingdom of God is never defined in abstract theological terms. Rather, the way to speak about God is to speak about the reality of political life and to open the hearer's mind and eyes about the injustice of the status quo under the empire. The invitation to hear or to compare is the invitation to realize the Shema: "Hear, O Israel, the LORD our God, the LORD is One..." (Deut 6:4). That means people are invited to realize that there is only one God for them, that God is king and not the emperor. People shall not submit to injustice and shape their life according to this one God's will.

A *MUJERISTA* HERMENEUTICS OF JUSTICE
AND HUMAN FLOURISHING

Ada María Isasi-Díaz

The starting place for all *mujerista* biblical interpretation is the liberation of Latina women living in the United States. Liberation for us refers to *la lucha*, our daily struggle for the flourishing of our own lives and fullness of life for all. *Mujerista* readings of the Bible, precisely because they are guided by *la lucha*, must contribute to our liberation. Therefore, any interpretation of the Bible that does not promote this goal is not accepted as valid, and any biblical text that impedes it is rejected. In other words, the biblical message is Word of God for us precisely because it contributes to our struggle for liberation.

A *mujerista* interpretation is rooted in Latinas' religious faith and the role it plays in our daily life experiences, in *lo cotidiano*. Such an interpretation begins with a critical cultural, sociohistorical, political, and economic analysis of our reality. This analysis also includes a thorough comprehension of our worldview, that is, of the values and goals that guide us and the hopes and dreams that motivate us. This interpretation of our reality is not a cold, analytical assessment from the outside but an analysis that starts with us and our understanding of ourselves. Because it is a critical analysis, this thorough study of our reality looks to move Latinas and society at large to understand what needs to be changed in order to enable our struggle for liberation.

Very intentionally, then, *mujerista* interpretation seeks to highlight biblical texts that refer to *lo cotidiano* and to favor interpretations that focus on the centrality and importance of everyday experience. We draw strength from the act of resistance of two ordinary midwives, Shiphrah and Puah (Exod 1:15–21); the daughter of Jephthah's decision not to be erased from history (Judg 11:39–40); the faithfulness and intimacy of Ruth and Naomi (Ruth 3:13–17); the need for Jesus to be touched and be taken care of by the woman who washed his feet with her tears (Luke 7:36–59); Jesus' sharing with others his self-understanding and his mission (Luke 9:28–36); the centrality of personal, bodily needs in the kin-dom of God (Matt 25:31–46); and the struggle for justice of the day workers (Matt 20:1–16). These account of the biblical *cotidiano* are central to a *mujerista* reading and interpretation of the Bible.

Lo cotidiano

To understand the complex concept of *lo cotidiano,* it is better to describe it at some length than to define it. *Lo cotidiano* constitutes the immediate space of our lives, the first horizon of our experiences, experiences that in turn are constitutive elements of our reality. *Lo cotidiano* is where we first meet and relate to the material world made up not only of physical realities but also of our relationship to that reality (culture) and our understanding and evaluation of it (history). *Lo cotidiano* is necessarily enmeshed in the material reality of life and is a key element of the structuring of social relations and their limits. *Lo cotidiano* situates us and grounds us in our experiences. It refers to our habitual judgments, including the tactics we use to deal with daily reality and with the practices and beliefs we have inherited. However, by *lo cotidiano* we do not refer to an uncritical acceptance of all we have been taught or to which we have become habituated. On the contrary, we understand by *lo cotidiano* that which is reproduced or repeated consciously. A conscienticized *cotidiano* is not one that supports this or that worldview but one that describes, relates to, and identifies the daily, ordinary reality of people's lives. This means that one can indeed talk about *lo cotidiano* of the rich as well as about *lo cotidiano* of the poor.[1]

Lo cotidiano has to do with the experiences we have lived and that have been analyzed and integrated into our understandings and behaviors. It is what makes the world of each one of us specific and, therefore, it is *in lo cotidiano* and *from lo cotidiano* that we live the multiple relations that constitute our humanity. It is the sphere in which our struggle for life is most immediate, most vigorous, most vibrant.

Another element of *lo cotidiano* is the manner in which we face it. The way we think and express ourselves and the impact economic status, gender, and race/ethnicity have on our routines and expectations are all a part of it. In no way should *lo cotidiano* be seen as belonging solely to the private world, for it interacts at all times with social systems, impacting their structures and mechanisms. It is made up of relations within families and among friends and neighbors in a community (Isasi-Díaz 2004, 92–106). It extends to our

---

1. Because *mujerista* biblical interpretation's goal is the liberation of Latinas, a marginalized and oppressed group in the United States, our focus is Latinas' *cotidiano*—the *cotidiano* of the poor and oppressed.

experience with authority and encompasses our central religious beliefs and celebrations (D. Levine 1992, 317).

RADICAL SUBJECTIVITY

Mujerista biblical hermeneutics is unapologetically and radically subjective. This in no way takes us outside rational discourse.[2] The arguments we use must carry weight, be persuasive, be clear, and not collapse under public scrutiny (Robb 1985, xv). Radical subjectivity is not about *ad libitum* claims that need not be argued. On the contrary, radical subjectivity is valid not because it is a given person's point of view or the view of some group of people but because it is straightforward. That is, it is understandable and can claim to be "common sense." It is understandable because it does not rely on proof from abstract arguments. It is valid because it is effective, productive, efficient, useful, and fruitful in guiding social and political processes of justice-making. Common sense refers to the human ability to discern, to establish criteria, and to make judgments not in an individualistic fashion but in ways that reverberate with others. Common sense deserves special consideration because it reflects human intuition. It is an intellectual activity that does not necessitate reasons or explanations for its importance but is recognized as valid because it resonates with the vast majority.[3]

Even so, radical subjectivity must be open and accountable to the critical claims of others. *Mujerista* biblical interpretation cannot serve just the liberation of Latinas; even less can it serve the liberation of Latinas at the expense of others. Openness to the critical claims of others immediately brings us face to face with our human sociality, which blankets all our claims, and with the radical need we have to be accountable for our own sake and the sake of society. Radical subjectivity does not allow hiding ourselves behind a veil of disinterestedness. Rather, it demands identifying and rendering account of our interests and privileges, thus opening ourselves to the claims of others. Tension between our own interests and those of others is what validates different subjectivities and makes it possible to bring as many of them as possible to bear on any given situation for the sake of the common good (Robb 1985, xv; Harrison 1985, 250).

---

2. I prefer to use "rational" to "logical" because logic has often been reduced to a syllogistic way of thinking, which is solely intent on exactitude and not on the social and historical conditioning of all truths.

3. My understanding and use of common sense is influenced by Geertz 1983. I am also indebted to the use of the term "human intuition" in Nussbaum 2000.

Another element of a *mujerista* understanding of radical subjectivity is the validity of claims emerging from daily experiences instead of from abstract ideas. First of all, claims of objectivity that ignore or denounce subjectivity have presupposed a grounding in no-place or in all-places that is simply not tenable given the particularity of all human knowledge. Furthermore, were such claims to universality feasible, the results would be abstractions that are useless in evaluating human institutions and practices. In order for claims to be constructive, they must identify the actual social context out of which they emerge (Young 1990, 4).

Exegetical Theories and Tools

Taking *lo cotidiano* seriously and owning up to our radical subjectivity, *mujerista* biblical interpretation follows primarily a line of inquiry called cultural criticism that has as its focus "the text as means, as evidence from and for the time of composition" (Segovia 1995a, 22). The emphasis is on the text "as a product and reflection of its context or world, with specific social and cultural codes inscribed, and hence a means for reconstructing the sociocultural situation presupposed, reflected and addressed" (22). *Mujerista* biblical interpretation searches for the meaning of a text by looking at the "world behind it, with analysis of text, author, and readers undertaken in terms of their relationship to and participation in that world" (22). Because *mujerista* biblical interpretation is particularly interested in *lo cotidiano* of the world of the biblical text, it emphasizes the personal, both in the private and the political spheres, as well as issues of gender, ethnicity-culture, anthropology, and ideologies. An important element of cultural criticism is that it is an eclectic method that does not preclude other methods such as sociohistorical critical method, form criticism, literary criticism, and rhetorical criticism. The openness of cultural criticism makes it possible to study the text from many different perspectives always in view of contributing a resource for Latinas' liberation.[4]

Parable of the Daily Workers: Initial Questions

Suspicion about Matthew's Interpretation

If, as has been repeated in the last forty years or so, the God of the Gospels opts for the poor and the oppressed and if the main message of Jesus' preach-

---

4. I am spurred on in my *mujerista* biblical interpretation by the work of Fernando Segovia, Leticia Guardiola, and Jean-Pierre Ruiz (2001).

ing was the establishment of the kin-dom[5] of God (in which the hungry are fed, the naked are clothed, the homeless are given shelter, those in prison are visited), then it makes absolutely no sense to us Latinas to say that the *patrón* is right and the day workers are wrong. We know what it means for the day workers that the *patrón* can decide what to do without taking anything into consideration except what he wants. How can he be the one we should listen to, the one whose doings we should support, the one we should identify with God? How can we accept and cheer for the way the *patrón* treats the day worker who protests, the one who dares to stand up for his honor and that of his fellow day workers, and for the worthiness and value of their work?[6] How can we not denounce the *patrón*'s attempt to turn some day workers against the others?

Principles used in selecting biblical texts as aids in moral guidance support our suspicion that it is impossible for this parable to be mainly about the *patrón* and his generosity. Three of these principles seem to be particularly relevant here. First, the text (or value or character or image) chosen to help analogically in moral choices and moral living has to be consistent with what is central to the biblical message at large. Second, the biblical text used has to be consistent with a theologically sound image of God. Third, it must be gauged against the whole of the story of Jesus (Spohn 1995, 120–21).[7] Seeing the *patrón* as an image of God contradicts all of these principles.

Rejecting Limitations Placed on the Meaning of Justice

Another question has to do with the insistence of scholars that this parable does not question today's order of justice. They insist that what the *patrón* does should be read as generosity or mercy or goodness (Donahue 1988, 85) but not as justice. Scholars have imposed reading this parable only in ways that do not question the order of justice based on "equal pay for equal work" (Donohue 1988, 81), as a moral judgment on the wage agreed on for a day's work, or as an example of proper labor-management relations (Nelson 1975, 289). This blindness to what the parable might very well be saying about the

---

5. For an elaboration of the meaning of kin-dom of God, different from the meaning of kingdom of God, see Isasi-Díaz 2004, 240–66.

6. With all due respect, I disagree here with most of the interpretations of this text offered by Hispanic theologian Pablo Jiménez (1997). I also disagree with two other Hispanic scholars: Rodríguez 1988; and González 1996, 118–19.

7. The other two are: the text should be appropriate to the situation under consideration; it must indicate a course of action that agrees with ordinary human morality.

meaning and order of justice seems an imposition by scholars that limits what could very well be the meaning intended originally by Jesus.[8]

As far as an ethical perspective is concerned, the vast majority of scholars, and preachers who have followed their lead, seem to consider other virtues less binding than justice. In their view, mercy, generosity, and goodness are the reasons why the *patrón* acted the way he did toward those hired last. They can accept this because they see these virtues as supererogatory, that is, beyond one's obligation. However, since scholars know that they cannot skirt the demands of justice, there seems to have been all along a great need to limit what justice means in this parable. To accept this parable as talking about a paradigm shift of the meaning of justice seems to demand too much, certainly beyond what the generally acceptable understanding of justice is today.

The scholars' insistence on not considering what happens in the parable as an issue of justice is suspicious. These qualms have led me to look further into what the parable might indeed be saying about justice. My contention is that the *patrón* is not just, but that does not mean that the parable does not question the present meaning and order of justice. It is not in the way the *patrón* acts but rather in the day workers' situation as portrayed in the parable, in the relationship between the *patrón* and the day workers, and in the way the day workers stand up for themselves and the value of their work that one indeed finds a radical shift in the meaning and order of justice.[9] This parable is not about supererogatory moral requirements but about what our obligation to be just entails. In order to discover what the parable says about justice, we must look at the day workers, not the *patrón*.

PRESENT REALITY OF LATINAS AND LATINOS AS CONTEXT FOR THIS STUDY

It is important for the reader to know a little more of the contemporary context of the Latina/o community in order to understand what motivates us to search for Jesus' parable and not to rest content with Matthew's interpretation.

Latinas and Latinos are at present faced with increasingly militant attitudes and actions from citizens and agents of the U.S. government. In the name of fighting terrorism (used since the 11 September 2001 terrorist attacks

---

8. It is important to note that Nelson, for example, sees the parable as indeed breaking "all previously held values, beliefs, judgements, and ideas of what is right and wrong, what is just and unjust, what is good and evil" (1975, 290). Yet he sees all of this as making room "for the inbreaking of grace," not for a new meaning and order of justice.

9. This will be explored further in my forthcoming book, *Justicia: A Reconciliatiory Praxis of Care and Tenderness*.

on the United States as a slogan to cover various belligerent behaviors), physical and verbal abuse is being leveled against Latinas and Latinos entering the United States by other than the sanctioned government ways. The attitude toward those among us who are undocumented has spread to the whole of the Latina/o community. Our community has responded with massive public demonstrations, and many different organizations have called for "comprehensive, and humane immigration reform" (ACHTUS 2006).

Large numbers of those who arrive in the United States without government-approved documents are employed as day workers. The attitude of many toward immigration of Latinas and Latinos is concretized in the way they treat day workers. Towns and cities have tried to forbid them congregating at "gathering places" where those in need of workers come to hire them. I see unemployed Latinos at parking lots and corners of small towns on the New Jersey side of the George Washington Bridge when I travel to work and at the corner of Flagler Street and the Palmetto Highway in Miami when I go there to visit my family. I meet Latino and Latina day workers every day. I meet them every time I stop to buy gasoline: always a different Latino pumps gasoline in a Korean-owned business. I see them painting buildings and replacing roofs all around my neighborhood. I buy flowers from them when my car stops for a red light in the streets of Manhattan. On the public bus that goes by my house, I meet women from many different countries of Latin America and the Caribbean who clean apartments up and down Fifth Avenue. They and their families, here or back in their countries of origin, depend on what they are paid for their labor. Their ability to work is the only thing they have. They have no safety net when it comes to meeting the bare essentials needed for living: housing, health, food. They have no bargaining power when it comes to setting their hourly wages.

It is not only the general message of the Gospels regarding Jesus' attitude toward the poor and the rich that makes me read this parable from the perspective of the day workers. It is this reality in the Latina/o community in the United States that pushes me to read from their perspective.[10] It is what has guided me to try to figure out why Jesus told this parable. What was he trying to say to the crowds that heard it? Is there a message different from the usual interpretations of the parable, including that of Matthew? Why did he tell this parable?

---

10. Pablo Jiménez likewise sees a direct correlation between the day workers in this parable and Latinas and Latinos in the United States. See Jiménez 1997, 36.

Searching for Jesus' Parable of the Day Workers[11]

There seem to be areas of general agreement among biblical scholars when it comes to what has been called the parable of the laborers in the vineyard in Matthew. First, in the words of the Jesus Seminar, "Jesus undoubtedly said this or something very like it" (Funk, Hoover, and the Jesus Seminar 1993, 36). The scholars of the Jesus Seminar and many others also agree that 20:16 is a later addition. This verse, "Thus the last shall be first and the first shall be last," was most probably added by Matthew to bring this parable in line with two other sections of the Gospel that revolve around the theme of "the first shall be last": 19:23–30, which immediately precedes this parable; and 20:20–26, where for the third time the issue of the "first being last" comes up. Verse 16 could also have been introduced at the end of the parable by Matthew to turn it into an example of Jesus' instruction to the disciples regarding rich people in the text immediately preceding (Herzog 1994, 79). Another possibility is that 20:16 is Matthew's way of "stitching his insertion back onto the Markan narrative fabric" (Herzog 1994, 80) that he had been following and had interrupted to insert this parable. Finally, reading this parable as a parable about the kin-dom of God is an attempt to fit this into the fourth narrative block of the Gospel of Matthew, 16:21–20:34, which deals with "life shaped by God's reign" (Carter 2000, 394).

With the opening verse of the parable, "For the kingdom of heaven is like a householder," and the concluding line, "the last shall be first," Matthew sets the theological framework and interpretation of the parable. In general, Matthew's interpretation has remained unchallenged regardless of the fact that it makes no sense in keeping with Jesus' understanding of the rich just a few verses earlier and the biblical theme of God's option for the poor. Jesus' parable emerges clearly once one identifies the later additions and Matthew's theological interpretation: that this parable has to do with life in the reign of God and the *patrón* is a God-figure. The parable then begins to make sense if one starts to read it from the perspective of the day workers.

To be able to find Jesus' parable, one has to read the narrative closely and not allow Matthew's theology and interpretation to interfere. Matthew's interpretation does not fit the parable.

> a look at the narrative structure suggests that an interpretation SIMPLY in terms of generosity will not do. If the parable were meant to focus on

---

11. I am most grateful to my colleague Melanie Johnson-De-Baufre for introducing me to the work of William R. Herzog II, whose basic insights are so important to what I present in this essay.

the generosity of the landowner, it would be told in a different order: those who were hired first would be paid first. Seeing them receive a denarius, those hired last would expect to receive about a tenth of a denarius. Imagine their joy and delight—and their sense of the landowner's generosity—when they also receive a denarius! Perhaps they would have protested: "But, sir, we didn't work as much as the others." And the landowner might have exclaimed, "That's all right. I want to give those who were hired last the same as those who were hired first." This seems to me a much more likely way to tell the story if the point of it is the generosity of the landowner, for then the surprise and the focus of the story would be on the generous act. (Lebacqz 1983, 34).

The Day Workers in Jesus' Parable

To read the parable of Jesus in place of Matthew's, one must recognize that the focus of this parable is the grumbling of the day workers (Lebacqz 1983, 34). Not only does a close reading indicate this, but also the fact that parables usually focus on the ordinary, the everyday, *lo cotidiano,* "a point often missed in scholar's tendency to distance the parables from everyday life by emphasizing the surprising, unusual, or even fantastic elements in them" (Hock 2002, 13). It is the reality of day workers and not the so-called generosity of the *patrón* that is ordinary and common.

A reading of this text, then, has to start by trying to understand the reality behind the parable, "the conventions of thought and behavior that governed the daily lives of people" (Hock 2002, 13–14). In this instance, most probably many of those who heard Jesus tell this parable had at some point been, were, or had friends and relatives who were day workers. Given the picture of Jesus' audiences in the Gospel, is it not far-fetched to believe that the majority of them were owners of vineyards or their friends?

So who are these day workers on whom Jesus' parable focuses? Day workers were, as they are today, an identifiable social group. They were drawn from among the peasants, who constituted 70 percent of the population at the time of Jesus (Herzog 1994, 63). They were mostly "children of peasant farmers who could not afford to divide their small patrimony. These farmers were forced to send their children into the streets as itinerant day workers who might work during harvest or planting season but had to beg the rest of the year" (Herzog 1994, 65). Day workers could also be peasants who had lost their land or simply peasants who had to supplement what their small plots produced (Herzog 2005b, 66).

Day laborers were so many, "between 5 and 10 percent of the population during normal times, but their number could swell to 15 percent during times of increased economic stress" (Herzog 1994, 64–65), that they were indeed cheap labor, with no bargaining power whatsoever. Scholars refer to them as "expendables," for that was the way society treated them.

> The presence of the expendable was the inevitable outcome of a system driven by unbridled greed. As the elites squeezed the dwindling resources of their peasant base, they forced households to exile their children into the most degrading and lethal form of poverty. For the expendables, life was brutal and brief; characteristically, they lasted no more than five to seven years after entering this class. (Herzog 1994, 66)

This parable gives today's reader a good sense of the reality of day workers at the time of Jesus. They were considered less valuable and, therefore, were less protected than slaves, since the latter were property. Their owners had "an interest in the profitability, that is, the ability to work and the life expectancy of slaves.... If the slave dies too soon or too quickly becomes incapable of working, the owner's capital account suffers. The day laborer, on the other hand, is a kind of slave working at his or her own risk" (Schottroff 2006, 213–14). Their only resource was their labor, the work they did for minimal pay, hopefully enough to keep them alive for one more day.

These are the people whom the *patrón* faces when he comes early in the morning into the center of the village where they gathered. Those chosen to go to the vineyard faced a long day of working under the sun, knowing that they would earn barely what they needed to eat. Those not chosen could only hope that another *patrón* would come into the marketplace and hire them. But that does not happen. So, when later in the day they are hired by the same *patrón* who hired the first ones, they must have thought that something was better than nothing.

THE *PATRÓN* IN THE PARABLE OF JESUS

Just like the day workers, the *patrón* belongs to an identifiable social group, the local elite, perhaps a member of the ruling class serving the "client kingship," through which Rome ruled Israel.

> Rome usually worked with local landed aristocracies, that is, local ruling classes who controlled large tracts of land, dominated the peasant cultivators, and extracted the yield for their own purposes, leaving the peasants under their control with little more than a subsistence living. Since these local elites were already in a predatory relationship with their peasants, they were willing to add Rome's demands for tribute to the tribute they were already extracting. Ruling aristocracies often extracted multiple layers of tribute from the same peasant base. (Herzog 2005a, 45)

The ruling elite to which the *patrón* in the parable belonged had probably squeezed peasant owners out of the land that now he so boastfully calls his. By having the *patrón* refer to the vineyard as "his" and noting that that *patrón* had a steward, Jesus lets his audience know in a few words what sort of man this character in the parable is. The extent of this *patrón*'s holdings is made clear by the fact that during the day he has to return to hire more and more day workers. "His imminent harvest is so great that even he cannot calculate accurately the amount of help needed" (Herzog 1994, 85).

The way the *patrón* deals with the day workers in the four trips he makes to the marketplace makes clear his power. In his first trip he tells the day workers he is going to pay them a denarius. The text speaks about an agreement between the day workers and the *patrón*, but since the denarius was the usual daily wage, it is far-fetched to think that there was any kind of negotiation. There are so many day workers unemployed, such a surplus of workers, that at the end of the day the *patrón* can still find men to hire. This is why on the second and third trips the *patrón* does not even have to agree to a wage. He simply tells them to go to work and he will decide at the end of the day what is right to pay them. His power over the day workers was absolute (Herzog 1994, 86).

What the *patrón* thinks about the day workers is also made amply clear by the way he talks to the group he hires at the eleventh hour. They had spent the day hoping that someone would hire them; there is nothing else they can do. But the *patrón* of this parable insults them by calling them lazy—foreshadowing what he will do later when he pays them. His "why do you stand here idle all day" (20:6b) cannot be ascribed to ignorance of the reality of day workers, for his business depended on knowing about them so he could exploit them. His way of talking to the day workers is a showing of his hand: what is behind this parable is not being generous but rather seeking to have tighter control over the day workers and exalting himself.

Yes, the *patrón* needs to call attention to his generosity, to locate "virtue in himself, a presumed moral goodness typical of aristocrats that subordinates were expected to accept without question" (Hock 2002, 36) The *patrón* is asking for the "deference and trust in his goodness that accrued to him simply as an aristocrat" (36).

One must examine this claim of generosity of the *patrón*. First, even if the denarius was the accepted pay for a day's work, given what has been said about how the elite exploited the peasant, one can hardly think that a denarius was a generous wage. It might have provided what a worker needed to survive but hardly what a person needed to have in order to be fit to work (Schottroff 2006, 211). Then there is the fact that a denarius might cover basic needs for a day, but since day workers did not find work every day, to be paid a denarius did not in any way alleviate their enormous need—it cannot in any way be considered a generous wage even for a few hours of work (Herzog 1994, 90). Third, a denarius might have covered the needs of a day worker, but it certainly was not enough income to provide for his family (Schottroff 2006, 211). What, then, did the generosity of the *patrón* consist of?

The other claim of the *patrón* that must be examined is in 20:15a, "Am I not allowed to do what I choose with what belongs to me? Well, the answer is no! Both Lev 25 and Deut 15 make it clear that the land belongs to God. In Israel, the so-called owners are only tenants who have to respond to God for how they manage the land (Herzog 2005a, 67). It is because the land does not belong to this or any other *patrón* but to God that the day workers have the right to expect to make a living by working the soil. This knowledge was perhaps what gave at least one of them the courage to complain about the way the *patrón* was treating the day workers.

The Confrontation

Insistence on reading the action of the *patrón* as a generous one is a conscious or unconscious attempt to distance any interpretation of the parable from questioning the ongoing order of justice. Also, because the *patrón* is identified with God, the readings attempt to present what he did not as an affront to the day workers first hired. They are an attempt "to exonerate the owner" (Herzog 1994, 91). But if these ideological readings are set aside, as one must do when searching for Jesus' parable behind Matthew's, the contrary is true: the orders the *patrón* gives his manager are seen by the day workers as an insult. The reversal in the order of paying the day workers, apparently a departure from what was customary, is an affront to the day workers who had been toiling since early morning.

By reversing the order of payment so that the last hired receive a wage equal to that of the first hired, he has told them in effect that he values their day-long effort in the scorching heat no more than the brief labor of the eleventh-hour workers. He has shamed their labor, and as day laborers who have nothing left to offer but their animal energy, they must respond to the provocation. If they consent to his judgment, namely, that their labor is worthless, then they have nothing left to offer (Herzog 1994, 91).

What can the *patrón* gain from insulting and shaming the day workers? First, he indulges his self-aggrandizement, his boasting about his generosity. Second, since the ability to work is all that day workers have, to shame their work by lessening its value humiliates and degrades them, a tactic used by the elites to control the poor and the oppressed. Even expendable or surplus people in society have their honor to protect, and for the day laborers the basis for their honor is the value of their work. They have to fight back or the last bit of their self-respect—their *dignidad*—will disappear.[12] "This explains why members of the lowest social class have the audacity to raise their voices in protest. They must defend their honor or die" (Herzog 1994, 92)!

The text already suggested that these are not the kind of day workers who will allow themselves to be insulted without responding. In 20:14b the ones hired at the eleventh hour defended themselves against the *patrón's* sly remark when he called them lazy. No matter how much they needed to work to be able to eat that very same day, they did not allow his insult to go unanswered. No, they are not lazy. They are not working because no one has hired them. They have been willing and able to work. That they are still sitting in the marketplace is not their fault.

Now those who had been hired at the beginning of the day feel insulted, and they will not stay quiet; they will also answer back; they will protest. The *patrón* picks one of them, most probably the leader, to address in order to make an example of him (20:13). In a condescending way (*hetaire*, the term he uses when addressing the day worker, is no friendly term) he alludes to "the pretense of bargaining" that took place in the marketplace between him and the day laborers. In 20:14a the *patrón* bans this one day worker, a chastisement that will certainly have negative repercussions for him beyond this one *patrón*: most probably he will not find work in the future in any of the surrounding vineyards (Herzog 1994, 92).

Not content with having shamed the day workers and banning their leader, the *patrón* seeks to validate his actions to the very men he has so gravely affronted and exploited and in so doing insults them even further. His "I choose to give" (20:14b) makes the denarius he is giving to those who were hired at the third, sixth, and eleventh hours not the payment due for their work but his own meritorious charity (Herzog 1994, 92). This is another indication of the true purpose of the *patrón* throughout the parable.

The parable draws to a close in the midst of the confrontation. The *patrón* has ineptly tried to defend his action as honorable but in reality has simply revealed who he is and his purpose in acting the way he has. The day workers have laid out their claim and in so doing have defended themselves the best way they are able. This does not change the actual fate of the day workers in the parable, but at least they still have their self-respect, their honor, their *dignidad*, and perhaps they even feel a bit better about themselves for having stood up to the *patrón*.

---

12. *Dignidad* and *honor* are key values and markers of self-understanding in Latina/o culture. See Garcia 1997.

Jesus' Purpose in Telling This Parable

Members of the elite like the *patrón* of this parable usually did not trouble themselves with the day-to-day operation of their vineyards. So the question why this *patrón* bothers to go to the marketplace personally to hire the day workers brings us to the purpose Jesus had in telling this parable. I have already indicated how it is far-fetched, out of character, and contrary to the general message of the Gospels to think that the purpose Jesus had in telling this parable was to praise the *patrón* or present him as a God-figure. The only other possibility is to postulate that, since his largest audience consisted of peasants, villagers, and fishermen, Jesus tells this parable to teach them, to enable and empower them to value their labor and to stand up for themselves. Is this not an opportunity for Jesus to make explicit the meaning of justice, the kind of social order that is needed so the hungry can be fed, the homeless sheltered, the sick cared for?

"Jesus' parables codify systems of oppression in order to unveil them and make them visible to those victimized by them. To disclose the source of exploitation, Jesus introduces a highly visible elite" (Herzog 1994, 87). The *patrón* himself comes to hire the workers to make him highly visible. Jesus' parable makes it very clear, to those who not only listen but indeed hear and understand, who the oppressor is. This, in turn, clarifies the injustice being committed by the *patrón*—injustice always being the starting place for the struggle for justice.

Parables follow closely nature and life. That is one reason why they are so powerful. But as a storyteller, Jesus tweaks this story to fit his purpose. The *patrón* could have remained a power behind the curtain while his manager was on stage, but actually Jesus brings the *patrón* on stage five times. This facilitates staging the confrontation scene, which is precisely where we have to look for the radical shift in the meaning and order of justice the parable proposes. Several key elements that need to be considered when talking about justice come to the fore when we look at the confrontation from the perspective of the day workers. The dynamics of power in the story become central. The issue of solidarity between the workers and the attempt of the *patrón* to break it also is made clear. Can we not easily imagine that, after Jesus told the parable, discussion about its meaning followed? What were the opinions of Jesus' audience about the *patrón*'s motives for banning the leader? Is it not highly probable that the audience praised the leader for what he did and that all learned from the eleventh-hour workers' response to the *patrón* the need to confront power and authority and not be intimidated? Comments may also have been raised about the need to hold on to *dignidad* regardless of any situation, for not to have self-respect and self-esteem is the surest way of being totally defeated.

Approaching Matt 20:1–16 with the intent of discovering as much as possible of the original text frees this parable from the interpretation of Matthew. By going back to Jesus' parable of the day workers, another way of reading the text becomes possible, a way that is guided by the attitude of Jesus toward the poor and the rich, as well as by the Gospel's overall message of a preferential option for the poor. The use of cultural criticism, social-historical method, and literary analysis makes possible a reading of this parable from the perspective of the day workers. Imagination, intuition, and emotion can balance scientific studies and subjective propositions (Reyes 2005, 31) and in the end can yield a rich reading of Matt 20:1–16, one that heartens Latinas and Latinos in the United States in our daily struggle—*la lucha cotidiana*.

Responses

LIBERATION HERMENEUTICS AND INDIA'S DALITS

Monica Jyotsna Melanchthon

INTRODUCTION

A major hurdle on the way to liberation of the Dalits[1] is "the body of knowledge known as Scripture" (Massey and Prabhakar 2005, 9). Scriptures control
and determine practically all aspects of the life of the believing community.
Hence, the canopy under which an examination of the Bible and Dalit experience should take place is the scripturality of the Dalit experience, namely,
the pervasiveness of scriptural legitimation of upper-caste consciousness by
Hindu scriptural mandates, for it reveals the context in which Dalits have had
to read and study any scripture, including the Bible. That reading and study
have not been uncontested. For centuries, Dalits have been and continue to
be involved in a struggle for canonical control of Hindu scriptures, which
sanctified and justified the hierarchical and discriminatory system of caste.
By being denied education, they were hindered from access to traditional
knowledge. Lack of access to Scripture has hindered them from making a
contribution to the interpretation of Scripture.

This scriptural rhetoric rested on the pillars of purity and pollution and
the determination of the upper castes to conquer through the forces of Hin-
dutva. This "scripturalism" (Marty 1987, 40) is not confined to the past but
continues to define in large degree contemporary Indian culture. The Hindu
scriptures have become the visceral vortex of deep-seated convictions about

---

1. The present application of the word can be traced back to the nineteenth century,
when Mahatma Jyotirao Phule, a Marathi social reformer and revolutionary, used it to
describe the outcastes and untouchables as the oppressed and broken victims of a caste-
ridden society. But it is also believed that it was Dr. Ambedkar who first coined this term.
The followers of the Panther Movement of Maharastra gave popularity to this term as a
constant reminder of their age-old oppression, denoting both the state of oppression as
well as the people who are oppressed. See Massey 1994, 4.

the nature of Indian reality and the survival of its customs and mores. As such, they function as a verbal icon whose power has little to do with the content of ancient scriptures but much more to do with the form of modern Indian life. It solidifies a national identity forged by the Hindu rhetoric of Brahmanical or caste supremacy and Dalit inferiority and untouchability (Melanchthon 2005a).

Dalit theology has arisen out of the Dalit movement, which found its inspiration in liberation movements in other parts of the world, particularly that of the Black Panther movement in the United States, the antiapartheid movement in South Africa, and the liberation movements in South America. Along with these communities oppressed by race and class, the Dalits, who are oppressed by caste, share the common historical experience of colonization, Christianization, and discrimination. Dalit Christian theology's affinity with other liberation theologies lies in its birth as a theological expression rooted in the historical experiences of those oppressed by caste in India and their encounter with the God of the Bible, who exhibits a preferential option for the poor and the oppressed and identifies with the suffering and agony of the marginalized through God's Son Jesus Christ. It is a theology that seeks to address caste not only as it functions within society but also the scandal of caste within the church.

The contours of Dalit theology are similar to that of other oppressed communities, since it has emerged among the people on the margins, the oppressed who see themselves as the contemporary counterparts of biblical victims and communities used by dominant caste communities. Therefore, when they hear the Bible offering hope and liberation to the oppressed of the ancient world, they hear hope and liberation being offered to them as the oppressed of the contemporary world (Wielenga 1998, 55–56). If God sided with the oppressed back then, they believe God continues to side with the oppressed Dalits here and now. This theology is critical in that it analyzes the Indian social structure and denounces the dominance of caste and its derogatory attitude toward Dalits and its concomitant effects on Dalit communities. It is constructive in the sense that it is cognizant of the absence of the Dalit voice, its history, and its experience in the articulation of an Indian Christian theology. Hence it envisions and works toward the building of an alternative social structure that is devoid of caste, one that is inclusive of Dalit traditions, history, and symbol system. It is collaborative in that it is open to work with other marginalized communities and their experiences to jointly seek liberation for all.

But Dalit theology as a liberation theology is different from its counterparts in other parts of the world because of its very long history of oppression that has contributed to the loss of most of Dalit history, land, culture, language, religion, and political/social rights. Dalits have to begin afresh, since much of what was theirs has now been appropriated and absorbed by the colonizers, and the Dalits themselves have become slaves of the dominant caste groups. The enslavement of Dalits is hence multifaceted, which unfortunately has also been interiorized by the Dalits themselves. The historical context of the Dalits reveals the peculiarity of their condition and differentiates them from other oppressed groups and their theology from that of other liberation theologies (Massey 2001, 84).

> We fought with crows,
> Never even giving them the snot from our noses.
> As we dragged out the Upper Lane's dead cattle,
> Skinned it neatly
> And shared the meat among ourselves,
> They used to love us then.
> We warred with jackals—dogs—vultures—kites
> Because we ate their share. (Dangle)

The essays contained in this volume uplift ideas and reflections that bear similarity with the views of Dalit theologians. I am unable to respond to all of them and hence attempt here to reflect on some issues related to the Dalit experience and their liberation as they have been presented in select essays in this volume.

Affirmation and Transformation of Life in All Its Wholeness

For example, Dalit theology also upholds the value and dignity of life and the rights of all people (Melanchthon 2005a, 56–57). The principle objective of reading the Bible, therefore, is not to interpret the Bible alone but to interpret life as well with the help of the Bible. The major preoccupation is not the quest for the meaning of the text in itself but the direction that the Bible suggests to the people of God within the specific circumstances in which they find themselves. Dalits are those who are struggling for life—a life free from fear, humiliation, rejection, want, and deprivation. They see God intervening on behalf of the victims whenever life is abused and destroyed, as in the case of Naboth, Abel, Uriah, the poor, and the widows.

The *talitha cum* hermeneutics of liberation described by Musa Dube based on the life of Kimpa Vita and the narrative of the woman with the issue of blood illustrated by the four African women's ways of reading the Bible for liberation appeals therefore to the Dalit reader and interpreter.

A major effort is being expended by Dalit interpreters to isolate and reclaim stories from their native religio-cultural resources, stories of heroes, men, women, and deities, that would function as exemplars of Dalit resistance and resilience against caste tyranny. Stories such as that of Madurai Veeran (Arul Raja 2006), of Goddess Ellaiyamman (Clarke 1998; Dietrich 2001), or Mariamman (Dietrich 2001, 246) are being uplifted because of their emancipatory potential, because they orient the reader or the Dalit to breaking the hegemonic barriers of the norms of untouchability; for them, "disobedience to the 'casteist norms' is part and parcel of their liberative struggle" (Arul Raja 2006, 104). They are stories of subversion and transgression, and such myths can be empowering for men and women if they are reread in a liberating process. By divinizing these characters and worshiping them, the community therefore engages continually in an act of denouncing caste hegemony and violating caste boundaries for the sake of life.

LAND: AT THE ROOT OF CASTE VIOLENCE

Schottroff's and Isasi-Díaz's submissions are related to parables. Schottroff reads the parables as "counterimages" to the "kingdom of God," and Isasi-Díaz understands the parable of the vineyard owner from a *mujerista* perspective. Both essay very effectively show the fallacy in Adolf Jülicher's dictum that every parable has one and only one central point based on allegorizing that imposes a fixed theological meaning upon each parabolic detail. On the contrary,

> the reduction of every parable to a single point (read: idea) renders it a mere illustration of more primary theological meanings. Lost is all sense of the parable's artistic integrity, its capacity to tell us something we do not know and could not come by in any other way, its ability to evoke experiences we have never had, and an awareness of realities we have not even guessed at before. (Wink 1980, 1062)

Interpreted from the perspective of oppressed minorities, and with the aid of liberation hermeneutics, the parables studied by these two women scholars bring to the fore an alternative meaning that is explosive and subversive in its intent and liberating as well. Matthew 20:1–16 (day laborers) and 21:33–44// Mark 12:1–12 (wicked tenants) are parables that involve land.

They remind me of the fact that, for example, eleven million Dalits live in Tamil Nadu, which represents 20 percent of the region's population. Further, 50 percent of the Dalits live below the poverty rate. Dalits are the backbone of an agrarian economy, as 72 percent of Dalits are land workers, but only 7 percent of the land belongs to them. In addition, 90 percent of Dalits own no land. With little land of their own to cultivate, Dalit men, women, and children numbering in the tens of millions work as agricultural laborers for a few kilograms of rice or Rs. 15–35 (U.S. 38–88¢) a day. Most live on the brink of destitution, barely able to feed their families and unable to send their children to school or break away from cycles of debt bondage that are passed on from generation to generation. At the end of day, they return to a hut in their Dalit colony with no electricity, kilometers away from the nearest water source, and segregated from all non-Dalits. Despite a host of land reforms, a great many Dalits lost even the little land they had and have no choice but to join the ranks of landless agricultural laborers. Land reforms are continually scuttled and violently undermined by lawless landlords who take the land back by brutal force with the connivance of the police. Other efforts by Dalits to acquire land through land reforms are met with social boycotts ostracizing them from buying or selling anything in the village. The implementation of ceiling laws has proceeded at a snail's pace and has been crippled by bureaucratic inertia. Division and competition is therefore created between individuals and communities.[2] At the root of violence against the Dalits is the issue of land.

How would these people respond to these parables? The landowner of the parable who pays all laborers, whether hired in the morning or later in the day, the same wage may be understood as a very generous employer. But the grumbling of those who were hired first and worked all day should not be minimized.[3] The grumbling of the workers is an expression of displeasure, and it provides a remarkable twist for the interpretation of the parable. As Donahue maintains with the help of a rabbinic parable, those who were hired later, although for a short time, worked immensely hard and accomplished as much as those who were hired in the morning and hence were paid a just wage. Those who grumbled were envious of the good fortune of the other workers and hence blind to the master's right to show justice and generosity (Donahue 1988, 82). "What began as an act of goodness to them and unfolded as an act of generosity to others blinded them to the goodness of the owner

---

2. Christian Dalits are currently not entitled to any of the privileges of affirmative action by the government. Their efforts to change this are being met with resistance not only by the government but also by other Dalit communities not wanting to share the little that they are entitled to.

3. See Kautsky 1982, 49–75, 230–46, 273–319, who argues that there was little conflict generated by peasants and artisans. He contends that peasants had few options or possibilities for resistance. He claims that they were afraid of starvation, a consequent result of resistance, and hence were calm by nature, accepting of their place in society and lacking in leadership skills. I do not agree. Dalit studies are replete with examples of subtle but effective Dalit resistance against caste supremacy. These are forms of resistance that aid the Dalit in coping with the marginalization and injustice. See Elisha 2002; J. Scott 1985.

and the good fortune of others" (83). Can this be real? Are such instances of employer generosity known in real life?

Another way to look at it that supports Schottroff's reading of the parable as "counterimage" and Isasi-Díaz's reading is as follows. An open and overt protest by the workers might deprive them of a job at the same site the next day. The parable does not inform us of what happens between the workers once they leave the workplace. The giving of equal wages by the owner to all the workers hired on that day actually creates animosity between workers. Is it possible to imagine that those who came first, unable to express any anger against the landowner, may have taken it out on those who came last, causing dissension and hostility and intensifying the spirit of competition among the workers? The worker's daily meal and that of his or her family is assured only through the wage that one earns on that day. Hunger and the responsibility to provide for the family and the insecurity that comes from not having a steady income would also contribute to envy, dissension, and rivalry among workers. By causing such ill feelings among workers, the landlord has better control over them.

The anger and violence of the tenants in the parable in Matt 21:33–44 seems to resonate once again with landless agricultural laborers in India, who are often forced to pay a high tenancy fee even before they are allowed to work on the land of the dominant castes. The Dalit experience is replete with cases of Dalit laborers reduced to bonded or slave labor because of their incapacity to pay their dues to landowners. Many in the recent past have succumbed to committing suicide in response to poor harvests or failure of crops, debt to landowners, and liberal economic policies of the government. In many cases tenancy is oral and informal, and hence even laws made for the security of tenants are ineffective. Landowners often take more of the share of the produce than what the law allows. Hence, tenant retaliation to years of abuse, extortion, and unfair treatment may result in responses similar to that of the tenants in the parable. The violence is regarded by some Dalit theologians as a sign of hope, because it indicates that they are no longer willing to accept their subjugation and are resisting the dominance of the landowner. But the power, as Schottroff maintains, the power to squelch the tenants and their resistance, to replace them with others more compliant with his demands, lies in the hands of the owner. The parable therefore leaves us with some uncomfortable feelings about owner-tenant relationships. Sallie McFague's comment is therefore helpful.

> A theology that is informed by parables is necessarily a risky and open-ended kind of reflection. It recognizes not only the inconclusiveness of all conceptualization when dealing with matters between God and human beings (an insight as old as religion itself), but also the pain and skepti-

cism—the dis-ease—of such reflection. Theology of this sort is not neat and comfortable; but neither is the life with and under God of which it attempts to speak. The parables accept the complexity and ambiguity of life as lived here in this world and insist that it is in *this* world that God makes his gracious presence known. A theology informed by the parables can do no less—and no more. (McFague 1975, 7)

Blessing

Jione Havea's essay on "Releasing the Story of Esau from the Words of Obadiah" was interesting reading. It succeeded in creating within me a soft spot for Esau but raised some questions for me with regard to the practice of blessing. I was reminded of a story in the *Mahābhārata* where Dhṛtarāṣṭra at the end of the great battle of Kurukshetra was overcome with grief and rage at the loss of his hundred sons. When the blind king met the Pandavas who had come to seek his blessing prior to ascending the throne, he embraced all of them. When it was Bhima's turn, Krishna knew that the king was blind and possessed the strength of a hundred thousand elephants from the boon granted by Vyasa. He was quick to move Bhima aside and push an iron figure of Bhima into Dhṛtarāṣṭra's embrace. When the thought entered Dhṛtarāṣṭra's mind that the man in his embrace had killed every one of his hundred sons without mercy, his anger rose to such a pitch that the metal statue was crushed into powder. Thus, Bhima was saved and Dhṛtarāṣṭrastra composed himself and gave the Pandavas his blessing (Hudson 2007).

Within the Hindu or Indian tradition and culture, blessings are central. They are good wishes or benedictions nurtured by the precepts of grace, energy, and the encountering and seeing of the divine. Blessings are often pronounced in response to the making of an offering, in the practice of pilgrimage, during initiation into something, or during other rites of passage. Blessings are considered to be positive utterances, pronouncements made for the good and prosperity of the receiver. A blessing is usually a deed performed by an older or authoritative person that is received by the one or those hearing it and hence can also be characterized as a "genre of power" that defines a kind of hierarchy of authority. Blessings perform functions, since they are "spoken acts." By pronouncing a blessing, the person receiving it is changed in religious or social status. While blessings help the receiver, those who pronounce the blessing are also helping themselves by legitimating and perpetuating their own position of auspicious and organizational priority and authority. Power and authority are constituent of blessings.

In the Bible, a blessing is depicted as a mark of God's relationship with a person or nation. When a person or group is blessed, it is a sign of God's grace upon them and perhaps even presence among them. To be blessed means that a person or people take part in God's plans for the world and humanity (Richards 1992). Commonly, an act of blessing links theology, liturgy, and ritual. Theology is involved because a blessing almost always involves the intentions of God. Liturgy is involved because a blessing often occurs in the context of liturgical readings. Ritual is involved because significant rituals occur when a "blessed" people remind themselves about their relationship with God, perhaps by reenacting events surrounding the blessing (Harrelson 1962, 1:446). Blessings also give insight about a person's life, may include promises of blessings, warnings about temptations or weaknesses, or counsel about how the person should live (see Gen 48).

Isaac gives Jacob the blessing (Gen 27:27–29), and the speech is delivered in the name of Yahweh, thereby suggesting that the blessing has its origin and effect in the power and purpose of Yahweh. Isaac kisses Jacob and then blesses him. Jacob is blessed with the dew of the heaven and the fatness of the earth and sovereignty over nations and his brothers. It is obvious that Jacob receives the main or primary blessing.

Havea argues that Isaac should have at least faked a blessing in response to Esau's plea for one. I agree that this would certainly have helped Esau, but Havea does not state how he understands Gen 27:39–40, which contain the words of Isaac to Esau. By not considering these verses, is Havea stating that these words do not constitute a blessing?

These words by Isaac are not introduced as a blessing but as an "answer" by Isaac to Esau's question and anguished plea, "Have you only one blessing, father? Bless me, me also, father!" How does one therefore classify verses 39–40? They contain no reference to the deity; there is no action by Isaac that accompanies these words pronounced upon Esau such as kissing, laying on of hands, or an embrace. Most translations of these verses render Esau as one who will be away from the fatness of the earth and the dew of the heavens, who will be a servant to his brother—words that are in complete antithesis to the blessing of Jacob. Hence this latter pronouncement does not seem to be a blessing when seen juxtaposed with verses 27–29.[4]

But a literal translation gives a different reading. Spina calls attention to the JPS rendering, which reads, "See, your abode shall enjoy the fat of the earth, and the dew of heaven above," which is positive in tone.[5] Yet Esau will

---

4. See Skinner 1912, 372–74, who wonders if what we have here in this J narrative is a residue of an original form of the curse. Gordon J. Wenham (1994) only highlights the ambiguity of the genre of these verses.

5. See Spina 2005, 20–21; Jewish Publication Society 1962, 48. Spina favors this rendering, which is contrary to the translations of most commentators. Spina therefore

experience all the harshness and pain of living but will have life (v. 40; see Westermann 1985, 443). This is therefore considered a blessing by some, albeit one that is secondary and less promising or inferior than the one given to Jacob (Westermann 1985, 443).[6] If this is so, could it be considered a "fake" blessing? Fake because it does not comply with traditional form? Because it is not pronounced in the right spirit and makes no reference to the deity or the power of the giver? Because it is not connected to the purpose of the giver? Esau was not too happy with what he heard, but he did not press Isaac again for a blessing! Esau did succeed in gaining prosperity for himself (Gen 33:9)!

While I am drawn to Havea's statement that "one will succeed because one has a blessing to uphold and materialize," there is still something about it that makes me feel uncomfortable. If it is up to the receiver to materialize the blessing, is it fair to fake one? What might be the psychological impact on the receiver when the blessing cannot be materialized? Blessings are also prayers in which a kind of power is thought to reside in those who say them, for they pray on behalf of others. They might function as a form of control because they express the desires of the giver. Indian women, for example, are traditionally blessed with "may you be a mother of a hundred sons." A woman is blessed with the phrase "*dheerga sumangali bhava*," meaning, "may you be in this condition of wearing ornaments and being a married woman for a long time" (eternal wifehood). The Hindu woman therefore prays and observes rituals and fasts seeking the longevity, well-being, and prosperity of her husband.[7] The prosperity portrayed in these blessings is one of a patriarchal ideal. The male has sons to continue his line, hold his property, and perpetuate the patriarchal organization. The women are important inasmuch as they are the source of children and are necessary to even conceive of the blessed life. When a woman is not able to bear sons, she is blamed and tormented. At the root of the ill treatment of Indian widows is this notion that the woman did not do enough to ensure her husband's life. Trying to materialize these standard and traditional blessings are a burden to women, and one wonders whether these are blessings or curses that enables me to appreci-

---

concludes that Esau and Jacob were both promised future prosperity. The difference lies only in the latter part of the pronouncement upon Esau, where unlike his brother he would be a servant but would experience liberation when he will be able to "break loose … break his yoke from your neck."

6. If this was a "blessing," why did the author not use the verb "blessed"? How do we explain this hesitation on the part of the author?

7. *Karwa chauth* is a festival/ritual observed by Hindu married women who on this day fast from sunrise to moonrise and pray for their husbands. There is no similar day of observance for Hindu men to benefit their wives.

ate the Hebrew term *brkh* and the ambiguity that surrounds its meaning and usage (as is the case in Job 2: 9).

The anguish and the pain that Esau is "blessed/cursed" with resonates with the cry of the Dalits whose rights to live on ancestral lands, whose subjectivity, and humanity has been taken away by the invading peoples, the architects of the caste system. They have been deprived to live lives far away from the fatness of the earth and away from the dew of the heavens.[8] They lives are characterized and impinged upon by the "sword," understood here as forces of death, violence, and pain. They are servants of their brothers. But they are striving toward that moment when they can "break loose" and "break the yoke from their neck." They are determined to annihilate caste and bring about a society free from its evils. They are like Esau, trying to uphold the blessing of life and to bring to realization life in its wholeness.

Sin of the Marginalized

Alejandro Botta's essay, "How to Hide an Elephant on Fifth Avenue: Universality of Sin and Class Sin in the Hebrew Scriptures," very effectively brings to the fore the fact of "class" in the Hebrew Scriptures in relation to sin. There is no doubt that the God of the Bible cares for and is on the side of the poor and expects the community also to care for the poor. However, that the Bible is the product of a certain class of people with a definite ideology has been proven beyond doubt. The texts were not produced on behalf of the poor. Rather, the texts represent the forms of domination and the interests of the dominant social classes that are similar to those of contemporary oppressors and exploiters.

If one were to look for insights within the Hebrew Bible for bridging the gap between the haves and the have-nots, one would notice that, while the Hebrew Bible contains narratives that depict the life and experiences of the poor, all instructions and prescriptions cited with regard to the poor or the oppressed seem to be addressed to the haves or the rich. The community is repeatedly told of its obligation to the poor and what it should do and should not do to remain in YHWH's favor. The onus to bridge the gap between the rich and poor or care for the poor seems to have been laid mostly on the rich. Despite this emphasis, the system does not seem to have worked very well, because one sees the concern expressed during all periods of Israelite

---

8. Water is a contested issue in Indian society, for Dalits are forbidden from drawing water from wells belonging to caste communities. Today, in the face of global warming, it is the Dalits who suffer most from lack of water for personal use and for their crops.

history in relative proportions. I wonder if this was the case because what was in practice was a situation of dependency on the part of the poor upon the rich, a top-down model of economics, contributing to a culture of receiving instead of ensuring an automatic sharing of resources or the creation of opportunities to become self-reliant, especially after the establishment of the monarchy. It is a model that is also intellectually and aesthetically satisfying to the middle-class mindset, apart from providing to that class a whole structure of privileges and status and lifestyles.

But the faults of the rich are, as Botta has shown, embedded in the language of universal sin, and the poor who do not have the capacity to commit such kinds of sin are also called to repentance and responsibility. Such universalizing or totalizing and unqualified understanding of sin is embedded in the logic of neocolonialist discourse (McCreight 1997, 421). Only a sociohistorical and postcolonial reading will bring to light that these deeds of injustice, exploitation, misuse, and abuse are those of the influential, propertied, and powerful class. The rich who collude with evil, defined as the systemic structures or patterns of oppression in economic, political, and social life, commit sin, for sin is "those free, discrete acts of responsible individuals that create or reinforce these structures of oppression" (Potter Engel 1990, 155). Sin is structural, and the unforgivable sin is the use of coercive power exercised through ecclesiastical and societal institutions to repress and quench the spirit of the marginalized, the poor, the women, Dalits, and other oppressed minorities.

While I agree with Botta's conclusions, I would like to point out that there is a way in which the poor and the marginalized collude with the sins of the rich and the powerful. Feminist scholars for some time now have categorized the sin of women as submissiveness, passivity, antifeminism, false humility, emotional dependency, and the like, which have been applied to all oppressed peoples in general without taking into consideration their variations based on race, class, caste, or gender. Dalit theologians have maintained that it is sin to oppress, but it also sin to allow oneself to be oppressed, and it has been contended by others as well that it is not only the oppressor who is sinful but the victim, too. While the sin of the oppressor is the oppression of the poor, the sin of the oppressed is identified as "the failure to take responsibility for self-actualization" (Goldstein 1960, 100–112; Plaskow 1980, vii). When the poor do not agitate or resist but acquiesce and are complacent to and appropriate the values of the oppressive dominant powers, they are sinning by perpetuating systems of power. Understood in this way, sin is, I guess, universal.

Psalms 5, 10, 14, and 53, which have been examined by Botta, are generally accepted by experts in the field to be of the lament genre, either individual or communal. It can be argued that resistance in these psalms is expressed in the form of an intercession or petition to God seeking God's intervention or punishment upon the evildoer (Pss 5:10; 10:12, 15) or through the words of hope and assurance (14:7; 53:5, 6). Prayer and lamentation are often covert means of resistance in a situation where there are no other means of resistance available to the poor and the marginalized. To be able to give voice to one's suffering, doubts, and anxieties and to seek retribution is an assertion of one's identity and self. The lament tradition of the Hebrew Scriptures gives visibility to this form of resistance in clear and obvious ways. It is a form of resistance and self-assertion that is rooted in a faith that is wrought out of suffering. It is a faith that finally satisfies one's thirst for justice that one's prayer for retribution and healing has been heard in the face of oppression and subjugation.

In Conclusion

The Bible is appealing to the Dalit because of its egalitarian message. This egalitarian message, though preached, is rarely practiced. The church has failed in its calling to be a sanctuary for the marginalized.[9] The church has been hesitant to challenge and critique structures and systems that contribute to poverty, oppression, and inhuman life conditions. Liberation theologies and liberation hermeneutics are met with resistance. Many of the churches emphasize an other-worldly piety and a theology of prosperity, thereby drawing people away from confronting the problem of marginalization. Power derived from the office of the church and its property is exercised in ways that stand in contradiction to the yearnings of the poor who are also victims of power abuse. Although the Christian community has gone on record for its exemplary and pioneering work among the poor, it has not dealt with the root causes of oppression and poverty, and it needs to do so if it desires to be a credible witness to the defense of the poor. I close with the following

---

9. "Though Catholics of the lower caste and tribes form 60 per cent of Church membership they have no place in decision-making. Scheduled caste converts are treated as lower caste not only by high caste Hindus but by high caste Christians too. In rural areas they cannot own or rent houses, however well-placed they may be. Separate places are marked out for them in the parish churches and burial grounds. Inter-caste marriages are frowned upon and caste tags are still appended to the Christian names of high caste people. Casteism is rampant among the clergy and the religious. Though Dalit Christians make 65 per cent of the 10 million Christians in the South, less than 4 per cent of the parishes are entrusted to Dalit priests. There are no Dalits among 13 Catholic Bishops of Tamilnadu or among the Vicars-general and rectors of seminaries and directors of social assistance centres" (Massey 1995, 82).

poem by a Dalit that powerfully expresses the frustrations of the Dalit with the church.

THE ELEVENTH COMMANDMENT

The time of his coming
Has become closer.

In the morning
On a rainy day
He descends.

He gathers
People drenched
On the pavements
And the people
Hunched together
In leaky huts
And walks
Towards the church.

Seeing it empty and locked
He commands in anger:
"Raze these useless churches to the ground."[10]

---

10. Poem by Ragasiyan, translated from the Tamil by Meena Kandasamy. See http://www.museindia.com/showconnew.asp?id=394.

Until Everyone Has a Place under the Sun

Lai Ling Elizabeth Ngan

I want to thank the contributors to this Semeia Studies volume on *The Bible and Liberation Hermeneutics*. Their essays have provided a rich matrix for conversation. The editors have brought together scholars with diverse perspectives and experiences from all over the world: Africa, Latin America, the Pacific Islands, Europe, and the United States. I am grateful for the opportunity to learn from these distinguished scholars from a global community that seeks liberty and justice for all.

My response to this collection of essays will be based on my social location as a Chinese American Christian woman from the Baptist tradition; therefore, ethnicity, gender, religion, and history will affect how I read. My reading approach can be broadly classified as an Asian American hermeneutics; I will say more about that in this response.

Let me first introduce myself. I was born in Hong Kong when it was a British colony. The citizens of Hong Kong were considered British subjects, but our passports stated very clearly that we had no right of abode in other parts of the United Kingdom. The only time that I was in London, I had an eight-hour wait for a connecting flight to Israel; the customs agent told me that I had no business to be in London and questioned why I could not simply stay in the airport. After more conversation, she grudgingly gave me permission to go into London. We were not really British after all.

I was born into a very devout Buddhist family, and through exposure from Christian schools I converted to Christianity as a teen and, after college graduation, chose to be a Baptist because of historical Baptist distinctives such as "soul competency," "priesthood of the believers," and "separation of church and state." I came to the United States at seventeen years of age and received all my subsequent schooling in this country. To make a long story short, I have become very Americanized and have since become a U.S. citizen.

Growing up in a traditional Chinese household, I experienced gender bias since childhood. Boys were important to the family because they were the ones who would carry on the family name; girls were considered "money-losing goods." Girls were objects for sale, and parents bemoaned that their investment in daughters would be a losing proposition. These experiences of being overlooked sensitized me to gender issues and the need for gender equality.

I had internalized racism as a colonized British subject. As with many Asians whose country had been colonies of Western powers, the sense of European might loomed large. We studied European history in school and read English authors such as Charles Dickens. The sign of sophistication was to embrace European culture and values and to become more like the Europeans in clothing, food choices, and mannerism. The stories of China's defeat at the hands of the European powers in the early part of the twentieth century made me ashamed to be a Chinese. Why were we humiliated over and over again? What happened to China's former glory?

I became aware of subtle racism after arriving in the United States. During my first semester in boarding school, a woman commented on the sneaky dark eyes of Asians. She quickly turned to me and said she did not mean me. Then whom was she talking about? I have those same sneaky dark eyes. I met a lot of nice people along the way who cared for me, and the internalized racism that belittled me blinded me to exploitations from schoolmates and the like. I did not think much about my racial identity. As a matter of fact, I thought I was white and acted the part. All my close friends were white, and I had very little to do with other students from Hong Kong except for speaking in Cantonese. The issue of my racial difference and of racial discrimination was less acute in the San Francisco Bay Area because of a large presence of Asians. Asian Americans and African Americans have strong voices and political clout. Coming to Texas was a different story. For the first time, I felt the full impact of not being white, not being male, and not being Texan. So who am I? My journey of self-discovery was painful but grace-filled. I rediscovered my roots and embraced the fact that I am an ethnic Chinese. My adopted country is the United States. I am no longer just Chinese. I am a Chinese American. My experience and history form the lens through which I read social realities, the Bible, and these essays. Issues of gender, race and justice as well as postcolonial and diasporic experience shape my understanding. In this response, I will explore the places of intersection between the liberation hermeneutics presented by the contributors and my reading as a Chinese American Christian woman.

Liberation Hermeneutics

"Liberation theology" became a prominent term in the late twentieth century because of social events and theological responses in Latin America. The movement is unsettling for many conservative Christians, especially those in the First World. Perhaps one of the reasons for the discomfort is due to reading Paul's injunction to submit to authorities literally without consideration to current social historical realities (Rom 13:1–5). A criticism often leveled against liberation theology is that violence is accepted as a legitimate Christian response to oppression. Erhard Gerstenberger notes in his essay that "Christians … have been very reluctant to oppose state authorities violently" (70), but we choose not to remember that even Bonhoeffer reached a point when he thought violence was the only possible response against Hitler.

The mention of liberation theology conjures up images from television reports of violent demonstrations, attacks, and counterattacks between students and workers and sometimes left-wing political factions and the forces of the established government. The chaos and bloodshed are more than we can stomach. We are quick to cite Gandhi's and Martin Luther King Jr.'s nonviolent resistance in their movements as the appropriate Christian response, forgetting to mention that Gandhi was not a Christian. I believe that, before criticisms can be raised, we need to see and understand the social realities that our fellow human beings have to endure in Latin America.

Most Christians in the First World do not live in abject poverty and suffer deprivations that the poorest of the poor experience. North Americans are very rich by the world's standard. Most of us do not live in cardboard "houses" that have no doors or windows or have to live off what food scraps we can gather from trash heaps. When suffering does not touch our own skin and flesh, I do not think we can chide others for how they react. It would be like Job's friends admonishing him to repent for his many sins. Desperate situations call for desperate reactions, and perhaps this is what our Latin American brothers and sisters see. It is a time for us rich Christians to see with, stand with, feel with, and be in solidarity with our Latin brothers and sisters. It is not time for the rich to castigate the poor. As Alejandro Botta points out, the indictment of sin in Scripture is, more often than not, a reference to class sin (105).

Out of the struggle against oppression and death-dealing forces and toward the goal of liberation and life-affirmation, the liberation movement in Latin America has provided the groundwork from which a whole host of reading methods has arisen. The image that I have for the liberation movement is a large rain forest with a huge canopy. Many life forms co-exist and flourish in this realm—colorful birds, well-adapted insects, mammals, and rodents. Different species of trees and shrubs provide medicine that can heal human diseases, replenish the humus, produce new generations of plant life, and provide food and shelter for the animals and insects within. All these life forms are unique and interdependent on each other. This old forest provides a space for diverse life forms to exist and thrive.

Under the canopy of liberation theology and hermeneutics, diverse reading approaches are being developed that enrich our interpretation and the meaning of the biblical texts. Methods such as contextual criticism, feminist readings, ideological criticism, postcolonial hermeneutics, and diasporic reading of the Bible are among those that can be gathered under liberation hermeneutics. Reading approaches from specific ethnic, racial perspectives and experiences can also be gathered under this canopy. The newer reading methods operate from a stance that there is no objective, value-free production or reading of texts. Texts are produced in particular contexts for particular intended audiences, and when they are read subsequently, the readers bring themselves and their contexts to the production of meaning.

ASIAN AMERICAN HERMENEUTICS

Asian American hermeneutics (AAH) are produced by persons who consciously identify themselves as Asians in America and/or Americans of Asian decent, but not all readings produced by Asian Americans can be designated as AAH. Readers and scholars may choose to use historical-critical methods or other forms of reading methods. My understanding of AAH is that it is based on Asian American experience and history in North America. AAH is still a relatively new endeavor. Two recent volumes that deal specifically with Asian American hermeneutics are *The Bible in Asian America* (*Semeia* 90–91), edited by Tat-siong Benny Liew and Gale A. Yee (2002); and *Ways of Being, Ways of Reading: Asian American Biblical Interpretation*, edited by Mary Foskett and Jeffrey Kah-Jin Kuan (2006). Like our Asian counterparts, AAH is contextual and highly diverse. The progressive reading of the Bible resists traditional interpretations that uphold the status quo, justify the maintaining of oppressive systems, and protect hierarchical and patriarchal structures at the expense of women, the poor, and the disenfranchised.

First, who are we? The term "Asian Americans" covers persons who are of Asian descent. She could be Indian, Pakistani, Tamil, Indonesian, Vietnamese, Chinese, Korean, or Japanese, to name just a few. She or her ancestors came from a continent that is diverse in its ethnic groups, cultural values, and religious beliefs and practices. Asians have been in the United States for more than two hundreds years and have made significant contributions to the building of this country. Students and merchants were welcomed at the beginning; then laborers were brought in to build railroads and work the gold mines. Congress quickly enacted laws to restrict Chinese immigration. The Chinese Exclusion Act of 1882 was the first anti-immigrant law based on ethnicity. Chinese men were not permitted to bring wives into the United States; those who stayed in China Towns essentially formed bachelor societies. Laws were also enacted to keep Chinese immigrants from taking jobs that white settlers wanted. These "Chinamen" were permitted to do only labor-intensive work that was deemed too low for white folk, such as agriculture, laundry, and being domestic servants. The Asians who came to this country endured tremendous hardship, humiliation, and racial and economic discrimination. A Chinese phrase that aptly describes their lot is "eating bitterness." Yet they endured, and their tenacity paved the way for future generations.

The term "Asian American" grew out of the pan-Asian movement as a unifier to boost political clout after the Vincent Chin incident. Chin was a twenty-seven-year-old Chinese American industrial draftsman in Detroit, Michigan. On 19 June 1982, the day before he was to get married, he was beaten to death with a baseball bat by two autoworkers who mistook him for Japanese. The autoworkers blamed Japanese carmakers for taking jobs away from American workers. The two perpetrators did not bother to find out what ethnic group Chin belonged to. They searched him out and killed him in front of a McDonald's. Though there were plenty of witnesses to the incident, the judge determined that the two white autoworkers, Ronald Ebens and Michael Nitz, were not the type of persons who should be in prison, so he sentenced them to two years' probation and $3,700 in fines each. The perpetrators never served a day in prison for murdering Vincent Chin. This event galvanized the Asian American communities into action and impressed on them the importance of unifying as a political force. Christine Ho reported at least two other cases of killing similar to Vincent Chin's had occurred. In July 1989, Jim Min Hai Loo was mistaken as Vietnamese and killed in Raleigh, North Carolina; then in April 1997, Kuan Chung Kao was shot to death by San Francisco police who assumed that, by holding a six-foot-long wooden stick, he must have been a martial arts expert and posed a threat to their safety (Ho). These killings were racially motivated.

Asian Americans are considered as perpetual foreigners even when their families have been in the United States for many generations. White immigrants from Europe and Russia can easily blend into the society. They are not as likely to be asked where they came from or be rounded up as illegal immigrants. Immigrants who do not have white skin could not fully integrate and be accepted in the same way. A common experience of Asian Americans is the questioning of where they came from. Maya Lin, the architect for the Vietnam Veterans Memorial, was born and raised in Athens, Ohio. When strangers asked her where she is from, she would answer, "Ohio." Inevitably, the stranger would insist, "No, no, but where are you from?" Even though Michelle Kwan was born in the United States, when she lost in a skating competition to a teammate, the sports announcer shouted excitedly, "American beat Kwan! American beat Kwan!" Such experiences are repeated a thousand times a day and remind us that we are perpetual foreigners.

Another issue that Asian Americans face is the myth of "yellow peril." Asians and, more recently, Middle Easterners must prove themselves twice as loyal as the average American. If there is any suggestion that one Asian may be a spy for a foreign country, all Asians immediately become suspected of disloyalty. For example, Wen Ho Lee, a naturalized U.S. citizen from Taiwan, was a scientist at the Los Alamos Nuclear Laboratory. In December 1999 he was accused of spying for the People's Republic of China. After nine months in prison waiting for his indictment, he pleaded guilty to a lesser charge of copying sensitive files and was released because federal authorities admitted that there was no evidence that Lee passed information to a foreign country. Co-workers who also copied files were never charged or arrested.

Asian Americans are expected to live into the stereotype that white society places on them. We are supposed to be smart, hardworking, geeks, socially awkward, passive; we are good workhorses but not management material. Asian American women are supposed to be the idealized Asian woman: exotic, feminine, the Madame Butterflies, the Suzie Wongs, the China dolls. When we do not act according to the prescribed script, we are castigated as inferior versions of the "authentic" natives (R. Chow 2002, 107–17). Chinese elders even taunt younger Chinese Americans as "bamboo sticks" that are closed on both ends. They would laugh at the younger generation as being unable to communicate effectively in Chinese language or American English, nor able to understand the cultures of the homeland or the adopted country (Ngan 2006, 72). We are not American enough, nor are we Chinese enough. We live in the space-between.

The sense of being an "other" and of belonging neither here nor there is a common experience of many immigrants, including Latino immigrants. Fernando Segovia first formulated the way of reading the Bible as immigrants as a "hermeneutics of the diaspora." It is a hermeneutics of "otherness" and "engagement" of both the text and the readers (1995b, 65–72). Diasporic hermeneutics is another way of reading that comes under the canopy of the liberation movement.

For me, a Chinese American woman, a first-generation immigrant who lives in the diaspora in the United States, the experience of colonialism, the internalization of Euro-American superiority and male dominance, and the reality of being an "other" who is on "racial display" (Yee 2006, 155) all produced the lens through which I read. Issues on racial justice and equality (Loury 2002, 136–41), immigrant rights, economic justice, gender equality, and inclusive diversity are important to me. For me, then, biblical interpretations that reinscribe bondage or subjugation of human beings need to be reread and reinterpreted. My intention is not to advocate reading in every which way or deny that some texts are difficult to interpret positively. Readings that bolster the status quo at the expense of the poor and the oppressed should be suspect of the veracity of the meaning. The world behind the text and the world of the text continue to be essential elements for our understanding of the sociohistorical contexts of its reception and production, but I am also interested in making meaning for the present, to look for what healing words the text may speak to my community.

I resonate with Musa Dube's *talitha cum* hermeneutics and Ada María Isasi-Díaz's *mujerista* hermeneutics, both of which aim for justice and liberation. The Gospel of Luke recorded that, when Jesus started his ministry, he read from the scroll of Isaiah: "The Spirit of the Lord is upon me, because he has anointed me to bring good news to the poor. He has sent me to proclaim release to the captives and recovery of sight to the blind, to let the oppressed go free, to proclaim the year of the Lord's favor" (Luke 4:18–19). In Isa 61:1d, the phrase is "to proclaim liberty to the captives." The word "liberty" (דרור) in the Hebrew Bible is used with passages that deal primarily with the release of the Sabbath Year or Jubilee Year. The liberty that is proclaimed extends beyond social, political freedom. It is economic freedom from debt and want, the freedom to be one's own person, the freedom from social structures that bind and maim, and the freedom to live life more abundantly.

Many Asian Americans have fared well in American society through educational opportunities and securing good jobs. The same cannot be said of our fellow immigrants who toil in stifling garment sweatshops or ethnic restaurants, immigrants who work sixteen to eighteen hours a day, seven days a week, immigrants who are ghettoized due to lack of language skills and education. Immigrants like these would welcome the rereading of the parables as suggested by Luise Schottroff and Ada María Isasi-Díaz. The traditional reading of the parables is an allegorized reading that always equates kings, rich men, and landowners with God. Even when the human characters in the parable act in arbitrary and demeaning ways toward others, an interpretation is often sought to justify why the king/rich man/landowner was right in how he acted because he is supposed to be the God-figure. How ironic that we biblical scholars strive to avoid allegorical interpretation of Scripture, yet when it comes to parables, we take an allegorized reading without question. If the parables are read as written, some of them can indeed be claimed as "horror stories" (Schottroff).

Immigrants who labor at menial, low-paying jobs could relate better to the parable of the vineyard owner and the day laborers (Matt 20:1–16) if it is seen through the eyes of the day laborers. The insults and mistreatment from the vineyard owner are humiliating experiences that immigrant workers know first-hand from the business owners for whom they work—docked paychecks, trumped up penalties, miscounted hours—and then to be chided that their work is not good enough. Immigrant workers often have to bite their tongues and apologize even when they did nothing wrong. Any hint of defiance would mean the end of the job and the risk of hunger and homelessness. They would "swallow a dead cat" by admitting to be at fault. For immigrant workers like these, they are "eating bitterness." I can hear the cheers rise from these workers when the day laborer in the parable talks back to the vineyard owner and stands up for his dignity. He would be the hero for the oppressed workers. No more kowtowing to the master. How differently would these immigrant workers experience this parable!

An Asian American liberation hermeneutics must address the social, economic injustice that immigrants face in this country. Many are paid far below the minimum wage for their labor. These are the poor and oppressed in our society, and we participate directly in their oppression. We enjoy the goods and services these immigrant workers provide, yet they are invisible to us. They do back-breaking work harvesting crops in the field; they toil behind locked doors and barred windows in garment sweatshops; they cook and clean in hot greasy kitchens; and they work into the wee hours of the night cleaning office buildings—but we do not see them and do not consider their plight. What does the Bible have to say about such exploitation? In the book of Amos, the rich folks of Samaria were indicted for abusing the poor and vulnerable. They sold people into slavery, possessed their property, and imposed fines on those who could not afford to pay (2:6–8). The rich women of Samaria contributed to the oppression by their incessant clamoring for more goods and more wine (4:1). Are we that different from the rich Israelites?

Liberation hermeneutics may not be as welcomed and accepted in Asian American Christian communities as we would hope. Many Asian American Christians are very conservative and tend to read the Bible literally. Even college graduates, scientists, and engineers in many Asian American churches set aside their scientific understanding of the world and embrace the notion of the inerrancy of the Bible. One of the conclusions of Hans de Wit's project bears this out. He states that:

> In contrast to what is sometimes suggested by liberation hermeneuticians, it appears that there is no significant correlation between social status (poverty) and the manner of reading and actualizing (liberation praxis). "The poor" read the Bible in diverse ways, in which the church and reading tradition they belong to frequently is much more important than their social status. (57)

Apparently, the social status and educational level of many Asian Americans are also not significant factors on how Asian American Christians read the Bible. The challenge this presents to the Asian American community was sounded by Jeffrey Kuan (2002, 54). Most Asian American Christians accept interpretation from their own pastors and from white conservative American pastors and commentators. The reading is often precritical and tends to be pietistic and devotional. Little consideration is given to the social context, the historical period, or the production of the Bible. They shun critical reading because it poses a threat to their faith.

The attitude that many Asian American Christians have toward the reading of the Bible is formed by Asian cultural values. In East and Southeast Asia, Confucian ethics continue to have a strong hold on everything from family structure, parent-sibling-spousal-friend relationships, and business dealings to relation to governing powers and more. The hierarchical structure that Confucius espoused set up a rigid structure that dictates how each person is supposed to act in this schema. Reference and obedience to persons in authority is a key component to keep society running smoothly, with those on the upper rings of the social pyramid wielding all the power. Translating this social structure into the church means that pastors, who more often than not are males, have the greatest say in what is the truth. When a pastor proclaims that God created in a literal seven-day week, it would be incredibly disrespectful to doubt an authority figure who represents God, and this questioning may even endanger one's salvation. Doubting is considered a lack of faith and is displeasing to God. If God is presented in Bible studies and sermons as an exacting and punishing deity, who would dare incite God's wrath?

This is no doubt a very unhealthy faith life, and persons under such a structure can be said to be captives. But do we believe Jesus' word that the truth will set us free? When interpretations bind, suppress, and oppress, can that be the true meaning of the text? Can that be the truth? For some Asian Americans, the oppression they experience is economic; for others, the oppression is social and spiritual. For many Asian American Christians, liberty comes when they are set free of spiritual and psychological manipulation, free from being forced to become who they are not, and free to define themselves and become the persons whom God has created them to be.

The Bible is very important for Asian American Christians because the story of God's people is our story (Kim 1994, 163). We so identified ourselves with the Israelites that our unbelieving relatives and neighbors are sometimes considered as "Gentiles." For many who read only the surface of the text, the patriarchs and the Israelites could do no wrong because they were the chosen people. For them, the New Testament church was the perfect church. The tendency is to try to re-create a world from two or more thousand years ago. Unfortunately, we pick and choose what we want to re-create, and the preferred selections reinscribe oppressive structures in favor of the powerful. We want to retain the cultural values from an ancient time, yet keep all the conveniences of a modern, technological society.

For many evangelicals, the mandate of evangelism is to save souls; when this is combined with a false dichotomy between "real gospel" and "social gospel," the result is an "unfleshed" spirituality (Bachmann, 125). A denomination such as the Southern Baptist Convention has moved its missionary work entirely to evangelism, that is, spreading of the gospel through preaching and church planting. Earlier mission work in agriculture, medicine, and education has been eliminated. It is not enough, however, to save the soul and neglect the body, nor is it enough to have orthodoxy without orthopraxis. Saint Francis is quoted as saying, "Preach the gospel at all times; if necessary, use words." The book of James states that

> What good is it, my brothers and sisters, if you say you have faith but do not have works? Can faith save you? If a brother or sister is naked and lacks daily food, and one of you say to them, "Go in peace; keep warm and eat your fill," and yet you do not supply their bodily needs, what is the good of that? So faith by itself, if it has no works, is dead. (2:14–17).

The Bible always couples faith and praxis. Those who claim to know God are supposed "to do righteousness and justice" (Gen 18:19). Right relationships are demonstrated through right behavior. To love God and neighbors is expressed by loving acts toward God and neighbors. Adherents of Asian American hermeneutics, like those of other liberation hermeneutics, read for liberation and advocacy. Though we cannot speak for the oppressed, we must stand with them and listen them to speech. We must speak up for every person's dignity and worth. We must lend physical support and aid to those in need. We must work beyond our own ethnic groups, even beyond North America. We live in a global village and must acquire a global vision for how to end injustice and poverty, to promote economic equality, and to be peacemakers in the world. Asian American hermeneutics share some common characteristics with other liberation hermeneutics: (1) we read with the poor and oppressed and stand in solidarity with them; (2) we read for life-enhancing power and against death-dealing forces; (3) we bring cultural contribution to our reading; (4) we read with an awareness of our history as peoples living in a diaspora in North America; (5) we read with a hermeneutics of otherness and engagement (Segovia 1995b, 65–72); and (6) we emphasize praxis that brings justice and equity.

Asian American Christians have a prophetic role in calling Asian American communities as well as the wider society to account. Those of us who have the luxury of "doing" Asian American hermeneutics are often in a privileged class. We are usually academics who speak, write, and travel. What about the poor and oppressed among us? Will their voices be heard, not through us speaking for them, but through their own voices? We cannot ignore our poorer brothers and sisters, nor can we avoid confronting our own complacency in their suffering. Like our Latin American counterparts, we must see injustice and exploitation for the evil that it is. We need a conversion experience much like that of Archbishop Oscar Romero of El Salvador, who went from a sheltered, bookish priest to one who became immersed in the pain of his people. We need to meet poor Asian Americans and other immigrant workers, to hear their stories empathetically in order to understand their plight. We need to hear how they read the Bible, if they read the Bible, and learn to see with their eyes.

CONCLUSION

Gerald West reminded us of Jesus' words, "You always have the poor with you" (Matt 26:11; Mark 14:7; John 12:8). Liberation hermeneutics is done at the service of the poor and oppressed of society. As long as there are the poor among us, the task of liberation hermeneutics is not finished. Ada María Isasi-Díaz said it well, "no one is truly liberated unless everyone is liberated" (quoted from the original abstract). The strength of a chain is measured by its weakest link. We cannot abandon the cause of the poor, for their cause is our cause and their welfare is intertwined with our welfare.

I find it helpful to look at liberation as the salvation of the whole person in every aspect of life. The Hebrew word *shalom* expresses this wholeness best. It is not just "peace," as in the cessation of conflict; it is not just health in the body. The translation of "peace" does not adequately express the encompassing nature of *shalom*. It is healing of the whole person, the wellness of body, mind, and spirit, of life circumstances and living environment, of relationship with God and other persons, of liberation from all that binds and kills. It is wellness of not only one person but whole communities and extends to the wellness of the entire world. To paraphrase the quote from Ada María Isasi-Díaz, "No one is whole until everyone is whole." Gerald West notes that, ten years after the end of apartheid in South Africa, the issues of liberation continue in other forms. For his country, it is currently unemployment and the HIV/AIDS crisis. As time and social issues change, liberation hermeneutics will adapt dynamically to address the issue of liberation for all. The canopy of the liberation movement is huge; it has room for more. The work of liberation hermeneutics is not done until everyone has a place under the sun.

LIBERATION HERMENEUTICS: A PASTORAL JOURNEY

Mortimer Arias

My response to this impressive selection of "liberation hermeneutics" around the world today is one of acclamation, appropriation, and interaction, sharing some questions that came up along the reading, out of my own experience, as a pastoral reader and interpreter of the biblical message and as a practical theologian engaged in theological education, both in Latin America and for a decade in the United States.

An outstanding feature of this volume is the emphasis on the participation of people in a liberating reading of the biblical text, from their own reality and in "interaction with one another." The strength of this unique volume is to surface the great richness of the voice of the "oppressed," in different contexts and ways: cultural identity suppression, socioeconomic-political oppression, racial and gender discrimination, academic and ecclesial traditions, and so on. It looks as if the authors consider their perspective and their work on the text as "liberation hermeneutics."

The struggle for human liberation has always been the need and the challenge of every generation. But why the Bible? The non-Christians who struggle for liberation do not go to the Bible for it. This volume of Semeia Studies, as it could not be otherwise, is about "Christian" hermeneutics—from Christians and for Christians. As Christians—even though the vision and the intention is inclusive and universalistic—the authors assume a starting point, an obligatory reference, namely, Jesus the Christ. Implicitly or explicitly.

THEOLOGICAL PRESUPPOSITIONS

The New Testament itself can be seen as a rereading or reading back to the Old Testament from the perspective of Jesus and the Christ event, as experienced by his followers and the early hermeneutical communities (i.e., Luke 24). The Gospel of John makes explicit the Christ-centered source of Christian hermeneutics, projecting it to the future with Jesus' promise of the *parákletos*, the "Intercessor, "the Advocate," the "Spirit of truth," "the Holy Spirit." In the Fourth Gospel, "to teach," "to bring to mind," "to guide," "to convince" are some of the verbs of the hermeneutical work of the Spirit: "The Holy Spirit will teach you everything and will call to mind everything I have told you" (John 14:26). The apostle Paul makes it explicit, once and again, that his rereading of the "Scriptures" is in the perspective of the crucifixion and the resurrection of Jesus Christ and that his interpretation is done "in Christ" and "in the Spirit" (1 Cor 1; 2; 15; Rom 6; 8; see also Col 3). It is christological and pneumatological hermeneutics!

Here comes the inevitable question for this reader: Where does Christ and the Holy Spirit enter into our "hermeneutical circle"? Is Jesus Christ the key to our "liberation hermeneutics"? Is there a place for the Holy Spirit in our interpretation? I believe it does, in any Christian hermeneutics, particularly in the ones represented here. There is, however, an aseptic way of not making our theological presuppositions explicit in our academic hermeneutics. I never found a mention of the hermeneutical role of the Holy Spirit—the Divine Hermeneut!—in liberation hermeneutics or any other. ...

In this volume of interpretations there is evidence that Jesus, and Jesus as the Christ, is the starting point and the central or final reference—implicitly or explicitly. The most touching one, for me, is the first essay on Kimpa Vita, the African woman who was crucified in 1706 because "she insisted that Jesus, his mother, and his disciples were black," a proclamation that eventually led to the launching of the African Indigenous Churches, which resisted both colonialism and patriarchy (Dube, 138). Four outstanding contemporary African women interpreters (Oduyoye, Madipoane, Dube, Okure) illustrate the *talitha cum* hermeneutics in the sub-Sahara region, looking for a healing that includes physical wounds, gender oppression, international relations, class, race, ethnic, age, and spiritual and environmental relations. Their "hermeneutics of life," while "recognizing other Christ figures," concludes that:

> Jesus of Nazareth, by counterculture relations he established with women, has become for us the Christ, the anointed one who liberates ... companion, friend, teacher, and true Child of Women.... Jesus is Christ—truly woman, for only God is the Compassionate One. (Dube, 141)

LATIN AMERICAN LIBERATION HERMENEUTICS

Latin American "liberation hermeneutics," born out of the "grassroots Christian communities" more than thirty years ago, is considered by Hans de Wit "the mother of all genitive hermeneutics," which discovered "a new hermeneutical space: the meeting between the people and the Bible." Since its beginning in the 1970s, according to de Wit, it was

> a completely new and extremely fertile creative period ... the most impres-
> sive examples of grassroots reading of the Bible ... with an enormous feeling
> of urgency and optimism ... a fundamental revolution ... militant herme-
> neutics.... The "people" is the new subject of this hermeneutics.... this
> involves liberation praxis as the access to the kerygma of the biblical texts....
> The text becomes a process.... the original text is interpreted and continued
> in a new event.... Texts are not objects but places of encounter. (41, 43, 45,
> 44, 60)

In de Wit's assessment, "The extent to which application or appropriation of biblical texts is successful *now* is not a standard for the quality of the exege-sis" (49). Does this not thereby give the hermeneutic circulation a closed and utilitarian nature? An observer of Latin American theology and hermeneutics for years, de Wit "revisits the fundamental presuppositions" of this libera-tion hermeneutics "to test some of its insights and pretensions." He makes an acute criticism of what he considers—from his European and academic perspective—the "pitfalls" of this hermeneutics, as represented by some of the leading Bible interpreters during a long period of three decades. It calls to the attention of this reader the absence of the one who articulated and developed more systematically than any other the "hermeneutical circle," namely, the late Uruguayan theologian Juan Luis Segundo, a pioneer both in praxis (with interdisciplinary groups in his native country since the end of the 1960s) and in academic theological and hermeneutical work.[1] Segundo would have something to say to de Wit's probing question.

I am a grateful beneficiary of this liberation hermeneutics done in Latin America during all this time. Of course, I would not taken all that has been done and said in the name of this "liberation hermeneutics." Actually, I share some of the critical observations made by de Wit in the area of textual inter-pretations, and surely I can subscribe to his plea for a plurality of methods in liberation hermeneutics. But I also can say that, after this process of "libera-tive rereading" of the Scriptures, we will never be the same, in terms of critical and committed reading of the Scriptures from our own reality.

---

1. Juan Luis Segundo (1925–96) was one of the pioneers in Bible study and theo-logical reflection, starting from praxis in the late 1960s, as shown in his series of *The Artisans of a New Humanity* (1974a–e). His books, originally in Spanish, *De la sociedad a la Teología* (1970) and *Liberación de la Teología* (1975), were more systematically devel-oped in his courses as a visiting professor at Harvard Divinity School and published in English (1976).

At this point, it is proper to stress that this reading and interpretation of the Scriptures in Latin America has been very much centered in Jesus and the Gospels, as can be seen in the theological literature coming up during the last four decades in the region.

CHRIST-CENTERED HERMENEUTICS

To begin, let us remember the early and well-known work of the Nicaraguan poet Ernesto Cardenal, *The Gospel from Solentiname* (1975–82), a recording of the reading of the Scriptures with the *campesinos* of a remote village in the archipelago of Solentiname. The community reading was on the Gospels, and Jesus was the center of their conversations, from their own situation.

Most of the Latin American theologians in that creative period of the 1970s have written their own Christologies: for instance, Leonardo Boff, from Brazil, *Jesus Cristo Libertador: Ensaio de cristologia crítica para o nosso tempo* (1972; 1978); Jon Sobrino, from El Salvador, *Cristología desde América Latina: Esbozo a partir del seguimiento del Jesús histórico* (1976; 1978); Hugo Echegaray, from Peru, *La práctica de Jesús* (1981; 1984); Juan Luis Segundo, from Uruguay, a three-volume superb work on *El hombre de hoy ante Jesús de Nazaret* (1982; 1984–88), among those translated from Spanish and Portuguese into English.[2] Probably there was a sort of interaction between hermeneutics, opening the way of access to the historical Jesus, and the academic work on the historical Jesus, providing a decisive key for hermeneutics (Schuurman 1977).

While writing this response, we received the news of the condemnation of Jon Sobrino to silence (prohibition of teaching and censorship of his publications) by Pope Benedict XVI (ex-Cardinal Ratzinger) and the Sacred Doctrine College (ex-Inquisition), precisely because Sobrino's Christology is not acceptable to the Vatican. Sobrino is a surviving member of the group of Jesuits assassinated during the military rule in El Salvador. He joins now with Leonardo Boff, Ivone Guevara, and other Latin Americans in the club of the silenced ones in the Roman Catholic Church. Since the times of Jesus—of Paul and Luther, for that matter—hermeneutics has become a dangerous job.

Reflecting on the relevancy of the historical Jesus quest in Latin America, Lambert Schuurman pointed out, back in 1977, the importance of Albert Nolan's *Jesus before Christianity: The Gospel of Liberation* (1976), coming from a peripheral country, South Africa, with its emphasis on a "more concrete and particular historical Jesus," as something to look at by the Latin American

---

2. See also an early collection on the "images of Christ in Latin America" (Bonino 1977).

interpreters. The surprising thing is that, ten years later, Gerald West, dealing with Albert Nolan's contribution to contextual theology in South Africa
(1986; 1988), identified him as one "who drew on elements of Latin American
Liberation Theology and re-contextualized and popularized them in South
Africa"! An unexpected bridge between South and South, back and forth. ...

Anyway, it is evident that liberation hermeneutics, in our part of the
world, has been built upon the historical Jesus, profiting from the scholars'
work for decades on the historical-critical method. In the last twenty years,
however, a network of biblical interpreters (*biblistas*) has been active and
productive, with a remarkable body of original material coming out of hermeneutical teachers from various theological schools from Latin America and
the Caribbean and published regularly in *RIBLA: Revista de interpretación
bíblica latino-americana* (http://www.ribla.org/). With three volumes a year,
RIBLA has already reached number 54. Some of the authors are among the
well known names, such as Pablo Richard, Milton Schwantes, Pablo R. Andiñach, Jorge Pixley, Néstor Míguez, Elsa Tamez, the late J. Severino Croatto,
together with a whole new generation of interpreters from different countries,
cultures, and theological orientations, with a growing number of women hermeneutical teachers, all of them using the best resources of the discipline and
great freedom and creativity in interpretation from Latin American, Caribbean, black, women and other perspectives.

Paul as an Anti-imperial Figure

Theodore W. Jennings Jr. begins his powerful presentation on "Paul against
Empire: Then and Now" with the affirmation that "[t]he question of a liberative reading of biblical texts has its origin in Latin America and, not
infrequently, has been developed in contradistinction to the traditional hermeneutical strategies of Europe and North America" (147). Interestingly,
notwithstanding, Jennings shows how today "the work of the Paul and Politics
Group of the SBL in the USA has produced considerable clarification of the
way in which Paul may be understood as developing counterimperial perspective in the context of the Roman Empire" (quoted from the original abstract).
Another discussion "has been underway for some time in contemporary continental thought that deals with Paul as a political thinker of importance for
contemporary radical politics."

His conclusion could be shared by most Latin American hermeneutical
colleagues:

> The acceleration over the intervening years of the rule of what have been
> called turbo capitalism or casino capitalism, together with the military

hegemony of the United States and its apparent determination to make the globe subservient to its own interests of certain classes of Americans, has evoked images of a new global empire.... It is in this context that renewed liberative (and especially counterimperial) reading of the Bible assumes something of a global significance, and it is here that the figure of Paul has come to have particular salience. (166)

Next to Jesus and the Gospels, the rereading of Paul in the context of the empire is crucial to our own hermeneutics in Latin America, from the inside of our imperial and globalization context. Two of the leading interpreters of the new generation, Elsa Tamez and Néstor Míguez, wrote their dissertations on Paul in the context of the Roman Empire (Miguez 1986; Tamez 1989).[3] RIBLA has had Paul in its hermeneutical agenda once and again. Issue 20 (1995) was dedicated totally to "Paul of Tarsus: Faith Militant," issue 48 (2004) to "Peoples Confronting the Empire."

In his essay "After the Empire: To Sustain the Biblical Hope in the Midst of Oppression," Néstor Míguez insists on the need to rebuilt, to reconstruct, the human subjectivity free from the empire hegemony." "The Empire of today, the postmodern 'empire,' manifests its power of oppression through the colonization of desire ... the colonization of subjectivity.... There is only one superpower ... but the economic center of postmodern civilization is, obviously, the total market.... The late financial capitalism is a net, a net fishing and destroying the resources of the world ... with the military power and the use of violence (and intelligence services).... The terror created by this imperial state is the worst terrorism (Miguez 2004b).

FEMINIST HERMENEUTICS

I would like to express in this comment my debt, my gratitude, and my tribute to feminist hermeneutics. For a quarter of a century I have benefited from feminist hermeneutics from north and south. I cannot read the Bible without women's eyes any longer. Thanks to God and to my sisters.

Again, the fifty-four issues of RIBLA give witness and offer resources for an inclusive perspective in the reading of the Scriptures, with the most original hermeneutical work done by women interpreters, opening up their critical and visionary perspective on life and lo cotidiano (everyday life and environment), the body, the community, gender and culture, and doing it

---

3. "El Imperio y los Pobres en el Tiempo Neotestamentario," RIBLA 5–6; Contra Toda Condena: La Justificación por la Fe desde los Excluidos, San José, C.R., DEI, 1991; see also "¿Cómo Entender la Carta a los Romanos?" RIBLA 20:75–97.

with all the resources of contemporary exegesis and hermeneutics. Some issues of *RIBLA* were totally written and edited by women interpreters, such as 15: "By Women Hands"; 37, "Gender in Everyday Life"; 41, "Women and Sexist Violence"; and 46, Mary."[4]

If I understand it correctly, liberation hermeneutics done by women in Latin America is not merely "feminist" or exclusively gender hermeneutics. It seems to be in line with the affirmation of Ada María Isasi-Díaz in "A *Mujerista* Hermeneutics of Justice and Human Flourishing": "*Mujerista* hermeneutics also seeks to make as specific as possible that of which liberation consist for Latinas, and the specifics of human flourishing for us as an oppressed group within the most powerful country in the world, *while always considering that our liberation cannot be at the expense of any other group, for no one is truly liberated unless everyone is liberated*" (quoted from the original abstract, emphasis added).

In the present volume we have an example of contemporary exegesis in Latin America by Mercedes L. García Bachmann in her analysis of the text of Isa 58, where the self-servicing religious piety of the oppressors is denounced in very strong terms.

Postliberation Hermeneutics

This volume of Semeia Studies allows us to pay due attention to what might be considered a "postliberation" situation, through the experience of South Africa and Germany.

South Africa

Gerald West, "after ten years of liberation, ten years of democracy, and ten years of the new Constitution," confirms that there was a liberation in South Africa, but not the final one:

> We have undergone a fundamental transformation in South Africa, one that can appropriately be designated as "liberation."... We "are, however, a society in transition, hopefully moving toward the full realization of these ideals" [nonracism, nonsexism, human dignity, equality, advance of human rights].... we still suffer from massive problems: poverty, unemployment, crime and corruption, HIV/AIDS, and lack of basic resources. (15)

---

4. *RIBLA* 15: "Por Manos de Mujer," Santiago de Chile, 1993; 37: "El Género en lo Cotidiano," Quito, Ecuador, 200/3; 41: "Las Mujeres y la Violencia Sexista"; 46: "María," Quito, Ecuador, 2003/3.

Is there any further role, then, for liberation theologies and hermeneutics in South Africa? Gerald West's own answer is, "while we no longer use the language of liberation, many of the concerns of liberation hermeneutics remain" (quoted from the original abstract).

The impressive bibliography listed about these topics looks like an answer to the question too: the fact of a constant mushrooming of theologies and hermeneutics—black, African, African women, local, cultural, contextual, and HIV-positive theologies.

GERMANY AND OLD EUROPE

Erhard Gerstenberger reviews the relationships of Christianity and European society in the last centuries, up to the times of the Nazi regime, the Communist rule in Eastern Germany, and after the Reunification. The author says that, in times of resistance, "the most powerful 'weapon' of dissenting Christians was, in fact, the Bible itself" (72; the Gospels, the Prophets, apocalyptic texts). Then "Christians took the lead in fighting peacefully for freedom.... Reunification was achieved among others by Christian grass-roots movement" (77). Also in contemporary Germany, "a biblical, prophetic, and Jesuanic wrestling with unjust conditions of life is underway everywhere to bring relief and hope to those who suffer.... Feminist interpretation of the Bible and the emancipation of women ... has been the most revolutionary development after the war" (80).

Furthermore, Gerstenberger is convinced that "critical reflection is hardly possible without harking back to the just causes enshrined in one's tradition, which for Christians include the kingdom of God, the preaching of Jesus Christ, and the suffering of the martyrs and saints.... Christian liberationists have to recur to the Bible and to read it as a guidebook in the valleys of death" (61).

His final words reflect the history of his own people and his personal understanding of the limits of liberation hermeneutics:

> situations of bondage and breaking bondages vary a great deal. Neither is there just one type of liberation envisioned in biblical testimonies. Mental, intellectual, emotional, and spiritual fetters are as real as economical, political, and legal ones.... Being human, though, we shamefully recognize the insufficiencies of all our liberation attempts. Further, as we study history, it becomes clear enough that successful strategies of liberation very soon may become oppressive themselves. Revolutions do swallow their own protagonists. (84)

LIBERATION FROM HERMENEUTICS?

So, it appears that not only society needs liberation (which, historically, is never complete) but hermeneutics needs to be liberated once and again! The amazing variety of hermeneutical perspectives shown in this volume, from different contexts and options, raises the question if "liberation hermeneutics" is not, after all, *the liberation from hermeneutics*! This is apparent in the representative selection we have before us. In most cases it is a matter of liberation from some former type of hermeneutics: traditional, missionary, European, American, cultural, male, academic, ecclesial hermeneutics.

One thing is clear: the Bible is not a manual for liberation. The Bible is more like the dry "bones of Joseph" (Gen 50:25; Exod 13:19) taken up by the people of Israel, while escaping from slavery and moving toward liberation and the Promised Land: a memory, a history, a witness, an interpellant, a vocation, a mission. Even more, the Bible is food and direction for the pilgrim people moving towards the reign of God.

WHILE LIBERATION IS NOT HERE

What has the Bible to say to us while liberation does not arrive? It is a fact of history that the faithful communities, and those working for human liberation, have to live most of their lives and for a whole generation without the coming of the liberative event. The Bible is not a handbook for liberation. Rather, the Bible has the word of assurance about God's love, God's presence in every human life, God's forgiveness and consolation in times of defeat and loss, and God's plan for humanity and for the world—the reign of God (Arias 1984).

The Scriptures are a source of hope and vision and strength to survive....

A PILGRIM PEOPLE AND A BOOK FOR PILGRIMS

We are part of a long and suffering line of a pilgrim people, always moving from captivity to liberation and fulfillment. Technical or partisan hermeneutics is not enough. We need the spirituality of survival and struggle, of love and hope, and solidarity in liberation.

Of course, the Bible—the text—has its own integrity. What is the first rule for hermeneutics? In the experience of the hermeneutical community (from the writers to the interpreters to the present readers), Scripture not only supports and inspires our actions, but also questions us and confronts us and our own expectations and commitments.[5]

---

5. Juan Luis Segundo has four rules for hermeneutics: (1) commitment to change and

The freedom to interpret and to appropriate the Scriptures is certainly ours (a gift that becomes a right), but it is also part of our outfit for the pilgrimage a sense of belonging. And, yes, accountability. Accountability toward the Book and accountability toward "the people of the Book." We are a pilgrim people with a Book for pilgrims.

It has been an unexpected and undeserved privilege to be invited to offer a "reader's response." To read carefully through this massive manuscript on liberation hermeneutics was not an easy task for this reader, but it has been a learning and illuminating experience. I am grateful for that. Surely, the readers of Semeia Studies will benefit from this daring effort by the editors.

---

improve the world; (2) awareness of ideological mechanisms; (3) turning theology into a serviceable tool for orthopraxis; and (4) "we must salvage the sovereign liberty of the Word of God if we are to be able to say something that is really creative and liberative in any given situation"(Segundo 1976, 39).

Bibliography

ACHTUS. 2006. Statement on Immigration Reform. Online: http://www.achtus.org/ImmigrationReform.html.

Agamben, Giorgio. 1998. *Homo Sacer: Sovereign Power and Bare Life*. Stanford, Calif.: Stanford University Press.

———. 2000. *Means without End: Notes on Politics*. Translated by Vincenzo Binetti and Cesare Casarino. Minneapolis: University of Minnesota Press.

———. 2005a. *State of Exception*. Translated by Kevin Attell. Chicago: University of Chicago Press.

———. 2005b. *The Time That Remains: A Commentary on Romans*. Stanford, Calif.: Stanford University Press.

Albright, William F. 1940. *From the Stone Age to Christianity; Monotheism and the Historical Process*. Baltimore: Johns Hopkins University Press.

———. 1963. *The Biblical Period from Abraham to Ezra*. New York: Harper & Row.

Alonso Schöckel, Luis, and Cecilia Carniti. 1994. *Salmos I*. Estella, Spain: Verbo Divino.

Alves, Rubem. 1969. *A Theology of Human Hope*. Washington: Corpus Books.

Amoah, Elizabeth, and Mercy A. Oduyoye. 1988. The Christ for African Women. Pages 35–46 in Fabella and Oduyoye 1988.

Andiñach, Pablo. 2006. *El Libro del Éxodo*. Salamanca, Spain: Sígueme.

Anzandula, Gloria. 1987. *La Frontera/Borderlands: The New Mestiza*. San Francisco: Aunt Lute Books.

Arias, Mortimer. 1984. *Announcing the Reign of God: Evangelization and the Subversive Memory of Jesus*. Philadelphia: Augsburg Fortress.

Arul Raja, A. Maria. 2006. Breaking Hegemonic Boundaries: An Intertextual Reading of the Madurai Veeran Legend and Mark's Story of Jesus. Pages 103–11 in *Voices from the Margin: Interpreting the Bible in the Third World*. Edited by Rasiah S. Sugirtharajah. 3rd ed. Maryknoll, N.Y.: Orbis.

Assman, Hugo. 1973. *Teología desde la praxis de liberación*. Salamanca, Spain: Sigueme.

Auffret, Pierre. 1991. "Qui donnera depuis Sion le Salut d'Israel?" Etude structurelle des Psaumes 14 et 53. *BZ* 35:217–30.

Badiou, Alain. 2002. *Ethics: An Essay on the Understanding of Evil*. Translated by Peter Hallward. London: Verso.

———. 2003. *Saint Paul: The Foundation of Universalism*. Translated by Ray Brassier. Stanford, Calif.: Stanford University Press.

──. 2004. *Infinite Thought: Truth and the Return to Philosophy.* Translated by Oliver Feltham and Justin Clemens London: Continuum.

──. 2005. *Being and Event.* Translated by Oliver Feltham. London: Continuum.

Bail, Ulrike, et al., eds. 2006. *Bibel in gerechter Sprache.* Gütersloh: Gütersloher Verlagshaus.

Bailey, Randall C. 1998. The Danger of Ignoring One's Own Cultural Bias in Interpreting the Text. Pages 66–90 in *The Postcolonial Bible.* Edited by Rasiah S. Sugirtharajah. Sheffield: Sheffield Academic Press.

──, ed. 2003. *Yet with a Steady Beat: Contemporary U.S. Afrocentric Biblical Interpretation.* SemeiaSt 42. Atlanta: Society of Biblical Literature.

Bal, Mieke. 1988. *Death and Dissymmetry: The Politics of Coherence in the Book of Judges.* Chicago: University of Chicago Press.

Balabanski, Vicky. 2002. Opening the Closed Door: A Feminist Rereading of the "Wise and Foolish Virgins" (Mt. 25.1–13). Pages 71–97 in Beavis 2002.

Balcomb, Anthony. 1993. *Third Way Theology: Reconciliation, Revolution and Reform in the South African Church.* Pietermaritzburg: Cluster.

Bartlett, John Raymond. 1969. The Land of Seir and the Brotherhood of Edom. *JTS* 20:1–20.

──. 1977. The Brotherhood of Edom. *JSOT* 4:2–27.

Beavis, Mary Ann, ed. 2002. *The Lost Coin: Parables of Women, Work, and Wisdom.* Sheffield: Sheffield Academic Press.

Bediako, Kwabena A. 1995. *Christianity in Africa: The Renewal of a Non-Western Religion.* Edinburgh: Edinburgh University Press; Maryknoll, N.Y.: Orbis.

Bethge, Eberhard. 1967. *Dietrich Bonhöffer: Eine Biographie.* Munich: Kaiser.

Blenkinsopp, Joseph. 2003. *Isaiah 56–66.* AB 19B. New York: Doubleday.

Blunt, Alison, and Gilian Rose, eds. 1994. *Writing Women and Space: Colonial and Postcolonial Geographies.* New York: Gilford.

Boesak, Allan. 1984. *Black and Reformed: Apartheid, Liberation, and the Calvinist Tradition.* Johannesburg: Skotaville.

Boff, Clodovis. 1978. *Teologia e prática.* Petrópolis, Brazil: Vozes.

──. 1980. *Teología de lo político: Sus mediaciones.* Salamanca, Spain: Sígueme.

──. 1987. *Theology and Praxis: Epistemological Foundations.* Maryknoll, N.Y.: Orbis.

Boff, Leonardo. 1972. *Jesus Cristo Libertador: Ensaio de cristologia crítica para o nosso tempo.* Petrópolis, Brazil: Vozes.

──. 1978. *Jesus Christ Liberator: A Critical Christology for Our Time.* Translated by Patrick Hughes. Maryknoll, N.Y.: Orbis.

Bonino, José Miguez. 1975. *Doing Theology in a Revolutionary Situation.* Philadelphia: Fortress.

──. 1976. *Christians and Marxists: The Mutual Challenge to Revolution.* Grand Rapids: Eermans.

──. 1977. *Jesús: Ni vencido ni monarca celestial.* Buenos Aires: Tierra Nueva.

Boureux, Christophe, and Christoph Theobald, eds. 2004. *Original Sin: A Code of Fallibility.* London: SCM.

Brah, Avtar. 2004. Diaspora, Border and Transnational Identities. Pages 613–34 in

Feminist Postcolonial Theory: A Reader. Edited by Reina Lewis and Sara Mills. New York: Routledge.

Brecht, Bertolt. 1967. *Dreigroschenroman*. Vol. 13 of idem, *Gesammelte Werke*. Frankfurt: Suhrkamp.

Bright, John. 1962. *A History of Israel*. London: SCM.

Brockman, Norbert C. 1994. Kimpa Vita (Dona Beatrice) c. 1682–1706: The Antonian Movement Congo/Democratic Republic of Congo/Angola. Online: http://www.dacb.org/stories/congo/kimpa_vita.html.

Brodkin, Karen. 1988. *How Jews Became White Folks and What That Says about Race in America*. New Brunswick, N.J.: Rutgers University Press.

Brueggemann, Walter. 1998. *Isaiah 40–66*. IBC. Louisville: Westminster John Knox.

Brunt, P. A. 1997. Laus Imperii. Pages 25–35 in Horsley 1997b.

Byamugisha, Gideon, et al., eds. 2002. *Journeys of Faith: Church-Based Responses to HIV and AIDS in Three Southern African Countries*. St Albans: TALC.

Cady, Linell E. 1986. Hermeneutics and Tradition: The Role of the Past in Jurisprudence and Theology. *HTR* 79:439–63.

Caputo, John. 1997. *Prayers and Tears of Jacques Derrida: Religion without Religion*. Bloomington: Indiana University Press.

Cardenal, Ernesto. 1975–82. *The Gospel from Solentiname*. Translated by Donald D. Walsh. 4 vols. Maryknoll, N.Y.: Orbis.

———. 1976–78. *Das Evangelium der Bauern von Solentiname*. Translated by Anneliese Schwarzer de Ruiz. Wuppertal: Jugenddienst.

Carter, Warren. 2000. *Matthew and the Margins: A Sociopolitical and Religious Reading*. Maryknoll, N.Y.: Orbis.

Chikane, Frank. 1985. The Incarnation in the Life of the People in Southern Africa. *JTSA* 51:37–50.

Childs, Brevard S. 2001. *Isaiah: A Commentary*. OTL. Louisville: Westminster John Knox.

Chopp, Rebecca. 1986. *The Praxis of Suffering: An Interpretation of Liberation and Political Theologies*. Maryknoll, N.Y.: Orbis.

Chow, John K. 1997. Patronage in Roman Corinth. Pages 104–25 in Horsley 1997b.

Chow, Rey. 2002. *The Protestant Ethnic and the Spirit of Capitalism*. New York: Columbia University Press.

Clarke, Sathianathan. 1998. Paraiyars Ellaiyamman as an Iconic Symbol of Collective Resistance and Emancipatory Mythography. Pages 35–53 in *Religions of the Marginalised: Towards a Phenomenology and the Methodology of Study*. Edited by Gnana Robinson. Delhi: Published for United Theological College, Bangalore, by Indian Society for Promoting Christian Knowledge.

Clévenot, Michel. 1978. *Lectura materialista de la Biblia*. Salamanca, Spain: Sigueme.

Cloete, Gerhard D., and Dirk J. Smit, eds. 1984. *A Moment of Truth: The Confession of the Dutch Reformed Mission Church 1982*. Grand Rapids: Eerdmans.

Cochrane, James R. 1991. Nation-Building: A Socio-theological View. Pages 51–75 in *Building a New Nation*. Edited by Willem S. Vorster. Pretoria: Unisa.

———. 2001. Questioning Contextual Theology. Pages 67–86 in Speckman and Kaufmann 2001c.

Cochrane, James R., and Gerald O. West. 1993. War, Remembrance and Reconstruction. *JTSA* 84:25–40.

Comblin, José. 1985. *Introdução General ao Comentário Bíblico: Lectura da Bíblia na perspectiva dos pobres*. Petrópolis, Brazil: Vozes.

Conrad, Joseph. 1899. *Heart of Darkness*. Edinburgh: Blackwood.

Croatto, José Severino. 1973. *Liberación y libertad*. Buenos Aires: Ediciones Mundo Nuevo.

———. 1978. Liberar a los pobres: Aproximación hermenéutica. Pages 15–28 in *Los pobres: Encuentro y compromiso*. Edited by José Severino Croatto et al. Buenos Aires: ISEDET.

———. 1981a. Befreiung und Freiheit: Biblische Hermeneutik für die "Theologie der Befreiung." Pages 39–59 in *Der Streit um die Theologie der Befreiung*. Vol. 2 of *Lateinamerika: Gesellschaft, Kirche, Theologie*. Edited by Hans-Jürgen Prien. Göttingen: Vandenhoeck & Rupprecht.

———. 1981b. *Exodus: A Hermeneutics of Freedom*. Maryknoll, N.Y.: Orbis.

———. 1984. Hermenêutica e lingüística: A hermenêutica bíblica à luz da semiótica e frente aos métodos histórico-críticos. *EstTeo* 24:214–24

———. 1985a. La contribución de la hermenéutica bíblica a la Teología de la Liberación. *Cuadernos de Teología* 6:45–69.

———. 1985b. L'Herméneutique biblique en face des méthodes critiques: Défi et Perspectives. Pages 67–80 in *Congress Volume: Salamanca, 1983*. Edited by J. A. Emerton. VTSup 36. Leiden: Brill.

———. 1986. *Crear y amar en libertad: Estudio de Génesis 2:4–3:24*. Buenos Aires: La Aurora.

———. 1987. De sociaal-historische en hermeneutische relevantie van de uittocht. *Concilium* 23:108–15.

———. 1994. *Hermenéutica Bíblica: Para una teoría de la lectura como producción de sentido*. Buenos Aires: Lumen.

———. 1995. *Historia de salvación: La experiencia religiosa del pueblo de Dios*. Estella, Spain: Verbo Divino.

———. 1997. *Exilio y sobrevivencia: Tradiciones contraculturales en el Pentateuco: Comentario de Génesis 4:1–12:9*. Buenos Aires: Lumen.

———. 2001. *Imaginar el futuro: Estructura retórica y querigma del Tercer Isaías*. Buenos Aires: Lumen.

———. 2002. *Hermenéutica práctica: Los principios de la hermenéutica bíblica en ejemplos*. Quito: Centro Bíblico Verbo Divino.

Dahood, Mitchell. 1976. The Chiastic Breakup in Isaiah 58:7. *Bib* 57:105.

Daneel, Inus. 1987. *The Quest for Belonging: Introduction to a Study on African Independent Churches*. Mambo, Zimbabwe: Gweru.

Dangle, Arium. The Cantonment Has Begun to Shake. Online: http://www.gowanusbooks.com/dalit.htm.

Davies, Graham I. 2004. A New Solution to a Crux in Obadiah 7. *VT* 27:484–87.

Davis, Thomas W. 2004. *Shifting Sands: The Rise and Fall of Biblical Archaeology*. New York: Oxford University Press

De Gruchy, John W. 1985. Christians in Conflict: The Social Reality of the South African Church. *JTSA* 51:16–26.

———. 1986. *Theology and Ministry in Context and Crisis: A South African Perspective.*
London: Collins.

De Gruchy, John W., and Steve De Gruchy. 2004. *The Church Struggle in South Africa:
25th Anniversary Edition.* London: SCM.

De Gruchy, John W., and Charles Villa-Vicencio, eds. 1983. *Apartheid Is a Heresy.*
Cape Town: David Philip; Guildford: Lutterworth.

De Gruchy, Steve. *See-Judge-Act: Putting Faith into Action.* Unpublished booklet.

Derrida, Jacques. 1989. *Of Spirit: Heidegger and the Question.* Translated by Geoffrey
Bennington and Rachel Bowlby. Chicago: University of Chicago Press.

———. 1990. The Force of Law: The Mystical Foundation of Authority. *Cardozo Law
Review* 11:919–1045.

———. 2001. *On Cosmopolitanism and Forgiveness.* Translated by Mark Dooley and
Michael Hughes. New York: Routledge.

———. 2005a. Justices. Translated by Peggy Kamuf. *Critical Inquiry* 31:689–721.

———. 2005b. *Rogues: Two Essays on Reason.* Translated by Pascale-Anne Brault and
Michael Naas. Stanford, Calif.: Stanford University Press.

Dietrich, Gabriele. 2001. Subversion, Transgression, Transcendence: "Asian Spiritual-
ity" in the Light of Dalit and Adivasi struggles. Pages 244–49 in *A New Thing on
Earth: Hopes and Fears Facing Feminist Theology.* Edited by Gabriele Dietrich.
New Delhi: ISPCK.

Donahue, John R. 1988. *The Gospel in Parable.* Philadelphia: Fortress.

Dube, Musa W. 1996. Readings of Semoya: Batswana Women's Interpretations of
Matt 15:21-28. *Semeia* 73:111–29.

———. 1997. Toward a Postcolonial Feminist Interpretation of the Bible. *Semeia*
78:11–26.

———. 1998. Savior of the World But Not of This World: A Post-colonial Reading of
the Spatial Construction in John. Pages 118–35 in *The Postcolonial Bible.* Edited
by R. S. Sugirtharajah. Sheffield: Sheffield Academic Press.

———. 2000. *Postcolonial Feminist Interpretation of the Bible.* St. Louis: Chalice.

———. 2001a. Fifty-Years of Bleeding: A Storytelling Feminist Reading of Mark 5:24–
43. Pages 50–62 in Dube 2001b.

———, ed. 2001b. *Other Ways of Reading: African Women and the Bible.* SBLGPBS 2.
Atlanta: Society of Biblical Literature; Geneva: WCC Publications.

———, ed. 2003a. *HIV/AIDS and the Curriculum: Methods of Integrating HIV/AIDS in
Theological Programmes.* Geneva: WCC Publications.

———. 2003b. Talitha Cum! Calling the Girl-Child and Women to Life in the HIV/
AIDS and the Globalization Era. Pages 71–93 in *African Women, HIV/AIDS and
Faith Communities.* Edited by Isabel Phiri. Peitermaritzburg: Cluster.

———. 2004a. *Talitha Cum!* A Postcolonial Feminist and HIV/AIDS Reading of Mark
5:21–43. Pages 123–38 in Dube and Kanyoro 2004.

———. 2004b. Twenty-Two Years of Bleeding and Still the Princess Sings. Pages 186–
200 in in Dube and Kanyoro 2004.

Dube, Musa W., and Musimbi Kanyoro, eds. 2004. *Grant Me Justice! HIV/AIDS and Gender Readings of the Bible.* Pietermaritzburg: Cluster.

Dube, Musa W., and Samuel T. Maluleke. 2001. HIV/AIDS as the New Site of Struggle: Theological, Biblical and Religious Perspectives. *Missionalia* 29:119–24.

Dube, Musa W., and Nyambura Njoroge, eds. 2001. *Talitha Cumi! Theologies of African Women.* Pietermaritzburg: Cluster.

Echegaray, Hugo. 1981. *La práctica de Jesús.* Lima: Centro de estudios y publicaciones.

———. 1984. *The Practice of Jesus.* Translated by Matthew J. O'Connell. Maryknoll, N.Y.: Orbis.

Eco, Umberto 1997. *Kant e l'ornitorinco.* Milan: Bompiani.

Elliott, Neil. 1997. The Anti-imperial Message of the Cross. Pages 167–83 in Horsley 1997b.

———. 2000. Paul and the Politics of Empire: Problems and Prospects. Pages 17–39 in Horsley 2000.

Elisha, James. 2002. Liberative Motifs in the Dalit Religion. *Bangalore Theological Forum* 34:78–88.

Erickson, Millard J. 1988. *Christian Theology.* 2nd ed. Grand Rapids: Baker.

Fabella, Virginia, and Mercy A. Oduyoye. 1988. *With Passion and Compassion: Third World Women Doing Theology.* Maryknoll, N.Y.: Orbis.

Fester, Gertrud. 1997. Women's Organizations in the Western Cape: Vehicles for Gender Struggle or Instruments of Subordination. *Agenda* 34:45–61.

Foskett, Mary F., and Jeffrey Kah-Jin Kuan, eds. 2006. *Ways of Being, Ways of Reading: Asian American Biblical Interpretation.* St. Louis: Chalice.

Frederiksen, Paula, and Adele Reinhartz, eds. 2002. *Jesus, Judaism, and Christian Anti- Judaism: Reading the New Testament after the Holocaust.* Louisville: Westminster John Knox.

Freedman, Harry. 1995. Jacob and Esau: Their Struggle in the Second Century. *JBQ* 23:107–15.

Freire, Paulo. 1973. *Pedagogue of the Oppressed.* 9th ed. Translated by Myra Bergman Ramos. New York: Seabury.

Frostin, Per. 1988. *Liberation Theology in Tanzania and South Africa: A First World Interpretation.* Lund: Lund University Press.

Funk, Robert W., Roy W. Hoover, and the Jesus Seminar. 1993. *The Five Gospels: The Search for the Authentic Words of Jesus.* New York: Macmillan.

Gadamer, Hans Georg. 1986. *Wahrheit und Methode: Ergänzungen.* Vol. 2 of idem, *Gesammelte Werke.* Tübingen: Mohr Siebeck.

———. 1989. *Truth and Method.* Translated by Joel Weinsheimer and Donald G. Marshall. New York: Crossroad.

Garcia, Ismael. 1997. *Dignidad: Ethics through Hispanic Eyes.* Nashville: Abingdon.

García Gutiérrez, M. 1983. La Biblia en la liberación del pueblo. *CHRISTUS* 571:29–33.

Garnsey, Peter, and Richard Saller. 1997. Patronal Power Relations. Pages 96–103 in Horsley 1997b.

Geertz, Clifford. 1983. *Local Knowledge.* New York: Basic Books.

Gennrich, Daniela, A. Gill, T. Hlatshwayo, M. Moleko, and L. Xaba. 2004. *Churches and HIV/AIDS: Exploring How Local Churches Are Integrating HIV/AIDS in the Life and Ministries of the Church and How Those Most Directly Affected Experience These.* Pietermaritzburg: PACSA.

Gerstenberger, Erhard. 1983. Enemies and Evildoers in the Psalms: A Challenge to Christian Preaching. *HBT* 5:61–77.

———. 1984. Exegese Vétero-testamentária e sua contextualizaçâo na realidade. *EstTeo* 24:303–19.

———. 1988. *Psalms, Part I: With an Introduction to Cultic Poetry.* FOTL 14. Grand Rapids: Eerdmans.

Girard, Marc. 1984. *Les Psaumes: Analyse structurelle et interpretation 1–50.* Paris: Cerf.

Goldstein, Valerie Saiving. 1960. The Human Situation: A Feminine View. *JR* 40:100–112.

González, Justo. 1996. *Tres meses en la escuela de Mateo.* Nashville: Abingdon.

Goodman, Martin. 1983. The First Jewish Revolt: Social Conflict. Pages 419–27 in *Essays in Honor of Yigael Yadin.* Edited by Geza Vermes and Jacob Neusner. Totowa: Oxford Centre for Postgraduate Studies.

Gordon, Richard. 1997. The Veil of Power. Pages 126–37 in Horsley 1997b.

Gorgulho, Gilberto. 1993. Biblical Hermeneutics. Pages 123–49 in *Mysterium Liberationis: Fundamental Concepts of Liberation Theology.* Edited by Ignacio Ellacuría and Jon Sobrino. Maryknoll, N.Y.: Orbis.

Gruber, Mayer I. 2004. *Rashi's Commentary on Psalms.* Brill Reference Library of Judaism 18. Leiden: Brill.

Guardiola, Leticia. 1997. Borderless Women and Borderless Texts: A Cultural Reading of Matthew 15:21–28. *Semeia* 78:69–81.

———. 2002. Border-Crossing and Its Redemptive Power in John: A Cultural Reading of Jesus the Accused. Pages 129–52 in *John and Postcolonialism: Travel, Space and Power.* Edited by Musa W. Dube and Jeffrey Staley. Sheffield: Sheffield Academic Press.

Gunkel, Hermann. 1998. *Introduction to the Psalms: The Genres of the Religious Lyric of Israel.* Translated by James D. Nogalski. Macon, Ga.: Mercer University Press.

Gutiérrez, Gustavo. 1973a. *Teologia de la liberación.* Salamanca, Spain: Sigueme.

———. 1973b. *Theologie der Befreiung.* Translated by Horst Goldstein. Munich: Kaiser.

Haddad, Beverly G. 2000. African Women's Theologies of Survival: Intersecting Faith, Feminisms, and Development. Ph.D. diss. University of Natal, Pietermaritzburg.

———. 2003. Synergies between Bio-medical and Social Science Research in the Context of HIV/AIDS. Pages 23–28 in *African Religious Health Assets Programme Report.* Pietermaritzburg Colloquium.

———. 2005. Reflections on the Church and HIV/AIDS: South Africa. *Theology Today.* 62:29–37.

Hanson, Paul D. 1975. *The Dawn of Apocalyptic.* Philadelphia: Fortress.

Hardt, Michael, and Antonio Negri. 2000. *Empire.* Cambridge: Harvard University Press.

Harrelson, Walter J. 1962. Blessings and Curses. *IDB* 1:446–48.

Harrison, Beverly W. 1985. *Making the Connections: Essasys in Feminist Social Ethics.* Boston: Beacon.

Harvey, David. 1999. *Limits to Capital.* London: Verso.

Havea, Jione. 2003. *Elusions of Control: Biblical Law and the Words of Women.* SemeiaSt 41. Atlanta: Society of Biblical Literature; Leiden: Brill.

———. 2004. Numbers. Pages 43–51 in Patte 2004.

———. 2006. Whoring Dinah: Poly-nesian reading Genesis 34. Pages 172–84 in *Voyages in Uncharted Waters: Essays on the Theory and Practice of Biblical Interpretation in Honor of David Jobling.* Edited by Wesley J. Bergen and Armin Siedlecki. Sheffield: Sheffield Phoenix.

Heard, R. Christopher. 2001. *The Dynamics of Diselection: Ambiguity in Genesis 12–36 and Ethnic Boundaries in Post-exilic Judah.* SemeiaSt 39. Atlanta: Society of Biblical Literature.

Heidegger, Martin. 1976. Only a God Can Save Us: *Der Spiegel*'s Interview with Martin Heidegger. Translated by Margaret Alter and John D. Caputo. *Philosophy Today* Winter:267–84.

Herzog, William R., II. 1994. *Parables as Subversive Speech: Jesus as Pedagogue of the Oppressed.* Louisville: Westminster John Knox.

———. 2005a. *Prophet and Teacher: An Introduction to the Historical Jesus.* Louisville: Westminster John Knox.

———. 2005b. Why Peasants Responded to Jesus. Pages 47–70 in *Christian Origins.* Vol. 1 of *A People's History of Christianity.* Edited by Richard A. Horsley. Minneapolis: Fortress.

Hillers, Delbert R. 1964. *Treaty-Curses and the Old Testament Prophets.* BibOr 16. Rome: Pontifical Biblical Institute.

Ho, Christine. *The Model Minority Awakened: The Murder of Vincent Chin. Parts 1–5.* Online: http://us_asians.tripod.com/articles-vincentchin.html.

Hock, Ronald F. 2002. Romancing the Parables of Jesus. *Perspectives in Religious Studies* 29:32–37.

Hofstede, Geert. 1995. *Allemaal Andersdenkenden: Omgaan met cultuurverschillen.* Amsterdam: Uitgeverij Contact.

Horsley, Richard A. 1987. *Jesus and the Spiral of Violence: Popular Jewish Resistance in Roman Palestine.* New York, Harper & Row.

———. 1989. *Sociology and the Jesus Movement.* New York: Crossroad.

———. 1997a. 1 Corinthians: A Case Study of Paul's Assembly as an Alternative Society. Pages 242–52 in Horsley 1997b.

———, ed. 1997b. *Paul and Empire: Religion and Power in Roman Imperial Society.* Harrisburg, Pa.: Trinity Press International.

———, ed. 2000. *Paul and Politics.* Harrisburg, Pa.: Trinity Press International.

Hudson, Emily. 2007. Listen But Do Not Grieve: Grief, Paternity, and Time in the Laments of Dhṛtarāṣṭra. Pages 35–52 in *Gender and Narrative in the Mahābhārata.* Edited by Simon Brodbeck and Brian Black. London: Routledge.

Huning, Ralf. 2005. *Bibelwissenschaft im Dienste populärer Bibellektüre: Bausteine einer Theorie der Bibellektüre aus dem Werk von Carlos Mesters.* SBB 54. Stuttgart: KBW.

Irvine, Stuart A. 1995. A Note on Psalm 14:4. *JBL* 114:463–66.

Isasi-Díaz, Ada María. 2004. *La Lucha Continues: Mujerista Theology.* Maryknoll, N.Y.: Orbis.

Jankélévitch, Vladimir. 2005. *Forgiveness.* Translated by Andrew Kelley. Chicago: University of Chicago Press.

Jayawardena, Kumari. 1986. *Feminism and Nationalism in the Third World.* London: Zed.

Jennings, Theodore W., Jr. 2005. *Reading Derrida/Thinking Paul: On Justice.* Stanford, Calif.: Stanford University Press.

Jeremias, Jörg. 1970. *Kultprophetie und Gerichtsverkündigung in der späten Königszeit Israels.* WMANT 35. Neukirchen-Vluyn: Neukirchener.

Jewish Publication Society. 1962. *The Torah: The Five Books of Moses—A New Translation of the Holy Scriptures according to the Masoretic Text.* Philadelphia: Jewish Publication Society.

Jiménez, Pablo. 1997. The Workers of the Vineyard (Matthew 20: 1–16): A Hispanic Homiletical Reading. *Journal for Preachers* 21:35–40.

Jones, Douglas Rawlinson. 1964. *Isaiah 56–66 and Joel: Introduction and Commentary.* London: SCM.

Jordaan, Roxanne. 1987. The Emergence of Black Feminist Theology in South Africa. *JTSA* 1:42–46.

———. 1991. The Emergence of Black Feminist Theology in South Africa. Pages 122–28 in *Women Hold Up Half the Sky: Women in the Church in Southern Africa.* Edited by Denise Ackermann, Jonathan A. Draper, and Emma Mashinini. Pietermaritzburg: Cluster.

Kairos theologians. 1986. *The Kairos Document: Challenge to the Church.* 2nd ed. Braamfontein: Skotaville.

Kant, Immanuel. 1784. Beantwortung der Frage: Was ist Aufklärung? *Berlinische Monatsschrift* 12:481–94.

Käsemann, Ernst. 1969. *New Testament Questions of Today.* Translated by W. J. Montague. Philadelphia: Fortress.

Kaufmann, Larry T. 2001. Good News to the Poor: The Impact of Albert Nolan on Contextual Theology in South Africa. Pages 17–32 in Speckman and Kaufmann 2001c.

Kautsky, John H. 1982. *The Politics of Aristocratic Empires.* Chapel Hill: University of North Carolina.

Kazantzakis, Nikos. 1960. *The Last Temptation of Christ.* Translated by P. A. Bien. New York: Simon & Schuster.

Keck, Leander E. 1977. The Function of Rom 3:10–18: Observations and Suggestions. Pages 141–57 in *God's Christ and His People: Studies in Honor of N. A. Dahl.* Edited by Jacob Jervell and Wayne. A. Meeks. Oslo: Universitetsforlaget.

Kee, Alistair. 2006. *The Rise and Demise of Black Theology.* Aldershot: Ashgate.

Keel, Othmar. 1969. *Feinde und Gottesleugner: Studien zum Image der Widersacher in den Individualpsalmen.* SBM 7. Stuttgart: Katholisches Bibelwerk.

Kemp, Amanda, Nozizwe Madlala, Asha Moodley, and Elaine Salo. 1995. The Dawn of a New Day: Redefining South African Feminism. Pages 131–62 In *The Chal-*

lenge of Local Feminisms: Women's Movements in Global Perspective. Edited by Amrita Basu, with the assistance of C. Elizabeth McGrory. Boulder, Colo.: Westview.

Kenyon, Kathleen M. 1957. *Digging up Jericho.* New York: Praeger.

Kessler, Rainer. 2004. From Bipolar to Multipolar Understanding: Hermeneutical Consequences of Intercultural Bible Reading. Pages 452–60 in de Wit, Jonker, Kool and Schipani 2004.

Kgosikwena, Kagiso B. 2001. Pastoral Care and the Dying Process of People Living with HIV/AIDS: Speaking of God in a Crisis. *Missionalia* 29:200–219.

Kim, Chan-Hie. 1994. Reading the Bible as Asian Americans. *NIB* 1:161–66.

Kingsolver, Barbara. 1998. *The Poisonwood Bible: A Novel.* San Francisco: Harper Perennial.

Koenen, Klaus. 1974–2006. "שָׁכַל." *TDOT* 14:112–28.

Kool, Marleen. 2004. Intercultural Bible Reading as a Practical Setting for Intercultural Communication. Pages 360–76 in de Wit, Jonker, Kool and Schipani 2004.

Kraus, Hans-Joachim. 1988. *Psalms 1–59: A Commentary.* Minneapolis: Augsburg.

Kretschmar, Louise. 1986. *The Voice of Black Theology in South Africa.* Johannesburg: Ravan.

Kritzinger, Johannes N. J. 1988. Black Theology: Challenge to Mission. Ph.D. diss. Pretoria: University of South Africa.

Krüger, René. 2003. *Arm und Reich im Jakobusbrief von Lateinamerika aus gelesen: Die Herausforderung eines prophetischen Christentums.* Amsterdam: Vrije Universiteit.

Kuan, Kah-Jin Jeffrey. 2002. My Journey into Diasporic Hermeneutics. *USQR* 56:50–54.

Kuss, Otto. 1963. *Der Römerbrief.* 2nd ed. Regensburg: Pustet.

Lacan, Jacques. 1992. *The Ethics of Psychoanalysis:The Seminar of Jacques Lacan Book VII.* Edited by Jacques-Alain Miller. Translated by Dennis Porter. New York: Norton.

———. 1998. *Encore: Seminar XX on Feminine Sexuality, the Limits of Love and Knowledge (1972–73).* Edited by Jacques-Alain Miller. Translated by Bruce Fink. New York: Norton.

Langa, Percy. 2006. Our Call to a Better Place. *Mail & Guardian* May 12. Online: http://www.mg.co.za/article/2006-05-17-our-call-to-a-better-place.

LaPoorta, Japie J. 1990. Evangelicalism and Apartheid. Pages 61–69 in *Listening to South African Voices: Critical Reflection on Contemporary Theological Documents.* Edited by G. Loots. Pretoria: Woordkor.

Lebacqz, Karen. 1983. Justice, Economics, and the Uncomfortable Kingdom. *Annual of the Society of Christian Ethics* 3.1:27–53.

Levine, Amy-Jill. 2002. Matthew, Mark, and Luke: Good News or Bad? Pages 77–98 in Frederiksen and Reinhartz 2002.

Levine, Daniel H. 1992. *Popular Voices in Latin American Catholicism.* Princeton: Princeton University Press.

Liew, Tat-siong Benny, and Gale A.Yee, eds. 2002. *The Bible in Asian America. Semeia* 90–91.

Loury, Glenn C. 2002. *The Anatomy of Racial Inequality. The W. E. B. DuBois Lectures.* Cambridge: Harvard University Press.

Luz, Ulrich. 1997. *Mt 18–25.* Vol. 3 of *Das Evangelium nach Matthäus.* EKKNT 1.3. Zürich: Benziger; Neukirchen-Vluyn: Neukirchener.

Maimela, Simon. 1991a. Black Theology and the Quest for a God of Liberation. Pages 141–59 in *Theology at the End of Modernity: Essays in Honor of Gordon D. Kaufman.* Edited by Sheila G. Devaney. Philadelphia: Trinity.

———. 1991b. Images of Liberation in Black and Feminist Theologies of Liberation. *Theologica Evangelica* 24:40–47.

Maluleke, Samuel T. 1996. Black and African Theologies in the New World Order: A Time to Drink from Our Own Wells. *JTSA* 96:3–19.

———. 1997a. Half a Century of African Christian Theologies: Elements of the Emerging Agenda for the Twenty-First Century. *JTSA* 99:4–23.

———. 1997b. The "Smoke Screens" Called Black and African Theologies: The Challenge of African Women's Theology. *Journal of Constructive Theology* 3:39– 63.

———. 1998a. African Traditional Religions in Christian Mission and Christian Scholarship: Re-Opening a Debate That Never Started. *Religion and Theology* 5:121–37.

———. 1998b. Black Theology as Public Discourse. Pages 60–62 in *Constructing a Language of Religion in Public Life: Multi-Event 1999 Academic Workshop Papers.* Edited by James R. Cochrane. Cape Town: University of Cape Town.

———. 2001a. African "Ruths," Ruthless Africas: Reflections of an African "Mordecai." Pages 237–51 in Dube 2001b.

———. 2001b. Theology in (South) Africa: How the Future Has Changed. Pages 364–89 in Speckman and Kaufmann 2001c.

Mandew, M. 1991. The Challenge of Black Feminist Theology in South Africa: A Black Male Perspective. Pages 129–44 In *Women Hold Up Half The Sky: Women in the Church in Southern Africa.* Edited by Dennise Ackermann, Jonathan A. Draper, and Emma Mashinini. Pietermaritzburg: Cluster.

Manoa, Pio. 1992. A Letter to My Storyteller. Pages 17–19 in *Trapped: A Collection of Writing from Fiji.* Edited by Séona Smiles and Sudesh Mishra. Suva: Fiji Writers Association.

Marty, Martin A. 1987. *Religion and Republic: The American Circumstance.* Boston: Beacon.

Masenya, Madipoane J. 1997. Proverbs 31:10–31 in a South African Context: A Reading for the Liberation of African (Northern Sotho) Women. *Semeia* 78:55–68.

———. 2001a. Between Unjust Suffering and the "Silent" God: Job and HIV/AIDS Sufferers in South Africa. *Missionalia* 29:186–99.

———. 2001b. A Bosadi (Womanhood) Reading of Proverbs 31:10–31. Pages 145–57 in Dube 2001b.

———. 2001c. Esther and Northern Sotho Stories: An African-South African Woman's Commentary. Pages 27–49 in Dube 2001b.

———. 2004. *How Worthy Is the Woman of Worth? Rereading Proverbs 31:10–31 in African-South Africa.* Bible and Theology in Africa 4. New York: Lang.

Massey, James. 1994. *Roots: A Concise History of Dalits.* Delhi: ISPCK.

————. 1995. *Dalits in India: Religion as a Source of Bondage or Liberation with Special Reference to Christian*. New Delhi: Manohar.

————. 2001. Movements of Liberation: Theological Roots and Vision of Dalit Theology. *CTC Bulletin* 17.2:76–86.

Massey, James, and Samson Prabhakar. 2005. Introduction. Pages 3–14 in *Frontiers in Dalit Hermeneutics*. Edited by James Massey and Samson Prabhakar. Bangalore: BTESSC/SATHRI.

Mbiti, John S. 1977. The Biblical Basis for Present Trends in African Theology. Pages 83–94 in *African Theology En Route: Papers from the Pan-African Conference of Third World Theologians*. Edited by Kofi Appiah-Kubi and Sergio Torres. Maryknoll, N.Y.: Orbis.

McCreight, Kathryn Greene. 1997. Gender, Sin and Grace: Feminist Theologies Meet Karl Barth's Hamartiology. *Scottish Journal of Theology* 50:415–32.

McFague, Sallie. 1975. *Speaking in Parables: A Study in Metaphor and Theology*. Philadelphia: Fortress.

McGovern, Arthur F. 1990. *Liberation Theology and Its Critics: Toward an Assessment*. Maryknoll, N.Y.: Orbis.

McKenzie, John L. 1968. *Second Isaiah*. AB 20. Garden City, N.Y.: Doubleday.

Mehlhausen, Joachim. 1977–2004. "Nationalsozialismus und Kirchen." *TRE* 24:43–78.

Melanchthon, Monica J. 2005a. Dalit Readers of the Word: The Quest for Hermeneutics. Pages 45–64 in Massey and Prabhakar 2005.

————. 2005b. Dalits, Bible and Method. *SBL Forum*. Online: http://www.sbl-site.org/ publications/article.aspx?articleId=459.

Messer, Donald. 2004. *Breaking the Conspiracy of Silence: Christian Churches and the Global AIDS Crisis*. Minneapolis: Fortress.

Mesters, Carlos. 1977. *El misterioso mundo de la Biblia: Estudio sobre la puerta de entrada al mundo de la Biblia*. Buenos Aires: Editorial Bonum.

————. 1981. The Use of the Bible in Christian Communities of the Common People. Pages 197–212 in *The Challenge of Basic Christian Communities: Papers from the International Ecumenical Congress of Theology, February 20–March 2, 1980, São Paulo, Brazil*. Edited by Sergio Torres and John Eagleson. Maryknoll, N.Y.: Orbis.

————. 1988. *A Bíblia lida pelo povo na atual renovação da Igreja Católica no. Brasil, 1964–1984*. Balanço de 20 Anos 7. São Leopoldo, Brazil: Centro de Estudos Bíblicos.

————. 2006. Mito e rito na Bíblia. Pages 86–93 in *Profecia e Esperança: Um tributo a Milton Schwantes*. Edited by Carlos Dreher. São Leopoldo, Brazil: Oikos Editora.

Michael, Walter B. 2006. *The Trouble with Diversity: How We Learned to Love Identity and Ignore Inequality*. New York: Henry Holt.

Miguez, Néstor. 1986. *No Como los otros que no tienen esperanza*. Buenos Aires: ISEDET.

————. 2004a. El Imperio y después: Sostener la esperanza bíblica en medio de la opresión. *RIBLA* 48:7–22.

————. 2004b. Reading John 4 in the Interface between Ordinary and Scholarly Interpretation. Pages 334–47 in de Wit, Jonker, Kool and Schipani 2004.

Miranda, José Porfirio. 1974. *Marx and the Bible: A Critique of the Philosophy of Oppression*. Maryknoll, N.Y.: Orbis.

Miscall, Peter D. 1991. Isaiah: The Labyrinth of Images. *Semeia* 54:103–21.

Mncube, Bernard Sr. 1984. Biblical Problems and the Struggle of Women. Paper presented at the Women's Struggle in South Africa: Feminist Theology conference, Hammanskraal.

Mofokeng, Takatso A. 1988. Black Christians, the Bible and Liberation. *Journal of Black Theology* 2:34–42.

Mosala, Bernardette I. 1984. Biblical Hermeneutics and the Struggle of Women. Paper Presented at the Women's Struggle in South Africa: Feminist Theology Conference, Hammanskraal.

———. 1985. African Independent Churches: A Study in Socio-theological Protest. Pages 103–11 in *Resistance and Hope: South African Essays in Honour of Beyers Naud*. Edited by Charles Villa-Vicencio and John W. De Gruchy. Cape Town: David Philips.

———. 1986. Black Theology and the Struggle of the Black Woman in Southern Africa. Pages 129–133 in *The Unquestionable Right to Be Free*. Edited by Itumeleng J. Mosala and Buti Tlhagale. Johannesburg: Skotaville.

Mosala, Itumeleng J. 1986a. Ethics of the Economic Principles: Church and Secular Investments. Pages 119–29 in *Hammering Swords into Ploughshares: Essays in Honour of Archbishop Mpilo Desmond Tutu*. Edited by Buti Tlhagale and Itumeleng J. Mosala. Johannesburg: Skotaville.

———. 1986b. The Relevance of African Traditional Religions and Their Challenge to Black Theology. Pages 91–100 in *The Unquestionable Right to Be Free: Essays in Black Theology*. Edited by Itumeleng J. Mosala and Buti Tlhagale. Johannesburg: Skotaville.

———. 1986c. The Use of the Bible in Black Theology. Pages 175–99 In *The Unquestionable Right to Be Free: Essays in Black Theology*. Edited by Itumeleng J. Mosala and Buti Tlhagale. Johannesburg: Skotaville.

———. 1987. Biblical Hermeneutics and Black Theology in South Africa. Ph.D. diss. University of Cape Town, Cape Town.

———. 1989. *Biblical Hermeneutics and Black Theology in South Africa*. Grand Rapids: Eerdmans.

———. 1992. The Implications of the Text of Esther for African Women's Struggle for Liberation in South Africa. *Semeia* 59:129–137.

Motlhabi, Mokgethi B. G. 1973. Black Theology and Authority. Pages 119–29 in *Black Theology: The South African Voice*. Edited by Basil Moore. London: Hurst.

———. 1986. The Historical Origins of Black Theology. Pages 37–56 in *The Unquestionable Right to be Free: Essays in Black Theology*. Edited by Itumeleng J. Mosala and Buti Tlhagale. Johannesburg: Skotaville.

Mudimbe, V. Y. 1988. *The Invention of Africa: Gnosis, Philosophy and the Order of Knowledge*. Indianapolis: Indiana University Press.

Muilenburg, James. Isaiah. *IB* 5:676–96.

Nadar, Sarojini. 2001. A South African Indian Womanist Reading of the Character of Ruth. Pages 159–75 in Dube 2001b.

———. 2003. *Power, Ideology and Interpretations: Womanist and Literary Perspectives on the Book of Esther as Resources for Gender-Social Transformation.* Pietermaritzburg: University of Natal.

Namer, Gérard. 1987. *Mémoire et société.* Paris: Méridiens Lincksieck.

Nelson, Diedrick A. 1975. An Exposition of Matthew 20:1–16. *Int* 29:288–92.

Ngada, Ndumisu H., ed. 1985. *African Independent Churches—Speaking for Ourselves.* Braamfontein: Institute for Contextual Theology.

Ngan, Lai Ling Elizabeth. 2006. Neither Here Nor There: Boundary and Identity in the Hagar Story. Pages 70–83 in Foskett and Kuan 2006.

Nieuwenhove, Jaques van. 1991. *Bronnen van Bevrijding: Varianten in de theologie van Gustavo Gutiérrez.* Kampen: Kok.

Nnaemeka, Obioma, ed. 1998. *Sisterhood, Feminisms and Power: From Africa to the Diaspora.* Trenton: Africa World Press.

Nogalski, James D. 1998. Obadiah 7: Textual Corruption or Politically Charged Metaphor? *ZAW* 110:67–71.

Nolan, Albert. 1976. *Jesus before Christianity.* Maryknoll, N.Y.: Orbis.

———. 1988. *God in South Africa: The Challenge of the Gospel.* Cape Town: David Philip.

———. 1994. Kairos Theology. Pages 212–18 in *Doing Theology in Context: South African Perspectives.* Edited by John W. De Gruchy and Charles Villa-Vicencio. Cape Town: David Philip.

Nussbaum, Martha C. 2000. *Women and Human Development: The Capabilities Approach.* Cambridge: Cambridge University Press.

Nzimande, Makhosazana. K. 2005. Postcolonial Biblical Interpretation in Post-apartheid South Africa: The *Gebirah* in the Hebrew Bible in the Light of Queen Jezebel and the Queen Mother of Lemuel. Ph.D. diss. Texas Christian University.

Oduyoye, Mercy A. 1983. Reflections from a Third World Woman's Perspective: Women's Experience and Liberation Theologies. Pages 246–55 in *Irruption of the Third World: Challenge to Theology.* Edited by Virginia Fabella and Sergio Torres. Maryknoll, N.Y.: Orbis.

———. 1990. The Search for a Two-Winged Theology. Pages 27–48 in Oduyoye and Kanyoro 1990.

———. 1995. *Daughters of Anowa: African Women and Patriarchy.* Maryknoll, N.Y.: Orbis.

———. 2001. *Introducing African Women's Theology.* Cleveland: Pilgrim.

———. 2004. *Beads and Strands: Reflections of an African Woman on Christianity in Africa.* Maryknoll, N.Y.: Orbis.

Oduyoye, Mercy A., and Musimbi R. A. Kanyoro, eds. 1990. *Talitha, Qumi! Proceedings of the Convocation of African Women Theologians 1989.* Ibadan: Daystar.

———, eds. 1992. *The Will to Arise: Women, Tradition, and the Church in Africa.* Maryknoll, N.Y.: Orbis.

Ogden, Graham S. 1982. Prophetic Oracles against Foreign Nations and Psalms of Communal Lament: The Relationship of Psalm 137 to Jeremiah 49:7–22 and Obadiah. *JSOT* 24: 89–97.

Okure, Teresa. 1988. *The Johannine Approach to Mission: A Contextual Study of John 4:1–42*. WUNT 2/31. Tübingen: Mohr Siebeck.

———. 1992. The Will to Arise: Reflections on Luke 8:40–56. Pages 221–30 in Oduyoye and Kanyoro 1992.

———. 1995. Reading from This Place: Some Prospects and Problems. Pages 52–69 in *Social Location and Biblical Interpretation in Global Perspective*. Vol. 2 of *Reading from This Place*. Edited by Fernando F. Segovia and Mary Ann Tolbert. Minneapolis: Fortress.

———. 2000a. First Was the Life, Not the Book. Pages 194–214 in Okure 2000b.

———, ed. 2000b. *To Cast Fire upon the Earth: Bible and Mission Collaborating in Today's Multicultural Global Context*. Pietermaritzburg: Cluster.

Parry, Geraint. 1969. *Political Elites*. New York: Praeger

Patte, Daniel, et al., eds. 2004. *Global Bible Commentary*. Nashville: Abingdon

Petersen, R. M. 1995. Time, Resistance, and Reconstruction: Rethinking Kairos Theology. Ph.D. diss. Chicago: University of Chicago.

Phiri, Isabel. A. 1997. Doing Theology in Community: The Case of African Women Theologians in the 1990s. *JTSA* 99:68–76.

Phiri, Isabel A., Beverly G. Haddad and M.n.M. Masenya, eds. 2003. *African Women, HIV/AIDS and Faith Communities*. Pietermaritzburg: Cluster.

Phiri, Isabel A., and Sarojini Nadar, eds. 2006. *African Women, Religion, and Health: Essays in Honor of Mercy Amba Ewudziwa Oduyoye*. Maryknoll, N.Y.: Orbis.

Plaatjie, Gloria K. 2001. Toward a Post-apartheid Black Feminist Reading of the Bible: A Case of Luke 2:36–38. Pages 114–42 in Dube 2001b.

Plaskow, Judith. 1980. *Sex, Sin and Grace: Women's Experience and the Theologies of Reinhold Niebuhr and Paul Tillich*. Washington, D.C.: University Press of America.

Potter Engel, Mary. 1990. Evil, Sin and the Violation of the Vulnerable. Pages 152–64 in *Lift Every Voice: Constructing Theologies from the Underside*. Edited by Susan Brooks Thistlethwaite and Mary Potter Engel. San Francisco: Harper & Row.

Procee, Hendrik. 1991. *Over de Grenzen van Culturen: Voorbij Universalisme en Relativisme*. Meppel: Boom.

Raabe, Paul R. 1996. *Obadiah: A New Translation with Introduction and Commentary*. AB 24D. New York: Doubleday.

Reyes, George. 2005. El desafío de la espiritualidad postmoderna en la lectura de la Biblia. *Signos de Vida* 38:26–31.

Richard, Pablo. 1982. La Biblia: Memoria histórica de los pobres. *Servir* 17:143–50.

———. 1984. Bíblia, memória histórica dos pobres. *Estudos Bíblicos* 1:20–30.

———. 1988. Leitura popular da Bíblia na América Latina. *RIBLA* 1:8–25.

———. 1998. The Hermeneutics of Liberation: Theoretical Grounding of Communitarian Reading of the Bible. Pages 272–82 in *Teaching the Bible*. Edited by Fernando F. Segovia and Mary Ann Tolbert. Maryknoll, N.Y.: Orbis.

Richards, Kent H. 1992. "Bless/Blessings." *ABD* 1:753–755.

Riches, John. 2004. Intercultural Hermeneutics: Conversations across Cultural and Contextual Divides. Pages 460–77 in de Wit, Jonker, Kool and Schipani 2004.

Ricoeur, Paul. 1970. Qu'est-ce qu'un texte? Expliquer et comprendre. Pages 181–200 in *Hermeneutik und Dialektik: Aufsätze. (Hans-Georg Gadamer z. 70. Geburtstag).* Edited by Rüdiger Bübner et al. Tübingen: Mohr Siebeck.

———. 1976a. Del conflicto a la convergencia de los métodos en exégesis bíblica. In *Exégesis y hermenéutica.* Madrid: Cristiandad.

———. 1976b. *El conflicto de las interpretaciones.* Buenos Aires: La Aurora.

———. 1986. Du Texte a l'action. *Essais d'herméneutique* 2:137–60.

———. 1991. *A Ricoeur Reader: Reflection and Imagination.* Edited by Mario J. Valdés. Toronto: University of Toronto Press.

———. 1998. Preface. Pages ix–xix in *Thinking Biblically: Exegetical and Hermeneutical Studies.* Edited by André Lacocque and Paul Ricoeur. Chicago: University of Chicago Press.

Robb, Carol S. 1985. Introduction. Pages xi–xxii in *Making the Connections: Essays in Feminist Social Ethics.* Edited by Beverly Wildung Harrison. Boston: Beacon.

Robinson, Robert B. 1988. Levels of Naturalization in Obadiah. *JSOT* 40:83–97.

Rodríguez, José David. 1988. The Parable of the Affirmative-Action Employer. *Apuntes* 8.3:51–59.

Ruiz, Jean-Pierre. 2001. Tell the Next Generation: Racial and Ethnic Minority Scholars and the Future of Biblical Studies. *JAAR* 69:649–71.

Sanneh, L. 1989. *Translating the Message: The Missionary Impact on Culture.* Maryknoll, N.Y.: Orbis.

Schmidt, Hans. 1934. *Die Psalmen.* Tübingen: Mohr Siebeck.

Schmithals, Walter G. 1988. *Der Römerbrief.* Gütersloh: Mohn.

Schottroff, Luise. 2006. *The Parables of Jesus.* Translated by Linda M. Maloney. Minneapolis: Fortress.

Schüssler Fiorenza, Elisabeth. 1998. *Sharing Her Word: Feminist Biblical Interpretation in Context.* Boston: Beacon.

Schwantes, Milton. 1987. Nuestra Vista Clareó: Lectura Bíblica en América Latina. *Presencia Ecuménica* 7:3–9.

———.1988. A presentação. *RIBLA* 1:5–6.

Scofield, Rodney. 1985. A Report: The Forum on Christianity in the Southern African Context. *JTSA* 51:51–54.

Scott, Bernard Brandon. 1989. *Hear Then the Parable: A Commentary on the Parables of Jesus.* Minneapolis: Fortress.

Scott, James C. 1985. *Weapons of the Weak: Everyday Forms of Peasant Resistance.* New Haven: Yale University Press.

Segovia, Fernando F. 1995a. "And They Began to Speak in Other Tongues": Competing Modes of Discourse in Contemporary Biblical Criticism. Pages 1–32 in *Social Location and Biblical Interpretation in the United States.* Vol. 1 of *Reading from This Place.* Edited by Fernando F. Segovia and Mary Ann Tolbert. Minneapolis: Fortress.

———. 1995b. Toward a Hermeneutics of the Diaspora: A Hermeneutics of Otherness and Engagement. Pages 57–73 in *Social Location and Biblical Interpretation in the United States.* Vol. 1 of *Reading from This Place.* Edited by Fernando F. Segovia and Mary Ann Tolbert. Minneapolis: Fortress.

Segundo, Juan Luis. 1970. *De la sociedad a la Teología*. Cuadernos Latinoamericanos 2. Buenos Aires: Carlos Lohlé.

——. 1974a. *The Community Called Church*. A Theology for Artisans of a New Humanity 1. Translated by John Drury. Maryknoll, N.Y.: Orbis.

——. 1974b. *Grace and the Human Condition*. A Theology for Artisans of a New Humanity 2. Translated by John Drury. Maryknoll, N.Y.: Orbis.

——. 1974c. *Our Idea of God*. A Theology for Artisans of a New Humanity 3. Translated by John Drury. Maryknoll, N.Y.: Orbis.

——. 1974d. *The Sacraments Today*. A Theology for Artisans of a New Humanity 4. Translated by John Drury. Maryknoll, N.Y.: Orbis.

——. 1974e. *Evolution and Guilt*. A Theology for Artisans of a New Humanity 5. Translated by John Drury. Maryknoll, N.Y.: Orbis

——. 1975. *Liberación de la Teologia*. Cuadernos Latinoamericanos 17. Buenos Aires: Carlos Lohlé.

——. 1976. *Liberation of Theology*. Translated by John Drury. Maryknoll, N.Y.: Orbis.

——. 1982. *El hombre de hoy ante Jesús de Nazaret*. 3 vols. Madrid: Cristiandad.

——. 1984–88. *Jesus of Nazareth Yesterday and Today*. Maryknoll, N.Y.: Orbis.

Setiloane, Gabriel. 1977. Where Are We in African Theology? Pages 59–65 in *African Theology en Route: Papers from the Pan-African Conference of Third World Theologians, Accra, December 17–23, 1977*. Edited by Kofi Appiah-Kubi and Sergio Torres. Maryknoll, N.Y.: Orbis.

Siegele-Wenschkewitz, Leonore, ed. 1988. *Verdrängte Vergangenheit, die uns bedrängt*. Munich: Kaiser.

Silva Gotay, Samuel. 1981. *El pensamiento cristiano revolucionario en América Latina y el Caribe: Implicaciones de la teología de la liberación para la sociología de la religión*. Salamanca, Spain: Sígueme.

Skinner, John. 1912. *A Critical and Exegetical Commentary on Genesis*. ICC. Edinburgh: T&T Clark.

——. 1917. *The Book of the Prophet Isaiah Chapters XL–LXVI: Revised Version with Introduction and Notes*. Cambridge: Cambridge University Press.

Smith, Paul A. 1995. *Rhetoric and Redaction in Trito-Isaiah. The Structure, Growth and Authorship of Isaiah 56–66*. VTSup 62. Leiden: Brill.

Smith, Wilfred Cantwell. 1993. *What Is Scripture? A Comparative Approach*. London: SCM.

Speckman, McGlory T., and Larry T. Kaufmann. 2001a. Editors' preface. Pages xi–xii in Speckman and Kaufmann 2001c.

——. 2001b. Introduction. Pages 1–14 in Speckman and Kaufmann 2001c.

——, eds. 2001c. *Towards an Agenda for Contextual Theology: Essays in Honour of Albert Nolan*. Pietermaritzburg: Cluster.

Spina, Frank Anthony. 2005. *The Faith of the Outsider: Exclusion and Inclusion in the Biblical Story*. Grand Rapids: Eerdmans.

Spohn, William C. 1995. *What Are They Saying about Scripture and Ethics?* New York: Paulist.

Steinberg, Stephen. 1989. *The Ethnic Myth: Race, Ethnicity and Class in America*. 2nd ed. Boston: Beacon.

Stendahl, Krister. 1976. The Apostle Paul and the Introspective Conscience of the West. Pages 78–96 in idem, *Paul among Jews and Gentiles, and Other Essays.* Philadelphia: Fortress.

Stern, David. 1981. Rhetoric and Midrash: The Case of the Mashal. *Prooftexts* 1:261–91.

———. 1991. *Parables in Midrash: Narrative and Exegesis in Rabbinic Literature.* Cambridge: Harvard University Press.

Stevens, I. D. 1985. The Role of the Church in Industry and Industrial Relations; Focusing on the Supportive Role with Worker Organisations, Especially the Independent Trade Unions in South Africa. Unpublished honors paper. University of Natal, Pietermartizburg.

Stoeßel, Frank. 1977–2004. Christenverfolgungen: Nationalsozialismus. *TRE* 8:48–51.

Stoffels, Hijme. 2004. *Bijbelbezit en bijbelgebruik in Nederland 2004.* Online: http://krizzz.nl/files/Bijbelbezit%20en%20bijbelgebruik%202004.doc.

Stooss, Andreas. 2002. Spreading Hope within the Outcasts of Society: How Contextual Bible Study Can Make a Powerful Contribution to the Struggle against HIV/AIDS and Possible Consequences for the Swiss Context. Unpublished honors paper. University of Natal, Pietermaritzburg.

Sundkler, Bengt G. M. 1961. *Bantu Prophets in South Africa.* London: Clarke.

Tacitus, Cornelius. 1952. *The Annals and the Histories.* Translated by Alfred J. Church and William. J. Brodribb. Chicago: Encyclopedia Britannica.

Tamez, Elsa. 1989. *La justificación como afirmación de la vida: Relectura desde América Latina.* Lausanne: University of Lausanne.

———. 1993. *The Amnesty of Grace.* Nashville: Abingdon.

Taubes, Jacob. 2004. *The Political Theology of Paul.* Edited by Aleida Assmann and Jan Assmann. Translated by Dana Hollander. Stanford, Calif.: Stanford University Press.

Terreblanche, Solomon J. 2002. *A History of Inequality in South Africa, 1652–2002.* Pietermaritzburg: University of Natal Press.

Thiselton, Anthony C. 1992. *New Horizons in Hermeneutics: The Theory and Practice of Transforming Biblical Reading.* Grand Rapids: Zondervan.

Thornton, John K. 1998. *The Congolese Saint Anthony: Dona Beatriz Kimpa Vita and the Antonian Movement, 1684–1706.* New York: Cambridge University Press.

Tlhagale, Buti. 1985. Culture in an Apartheid Society. *JTSA* 51:27–36.

Tutu, Desmond M. 1979. Black Theology/African Theology: Soulmates or Antagonists? Pages 483–91 in *Black Theology: A Documentary History, 1966–1979.* Edited by Gayraud. S. Wilmore and John. H. Cone. Maryknoll, N.Y.: Orbis.

———. 1983. *Hope and Suffering: Sermons and Speeches.* Johannesburg: Skotaville.

Ukpong, Justin S. 2000a. Developments in Biblical Interpretation in Africa: Historical and Hermeneutical Directions. *JTSA* 108:3–18.

———. 2000b. Developments in Biblical Interpretation in Africa: Historical and Hermeneutical Directions. Pages 11–28 in West and Dube 2000.

United Methodist Church. 2004. *The Book of Discipline of the United Methodist Church.* Nashville: Abingdon.

Urbach, Ephraim E. 1979. *The Sages, Their Concepts and Beliefs.* Translated by Israel Abrahams. Jerusalem: Magnes, 1969. Repr., Cambridge: Harvard University Press: 1987.

Vendrell, Angel S. 2008. Missiological Interpretation of the Work of Richard Shaull in Latin America. Th.D. diss. Boston University School of Theology.

Vilar, Pierre. 1980. *Iniciación al vocabulario del análisis histórico.* Barcelona: Crítica.

Villa-Vicencio, Charles. 1988. *Trapped in Apartheid: A Socio-theological History of the English-Speaking Churches.* Maryknoll, N.Y.: Orbis; Cape Town: David Philip.

Water, Des van der. 2001. A Legacy for Contextual Theology: Prophetic Theology and the Challenge of the Kairos. Pages 33–64 in Speckman and Kaufmann 2001c.

Wegner, Uwe. 1998. *Exegese do Novo Testamento: Manual de Metodología.* São Leopoldo, Brazil: Sinodal; São Paulo: Paulus.

Weiser, Artur. 1962. *The Psalms: A Commentary.* OTL. Philadelphia: Westminster.

Weissblueth, Schlomo. 1983–84. Ps 14 and Its Parallel Ps 53. *Beth Mikra* 29:133–38.

Wenham, Gordon J. 1994. *Genesis 16–50.* WBC 2. Waco, Tex.: Word.

West, Cornel. 1984. Religion and the Left: An Introduction. *Monthly Review* 36:9–19.

West, Gerald. O. 1993. *Contextual Bible Study.* Pietermaritzburg: Cluster.

———. 1995. *Biblical Hermeneutics of Liberation: Modes of Reading the Bible in the South African Context.* 2nd ed. Maryknoll, N.Y.: Orbis; Pietermaritzburg: Cluster.

———. 1999. Being Partially Constituted by Work with Others: Biblical Scholars Becoming Different. *JTSA* 104:44–53.

———. 2000. Contextual Bible Study in South Africa: A Resource for Reclaiming and Regaining Land, Dignity and Identity. Pages 595–610 in West and Dube 2000.

———. 2003a. *The Academy of the Poor: Towards a Dialogical Reading of the Bible.* Pietermaritzburg: Cluster.

———. 2003b. Reading the Bible in the Light of HIV/AIDS in South Africa. *The Ecumenical Review* 55:335–44.

———. 2004a. Early Encounters with the Bible among the BaTlhaping: Historical and Hermeneutical Signs. *BibInt* 12:251–81.

———. 2004b. The Open and Closed Bible: The Bible in African Theologies. Pages 162–80 in *African Christian Theologies in Transformation.* Edited by Ernst M. Conradie. Stellenbosch: EFSA.

———. 2005a. Articulating, Owning and Mainstreaming Local Theologies: The Contribution of Contextual Bible Study. *JTSA* 122:23–35.

———. 2005b. Shifting Perspectives on the Comparative Paradigm in (South) African Biblical Scholarship. *Religion and Theology* 12:48–72.

———. 2006. Contextual Bible Reading: A South African Case Study. *Analecta Bruxellensia* 11:131–48.

———. 2009. The Not So Silent Citizen: Hearing Embodied Theology in the Context of HIV and AIDS in South Africa. Pages 23–42 in *Heterotopic Citizen: New Research on Religious Work for the Disadvantaged.* Edited by Trygve Wyller. Göttingen: Vandenhoeck & Ruprecht.

West, Gerald O., and Musa W. Dube, eds. 2000. *The Bible in Africa: Transactions, Trajectories and Trends.* Leiden: Brill.

West, Gerald O., and Bongi Zengele. 2004. Reading Job "Positively" in the Context of HIV/AIDS in South Africa. *Concilium* 4:112–124.

———. 2006. The Medicine of God's Word: What People Living with HIV and AIDS Want (and Get) from the Bible. *JTSA* 125:51–63.

Westermann, Claus. 1969. *Isaiah 40–66: A Commentary.* Translated by David M. G. Stalker. OTL. London: SCM.

———. 1985. *Genesis 12–36: A Commentary.* Translated by John. J. Scullion. London: SPCK.

———. 1994. *Genesis 1–11: A Continental Commentary.* Translated by John J. Scullion. Minneapolis: Fortress.

Whybray, Roger N. 1975. *Isaiah 40–66.* NCBC. Grand Rapids: Eerdmans; London: Marshall, Morgan & Scott.

Wielenga, Bas. 1998. *It's a Long Road to Freedom: Perspectives of Biblical Theology.* 3rd ed. Madurai: TTS.

Wieringa, Saskia. 1995. *Subversive Women: Women's Movements in Africa, Asia, Latin America and the Caribbean.* London: Zed.

———, ed. 1998. *Women's Struggles and Strategies.* Aldershot: Gower.

Wiesel, Elie. 1998. Supporting Roles: Esau. *Bible Review* 14.2:26–27.

Wilckens, Ulrich. 1978. *Der Brief an die Römer.* Zürich: Benziger; Neuckirchener-Vluyn: Neukirchener.

Wink, Walter. 1980. *Letting Parables Live. ChrCent* 97:1062–64.

Wit, Hans de. 1991. *Leerlingen van de Armen.* Amsterdam: VU-uitgeverij.

———. 2000. Leyendo con Yael: Un ejercicio en hermenéutica intercultural. Pages 11–66 in *Los caminos inexhauribles de la Palabra: Escritos festivos para José Severino Croatto.* Edited by Guillermo Hansen. Buenos Aires: Lumen-ISEDET.

———. 2002. *En la dispersión el texto es Patria: Introducción a la hermenéutica clásica, moderna y posmoderna.* San José: Universidad Bíblica Latinoamericana.

———. 2004a. Codes and Coding. Pages 395–436 in de Wit, Jonker, Kool, and Schipani 2004.

———. 2004b. Intercultural Bible Reading and Hermeneutics. Pages 477–92 in de Wit, Jonker, Kool, and Schipani 2004.

———. 2004c. Through the Eyes of Another: Objectives and Backgrounds. Pages 3–53 in de Wit, Jonker, Kool, and Schipani 2004.

———. 2006. Caminho dum dia (Jonas 3.4): Jonas e a memoria social dos pequenos. Pages 283–313 in *Profecia e Esperança: Um tributo a Milton Schwantes.* Edited by Carlos Dreher et al. São Leopoldo: Oikos Editora.

Wit, Hans de, Louis Jonker, Marleen Kool, and Daniel Schipani, eds. 2004. *Through the Eyes of Another: Intercultural Reading of the Bible.* Elkhart, Ind.: Institute of Mennonite Studies; Amsterdam: Vrije Universiteit.

Wittgenstein, Ludwig. 1958. *Philosophical Investigations.* New York: Macmillan.

Witvliet, Theo. 2004. The Ecumenical Relevance of Intercultural Bible Reading. Pages 493–502 in de Wit, Jonker, Kool and Schipani 2004.

Wolff, Hans Walter. 1986. *Obadiah and Jonah: A Commentary.* Translated by Margaret Kohl. Minneapolis: Augsburg.

Yee, Gale A. 2006. Yin/Yang Is Not Me: An Exploration into an Asian American Biblical Hermeneutics. Pages 152–63 in Foskett and Kuan 2006.

Young, Iris Marion. 1990. *Justice and the Politics of Difference.* Princeton: Princeton University Press.

Žižek, Slavoj. 1999. *The Ticklish Subject: The Absent Center of Political Ontology.* London: Verso.

———. 2000. *The Fragile Absolute: Or, Why Is the Christian Legacy Worth Fighting For?* New York: Verso.

———. 2003. *The Puppet and the Dwarf: The Perverse Core of Christianity.* Cambridge: MIT Press.

CONTRIBUTORS

Pablo R. Andiñach is Professor of Old Testament, Instituto Universitario ISEDET, Buenos Aires. He was born in Argentina and received his Doctorate in Theology from ISEDET. He is currently President of the Faculty of Theology at ISEDET and Director of the journal *Cuadernos de Teología*. His publications include a commentary on Song of Songs (1997), "Zechariah" in the *International Bible Commentary* (1999), "Joel" in the *Global Bible Commentary* (2005), "Génesis" and "Tobías" in the *Comentario Bíblico Latinoamericano* (2005), *El libro del Éxodo* (2006), *Ser Iglesia* (2007), *Éxodo: Comentario para su traducción* (2009). He is an ordained pastor in the Methodist Church in Argentina.

Mortimer Arias is Bishop Emeritus of the Bolivian Methodist Church. He was born in Uruguay and studied theology at the Facultad Evangélica de Teología in Buenos Aires (now ISEDET) and Perkins School of Theology. In 1980, he was was kidnapped and incarcerated by the Bolivian military regime for his ministry among the poor. After a short exile in Brazil, Arias accepted a teaching position at Claremont School of Theology and a professorship at Iliff School of Theology. Among his many publications are *Venga tu Reino: La Memoria Subversiva de Jesús* (1980), translated as *Announcing the Reign of God: Evangelization and the Subversive Memory of Jesus* (1984); *The Great Commission: Biblical Models for Evangelism* (1992); and *La Gran Comisión: Relectura desde América latina* (1994).

Alejandro F. Botta is Assistant Professor of Hebrew Bible, Boston University School of Theology. He was born in Argentina and earned his doctorate from the Hebrew University of Jerusalem in Israel. He has taught and lectured in Argentina, Mexico, Israel, Venezuela, Spain, and the United States. Among his publications are *The Aramaic and Egyptian Legal Traditions at Elephantine: An Egyptological Approach* (2009); *Los Doce Profetas Menores* (2006); *Cultura material, evolución demográfica y cambio político en Palestina durante la dominación egipcia* (1995). He also contributed articles to *The New Interpreter's Bible Dictionary*, *The Dictionary of Early Judaism*, and others collective works.

Musa W. Dube is Professor of Religious Studies at the University of Botswana, at Gaborone, Botswana. She was born in Botswana and completed her Ph.D. at Vanderbilt University. She is actively involved with the Circle for Concerned African Women Theologians, where she has served as the chair of biblical research and publication for the association. Among her publications are *The HIV and AIDS Bible: Selected Essays* (2008); *Feminist New Testament Studies: Global and Future Perspectives* (co-editor, 2005); *Talitha cum! Theologies of African Women* (co-editor, 2001); *Postcolonial Feminist Interpretation of the Bible* (2000); and *The Bible in Africa: Transactions, Trajectories, and Trends* (co-editor, 2000).

Mercedes García-Bachmann is Professor of Old Testament, Instituto Universitario ISEDET, Argentina where she is also co-coordinator of the Forum for Theology and Gender Studies. She was born in Argentina, studied theology at ISEDET in Buenos Aires, spent a year at the Swedish Theological Institute (Jerusalem), and then completed a Ph.D. in Old Testament at the Lutheran School of Theology at Chicago. She is an ordained minister of the Lutheran Church (Argentina-Uruguay, IELU) and has published, among other works, "La ley y el orden. Una apreciación del material legal y cultual en el libro del Éxodo," in *Relectura del Éxodo* (2006); "A la búsqueda de trabajadoras en la Biblia hebraica: Algunos problemas metodológicos," *RIHAO* (2005–6); and "Deuteronomy" in the *Global Bible Commentary* (2004).

Erhard Gerstenberger is Professor Emeritus of Old Testament at the Philipps-Universität Marburg. He studied at the universities of Marburg, Tübingen, Bonn, and the seminary of Wuppertal and taught at the Lutheran seminary of São Leopoldo, Brazil, at Giessen University, and at Marburg University. He has published widely in the areas of biblical theology and Old Testament in German, English, and Portuguese, including *Psalms, Part 1 (Ps 1–60) with an Introduction to Cultic Poetry* (1988); *Psalms, Part 2 (Ps 61–150) with Lamentations* (2001); *Das 3. Buch Mose, Leviticus* (1993), translated as *Leviticus: A Commentary* (1996); *Theologien im Alten Testament: Pluralität und Synkretismus alttestamentlichen Gottesglaubens* (2001), translated as *Theologies of the Old Testament* (2002); and *Israel in der Perserzeit: 5. und 4. Jahrhundert v. Chr.* (2005).

Jione Havea is Lecturer in Biblical Studies at the School of Theology, Charles Sturt University, and United Theological College, North Parramatta, NSW, Australia. He is a Researcher with the Public and Contextual Theology (Charles Sturt University) and an Assistant Chaplain at Parklea Prison. His most recent publications include *Elusions of Control: Biblical Law on the Words of Women* (2003); "'*Unu'unu ki he loloto*: Shuffle Over into the Deep, into Island-Spaced Reading," in *Still at the Margins: Biblical Scholarship Fifteen Years after* Voices from the Margin (2008); "Telling as If a Local: Toward Homing the Bible out-side Western [Main]streams," *Joskiran: Journal of Religion and Thought* (2008); and "Who Is strange(r)? A Pacific Native Muses Over Mission," *JTCA: Journal of Theologies and Cultures in Asia* (2008).

Ada María Isasi-Díaz is Professor of Ethics and Theology at The Theological School, Drew University. She was born and raised in La Habana, Cuba, and came to the United States in 1960 as a political refuge. She earned a Ph.D. in Theology in 1990 from Union Theological Seminary and has taught in Perú, Cuba, Korea, and Spain and lectured around the globe. She has published several books, more than forty chapters in books, and more than thirty articles in magazines and journals. Among her publications are *La Lucha Continues—Mujerista Theology* (2004); *Mujerista Theology: A Theology for the 21st Century* (1996); and *En La Lucha-A Hispanic Women's Liberation Theology* (2nd ed., 2003). She is complet-ing *Justicia: A Reconciliatory Praxis of Care and Tenderness*.

Theodore W. Jennings Jr. is Professor of Biblical and Constructive Theology at Chicago Theological Seminary. After completing a Ph.D. at Emory University, he served as a local pastor and taught for three years at the Methodist Seminary in Mexico City and served as a consultant with the United Methodist Church on issues related to commitment to the poor. Among his publications are *Jacob's Wound: Homoerotic Narrative in the Literature of Ancient Israel* (2005); *Reading Derrida, Thinking Paul: On Justice* (2005); *The Man Jesus Loved: Homoerotic Narratives from the New Testament* (2003); *Santidad bíblica* (2002); *Loyalty to God: The Apostles Creed in Life and Liturgy* (1992); *Good News to the Poor: John Wesley's Evangelical Economics* (1990); and *Beyond Theism: A Grammar of God-Language* (1985).

Monica Jyotsna Melanchthon is Professor at Gurukul Lutheran Theologi-cal College and Research Institute, Chennai, India. She was born in India and attended Lutheran School of Theology at Chicago, where she received a M.Th. degree in 1990 and a Ph.D. in Old Testament in 1995. She has served on various study teams of the Lutheran World Federation and the LWF Assembly Study Book (2007); as a member of the editorial council of *Dialog*; and as co-editor of the International Voices in Biblical Studies, a new online series of the SBL Inter-national Cooperation Initiative. Among her publications is *Rejection by God: The History and Significance of the Rejection Motif in the Hebrew Bible* (2001). Her current research projects involve the Bible in conversation with issues of gender and caste.

Lai Ling Elizabeth Ngan is Associate Professor of Christian Scriptures at George W. Truett Theological Seminary, Baylor University. She was born in

Hong Kong and has earned degrees from California Baptist University, Loma Linda University, and Golden Gate Baptist Theological Seminary (Ph.D.). She joined the faculty of Truett Seminary in the fall of 1996 from Golden Gate Seminary, where she taught for three years. She has served in a number of church ministry positions in Chinese churches in California and has continued to pulpit supply and lead conferences since coming to Truett Semianry. She has contributed articles to *The New Interpreter's Bible Dictionary*, the *Global Bible Commentary*, and others and is interested in Asian American women's biblical interpretations.

Luise Schottroff is Professor Emeritus of New Testament at the Institut für Evangelische Theologie, Universität Kassel. She has authored more than twenty books on the New Testament and feminist theology; among her publications are *The Eucharist: Bodies, Bread, and Resurrection* (with Andrea Bieler, 2007); *Die Gleichnisse Jesu* (2005); *The Parables of Jesus* (2006); *Jesus of Nazareth* (with Dorothee Soelle, 2002); *Lydia's Impatient Sisters: A Feminist Social History of Early Christianity* (1995); and *Let the Oppressed Go Free: Feminist Perspectives on the New Testament* (1993). She taught at Mainz, Kassel, Berkeley (U.S.), and New York. In 2007, she received an Honorary Doctorate from the Fachbereich Evangelische Theologie of the Philipps-Universität Marburg.

Gerald O. West is Professor of Biblical Studies in the School of Religion and Theology at the University of KwaZulu-Natal, South Africa, and Director of the Ujamaa Centre for Community Development and Research. A native of South Africa, he completed a Ph.D in Biblical Studies from the University of Sheffield. Among his publications are *Biblical Hermeneutics of Liberation: Modes of Reading the Bible in the South African Context* (2nd ed., 1995); *The Academy of the Poor: Towards a Dialogical Reading of the Bible* (1999); *Reading Other-wise: Socially Engaged Biblical Scholars Reading with Their Local Communities* (editor, 2007); *The Bible in Africa: Transactions, Trajectories, and Trends* (co-editor, 2000); and *African and European Readers of the Bible in Dialogue: In Quest of a Shared Meaning* (co-editor, 2008).

Hans (J. H.) de Wit is Professor on the Faculty of Theology, VU University Amsterdam, The Netherlands. From 1980 to 1989 he worked at the Comunidad Teológica Evangélica de Chile as Professor of Old Testament and Biblical Hermeneutics. De Wit is one of the initiators of a new international project called *Through the Eyes of Another: Intercultural Reading of the Bible* (co-editor, 2004). Among his other publications are *Libro de Daniel: Una Relectura desde América Latina* (1990); *En la dispersión el texto es patria: Introducción a la hermenéutica clásica, moderna y posmoderna* (2002); and *African and European Readers of the Bible in Dialogue: Towards a Shared Meaning* (co-editor, 2008).

Breinigsville, PA USA
17 September 2009
224290BV00002B/1/P

9 781589 832411